Professional Competencies of Social Workers

Professional Competencies of Social Workers

Authors
Dr. S. Sudarmathy
Dr. K. Sathyamurthi

ALLIED PUBLISHERS PVT. LTD.
Noida • Mumbai • Kolkata • Chennai • Bangalore

ALLIED PUBLISHERS PRIVATE LIMITED

D-5, Sector-2, **Noida**–201 301
Ph. Nos.: 0120-4320295/2542557/4352866 • E-mail: delhi.books@alliedpublishers.com

17 Chittaranjan Avenue, **Kolkata**–700072
Ph.: 033-22129618 • E-mail: cal.books@alliedpublishers.com

15 J.N. Heredia Marg, Ballard Estate, **Mumbai**–400001
Ph.: 022-42126969 • E-mail: mumbai.books@alliedpublishers.com

No. 25/10, Commander-in-Chief Road, Ethiraj Lane (Next to Post Office)
Egmore, **Chennai**–600008
Ph.: 044-28223938 • E-mail: chennai.books@alliedpublishers.com

P.B. No. 9932, No. 15, 3rd Floor (Next to Vijaya Bank), 5th Cross, Gandhinagar, Karnataka, **Bangalore**–560009, Ph.: 080-41530285 / 22386239
E-mail: bngl.books@alliedpublishers.com

Website: www.alliedpublishers.com

ISBN: 978-93-89934-46-5

Published by Sunil Sachdev and printed by Ravi Sachdev at Allied Publishers Pvt. Ltd., D-5, Sector-2, Noida–201 301

Preface

Social Work is a profession that aims to help the helpless by helping them solve their problems. This process is made more impactful by assuming a scientific and factual basis. Its main purpose is to make them become more cognizant of their situation and find a solution to their problems.

Social Work Professional is the one who dedicated his full time to accomplishing social work practice. This has been clearly stated that a professional is the one who dedicates his entire time to particular activity than a person who is engaged in such activities for a short period (Flexner, 2001). Hence the profession is complete and focuses on a particular field and the professionals are intellectuals in their field and learned as well. But no profession is showed efficient unless they practice in their life.

The most common misunderstanding about Social Work is that people mistake charity, almsgiving, and volunteer activities for Social Work. However, this is not Social Work because it does not provide a definitive answer to a person's situation and does not embolden a person to face his or her problems on his or her own. The goal of social work is to help people become self-sufficient.

The nuances of Social Work have always existed in society. However, a scientific basis was established during the latter part of the 19th century. While the roots of it were laid in the form of social service in India, it assumed a professional outlook that has evolved from the west. Individuals and institutions are driven by the religious notions of seeking salvation through service, helped people in distress. These institutions and individuals valued human dignity and social welfare and campaigned for the same through their service.

Social Work seeks to investigate the possible causes underlying the problems and solve them scientifically. As a result, it is discerned that Social Work is a scientific process for assisting those in need who are suffering from poverty, developmental disorders, mental illnesses, emotional difficulties, and so forth, by employing knowledge of human relationships, as well as methods and skills for dealing with them. In essence, Social Work aims to assist individuals, families, social groups, and communities in identifying and permanently resolving personal and social problems through a structured approach.

However, as time has passed, the professional quality of Social Work has deteriorated, and the profession's ultimate goal has been distorted. Currently, the number of professional Social Workers is expanding while the number of competent Social Work students is dropping. The reason for this is that there are more colleges than ever before. Before the last two decades, it was quite difficult for a student who had completed his or her PG in Social Work to get work. However, a decade later, there are numerous prospects in NRHM, multinational corporations, medical and psychiatric social work departments, and so on. Because it is such a vast area, there are several opportunities to engage in a global arena. However, the competence of Indian Social Work students falls short of worldwide expectations. Even though numerous Indian and foreign social workers and social scientists have detected it, there has been no progressive change. For a scientific knowledge and basis to be sound, it is essential that the person practicing Social Work adopt the principles, values, and skills of the profession, and become competent in their field of work.

Although Social Work courses are available at the undergraduate, graduate, master's, and doctoral levels, the profession is not well-known in rural and semi-urban regions. The simpleton's conceptions of social work, as well as the misunderstanding that social work is a form of social service, persist. Few urban residents understood the importance of social work and encouraged their children to choose their careers in social work. Furthermore, it may be alarming to note that many students to enroll in Social Work because they have no other options for their grades. Meanwhile, as the need for social workers in the corporate sector has grown, many people have resigned from their jobs and enrolled in M.S.W. programs. Their major goal is to find a job that pays well and which is not too tough to obtain.

In India, social work can best be defined as a semi-profession, as Etzioni puts it. In nations like the United States and the United Kingdom, social work and social workers are legally protected. In India, however, this is never feasible. Professional social work will coexist alongside social work, with the latter having a lesser standing.

As a result, the profession of social work is currently losing its professionalism. In today's world, social workers are assisting people without the necessary skills, expertise, or experience. Many students are admitted without qualifications and leave with naught after finishing college.

This highlights the need for a competency-based approach in social work. Social workers are fundamentally capable of assisting an individual as well as society. Students pursuing a degree in social work must be evaluated on their abilities, values, and understanding of the field.

Contents

Preface ..... *v*

CHAPTER 1: Introduction 1

CHAPTER 2: Professional Competency Frame Work for Social Work 9

CHAPTER 3: Theoretical Frame Work 17

CHAPTER 4: Psycho Metric Assessment of Professional Competencies for Social Work 25

CHAPTER 5: Demographic Profile 31

CHAPTER 6: Demographic Variables of the Respondents... 45

CHAPTER 7: Level of Professionalism Competency 69

CHAPTER 8: Level of Values and Ethical Competency 85

CHAPTER 9: Level of Engage Diversity and Equality Competency 101

CHAPTER 10: Level of Rights, Justice and Economic Wellbeing Competency 119

CHAPTER 11: Level of Knowledge about Human Behaviour Competency 137

CHAPTER 12: Level of Critical Thinking and Analysis Competency 155

CHAPTER 13: Level of Intervention and Skills Competency 173

CHAPTER 14: Level of Contexts and Organisation Competency .. 189

CHAPTER 15: Level of Professional Leadership Competency 205

CHAPTER 16: Level of Professional Competencie 223

CHAPTER 17: Intervention 239

References 243

CHAPTER 1

Introduction

Educational Competencies in Social Work curricula can purposefully, intentionally, and professionally integrate and apply Social Work knowledge, beliefs, and skills to practice settings to enhance individual and societal well-being.

The evaluation of student learning outcomes is an important part of competency-based education. The assessment indicates that students have proven the level of competence required to join the professional practice, indicating that programs are meeting their objectives. In Social Work Education, a student's competency may be determined by assessing their degree of knowledge about Social Work values, principles, techniques, and skills, among other aspects. The competence of a Social Worker is viewed as progressive and dynamic, developing over time in response to ongoing learning. The assessment methods employed by programs and the data collected may differ by setting, making it critical to comprehend social work practice.

The program must define skills and their component elements, as well as relate them to tools, to build a meaningful competence assessment. Multiple assessments of each overall skill are required by current Social Work certification requirements. Knowledge competency is tested in Social Work education through class tests and assignments, whereas practice competency is assessed through field assessments. However, this is insufficient to establish the validity of social work as a career.

Thus the authors aims to understand the professional competencies of a Social Worker concerning the nine competencies, that are professionalism, values and Ethical, engaging in engage diversity and equality, rights, justice and economic well-being, knowledge about human behaviour, intervention and skills, critical thinking and analysis, contexts and organization and professional leadership. Ratings of individual competence must establish a range of competence from beginner to expert. This book mainly focuses on the Social Worker to bring an understanding about their Social Work Educational Competence and to enhance the area in which they are lacking. The periodic assessment helps the Social Worker to enhance their professionalism as a result the worker's competency will increase.

Competency

Kristin A. Jones *et al.* (2017) wrote a chapter on Building competencies among post-secondary education and the historical perspective of competency-based education. It was mentioned that CBE is rooted deeply in decades – old pedagogical philosophies. But recently it gained attention in post-secondary education. A smaller actionable statement to measure is termed as competency. Competency based education was defined as an instructional approach that places more control over the learning process with the student, rather than the instructor making all learning decisions regarding the course or program. Students demonstrate the ability to meet competencies set by the program or school. In response, over the past three years, there has been a dramatic shift in higher education practices. Colleges and universities are implementing programs that emphasize demonstration of skills and knowledge acquired through work or life experience or through prior learning activities. These programs are generally referred to as competency-based education, as well as standards-based education, outcomes-based education, inquiry-based education, and problem-based learning. While there are similarities among these terms, there are also differences that require elaboration for their distinctions to be understood. (Olswang, 2017).

Professional Competency

Competence in a professional setting differs from competency in a general sense. Professional competency is the broad professional knowledge, attitude, and skills required to work in a specialized area or profession, whereas competency is generally viewed as the effective application of skills. When a person is accountable and capable in a career, he or she is competent.

Professional competence is described as the capacity to produce sustained effective (worthy) performance (including problem-solving, achieving innovation, and implementing change) in a certain learning domain, profession, role, organizational environment, and task circumstance. Professional competence does not relate to a single skill; rather, it encompasses many skills. Professional competencies are knowledge, abilities, and attitudes that may be used in a certain field. In a crime scene investigation, for example, a forensic expert must create a DNA profile of a piece of evidence. It necessitates disciplinary knowledge, abilities (artifact handling), and attitudes (accuracy, coping with pressure, integrity). All of this adds up to professional competence.

In the eyes of the educational system, a person who completes a bachelor's degree is competent, because many companies regard a bachelor's degree to be a competent prerequisite.

Professional competence is a component of that because, without it, the professional would be unable to perform the position in the issue. However, this is not the same as claiming that the role is a defining feature of competence. It's the contrary—competencies are performance requirements without which professionals would be unable to function successfully in their professional environments. Competence includes knowledge, skills, and attitudes.

Social Work Education

Social work is a people-centered profession that recognizes that each person is unique. It promotes the development of social change, cohesion, and the empowerment of individuals and communities. All elements that make the core fabric of society are to be significantly comprehended to practice this profession. Social Work is the only profession that helps people of different castes, religions, and ethnicity.

Mahesh Palloor, and Dr. F. Carter Premraj (2017)conducted a case study and found that the major reasons for reduced social workers recruitment are No Effective Aptitude Test, Students are opting their specialization not based on their personal capacity or personal wish it is based on the interest of facilitator and the demand of market/job opportunities the students are only concentrating to complete their course, The facilitators are guest faculties and not much firm in some of the aspects such as submission of research and Field Work Report, failure in Selection of Training and Placement Agency, No trainers in the Placement Agency, sympathetic approach towards the students, etc. To protect the dignity of social work profession, this is the right time to develop the skills of the students. Every institution has to awake and to provide training centered education to the professional social work students. (Premraj, 2017).

Devi Prasad (2014) identifies five deficits of professional social work in India. These are knowledge deficit, competency deficit, professional deficit, governance deficit, and ideological deficit. Lack of academic work ethic and scholarship, and lack of ability to use social work lens to examine social issues are two important aspects under knowledge deficit. By competency deficit, he means knowledge and skill set deficit. Deteriorating quality of professional social work education and consequently, the decline in the quality of social work profession; commercialization of social work education; and the extensive variation in the curricula in the different schools are the main components of professional deficit. Social work education under varied affiliations and the inadequate capacity of a majority of social work educational institutions in the country are examples of governance deficit. Devi Prasad laments the ideological deficit, that is, the absence of any discussion on the kind of "desirable society" that social workers envision. (T.K. Nair, 2015)

E.F. Lymbery (2003) Social Work education in Britain has recently been dominated by a competence-based frame of reference, which has proved to be inadequate in preparing Social Workers for the professional judgements that have to be applied in practice. At the same time the concept of reflective practice, which emphasizes the need for professionals to demonstrate creativity in their practice, has gained currency. This article explores the possibility of reconciling the two principles of competence and creativity within Social Work education. The article concludes that it is possible to see competence as a necessary stage to the development of the level of creativity that should characterize highly skilled Social Work practice. This implies the need for more systematic development of post-qualifying education that is directly aimed at the enhancement of practitioners' creativity. (E.F.Lymbery, 2003)

H.Y. Siddiqui, attempt to highlight issues which have resulted in making social work education uncertain about its goals and, as a result, ineffective in producing competent professionals. Besides identifying the issues which have hitherto led to confusion about the scope and boundaries of social work practice, posing problems both for social work educators and students, the need for identifying specific objectives and gearing social work education to these objectives, in order to develop specific professional skills, has been emphasized. It has been argued that efforts at identifying the skills, developing suitable methods for teaching them and developing tools to assess the level of their development in students, has been rather a weak trend in most schools of social work, particularly in India. It was concluded, that a competency-based model for social work education must begin by identifying specific tasks, developing a suitable theoretical framework for performing these tasks and, lastly, provide adequate inputs to develop a core of facilitative skills. (H.Y. Siddiqui).

Social Work and Competency

The educational system is currently shifting toward a competency-based educational framework. The authors from various disciplines define competency in a variety of ways.

In general identifying and analysing what student's exhibit in practice is referred to as a competency-based approach. This technique is used in social work to evaluate students' capacity to exhibit the skills defined in the curriculum. It is defined as the permanent distinguishing characteristics and traits that determine performance; distinctive characteristics which differentiate the successful performer from the rest; an ability to reach goals; inner personality traits that allow a person to cope better with a given task, role or situation; knowledge, skills, abilities and other characteristics demonstrated at work, etc. As a result, no one specific definition of competency exists.

According to the European Qualification Framework, competence denotes the proven ability to employ knowledge, skills, personal, social, and/or methodological abilities in work or study circumstances, as well as in professional and personal development. IEEE Reusable Competency define Competence as any kind of knowledge, skill, attitude, ability, or educational aim that may be articulated in a framework of learning, education, or training (RCD).

David Mc Clelland, widely regarded as the originator of the contemporary competency movement (1973), was the first to talk about competence. He added a new dimension to students' understanding of competency. He was a firm believer that a person's ability cannot be measured just by their school grade. He went on to say that a student's grades have no actual value in forecasting competency in real-life situations.

Though social work began as a charitable endeavor, it has evolved into a rigorous profession with a scientific approach, necessitating skill. Society expects ethical and successful social workers to provide quality social work to those in need. Social work schools must develop competent graduates who can successfully cope with society's challenges. Competence is defined as the combination of knowledge, values, and skills that leads to effective practice. To provide professional services in social work, knowledge, values, and abilities must be transferred into practice. This has been researched and clearly emphasizes social workers' professional abilities.

Competence deficit has been documented as one of the professional social work deficiency in India. This has been referred to a lack of knowledge and skills. The major components of professional deficit include diminishing quality of professional social work education and, as a result, a deterioration in the quality of the social work profession; commercialization of social work education; and considerable engage diversity in curricula between institutions (Devi Prasad, 2014).

According to an Indian study on social welfare manpower, graduates deemed the training beneficial since it equipped them with job knowledge and abilities (Pathak, 1983). The research, on the other hand, did not specify the skills the graduates learned. Even though these criticisms raise several difficult problems, social work educators must assess whether social work education is accomplishing its main aim of allowing students to achieve the level of competence required for responsible professional practice.

Competency-based education should be delivered to benefit students by addressing fundamental information, abilities, and attitudes in a unified model. The professional competence necessitates the acquisition of appropriate information on the one hand, as well as the capacity to apply it in practice on the other. At each level of social work education, an inventory should be created in line with the particular objectives of the training program, in which social workers should be competent and make a concerted effort to acquire the skills required. A competency-based approach for social work education must begin by defining specific activities, establishing an appropriate theoretical framework for executing these tasks, and then providing enough inputs to create a core of facilitative abilities, according to the findings (H.K. Siddiqui).

CHAPTER 2

Professional Competency Frame Work for Social Work

Selwyn Stanley *et al.* (2020) Social work education and training seeks to develop professional competence in students in terms of knowledge, values and skills. Emotional intelligence, reflective ability and empathy assume significance in this regard. This study investigated the manifestation of these competencies in women social work students in India using a longitudinal design (n = 34) Findings revealed that reflective ability scores significantly predicted the manifestation of emotional intelligence. No statistically significant change in the manifestation was evidenced as students progressed from course entry to completion. (Social work education, the international Journal 2020)

Britany Swinton (2019) in an article mentioned that competence allows us to absorb knowledge, apply theoretical concepts, assess, and intervene with accuracy. It is measurable and gets the job done. However, as Social Workers, we are more than a job. We are encouragers, educators, connectors, innovators, and change agents. These roles demand that we go beyond simply meeting the criteria. Competence is not stagnant; it is a never-ending push for personal and professional excellence. The challenge is to be better than the day before, while promoting the rights, values, and respect of those we serve. (Britany Swinton, 2019).

Larisa Alexandrovna Darinskaia *et al.* (2019) wrote a chapter on the problem of preparing a graduate of a classical university, possessing both professional and special competencies, which include expertise, knowledge, and skills obtained in the study of pedagogical disciplines. It was mentioned that the effectiveness of student preparation largely depends on the results of their independent work, which is given a significant amount of academic time. At the same time, the teacher's task is to accompany the student's independent work and to draw up a system of non-standard tasks that develop communicative and creative skills, skills of working with scientific texts and project activities. They defined Professional Competencies as the broad professional knowledge, attitude, and skills required in order to work in a specialized area or profession. (Molodtsova, 2019).

Frazier *et al.*, 1994–2020, mentioned that, Competence includes skill, knowledge, and a positive attitude that empowers. That which expands personal development inherently affects professional development. Social Workers who engage in self-help education, self-care, mentorship, therapy, spiritual practices, and sound financial management can potentially build a strong personal foundation. It is in grounding oneself that we become the best version of self; thus, we become models, mentors, and educators for clients. We live in a society of engage diversity where there is constant change. Competence should not be limited to the working professional but should expand to equip all humans with knowledge. To effectively have an impact on the lives of others, one must develop deeply into knowledge and expertise to serve the vulnerable most effectively. Competence is not given; it must be earned through constant research, reading, reflection, and expanding education. Social Workers are charged with a responsibility to self and others to advance learning to ensure exceptional delivery of service. Building trust, respect, and discipline requires us, as Social Workers, to elevate competence, so it becomes a mind-set and a passion that drives us to merge authenticity with knowledge.

YuGuo *et al.,* (2018), this study explored the competency-based education and assessment in the process of creating a social work student to become a competent professional, with a quantitative examination of Chinese student's core competencies. Core competencies are grouped into two, namely conceptual and professional competencies. It was found that curriculum content satisfaction, preference for the social work, field experience and knowledge of career outlook are positively related to students conceptual, professional and comprehensive competencies. Gender and willingness for further study also relate positively to both conceptual and comprehensive competencies. Grade is positively associated with professional competencies. (Yu Guo, 2018).

Jasmine Sarah Alexander (2017) in his article attempts to introduce a competency-based framework to social work education in India. This framework adopts a Competency Based Education (CBE) approach by drawing directly from social work practice in India. The framework purports to address the shortcomings of the present model by being more relevant to Indian social realities, creating a strong link between theory and practice, and fostering greater commitment to the profession. It also hopes to be useful, to both social work schools and social welfare institutions, in setting standards of training for social work students and practitioners. (Alexander, 2017)

George Karpetis (2017) Using the keywords 'social work' and 'skills', an electronic data- base search extracted peer-reviewed articles from the last ten years. The thematic analysis of the twenty-three articles retrieved revealed that the publications adopted the humanistic, critical, behavioural, psychodynamic, managerial and eclectic theoretical perspectives. Even though the clear majority of authors refrained from explicitly identifying the theories underlying specific skills, most implicitly espoused either the managerial perspective that neglects the holistic bio-psycho-social assessment of clients or the practice ambiguous eclectic theoretical perspective.

EDrisko, James W. (2016) stated in his article that competence may be broken down into component parts. In social work and in many related professions, competence is widely viewed as including knowledge, values, and skills. This trio has been formalized in the accreditation requirements set by CSWE (2008) and in the core ethical values established by the National Association of Social Workers (NASW; 2008). Specific knowledge is a vital part of professional competence. Having requisite knowledge is as a central part of many competencies. It is important to note that social workers also identify competence as a core professional value. The authors of the Code stated, "social workers practice within their areas of competence, and develop and enhance their professional expertise. Social workers continually strive to increase their professional knowledge and skills and to apply them in practice" (NASW, 2008, Ethical principles). In social work, skills are evident in the application of knowledge, integrated with core values, to a specific client in a specific situation. Identifying what is important to the client in a particular situation requires both knowledge and judgment. These intersecting and overlapping definitions suggest that breaking competencies down into component parts reflecting knowledge, values, and skills is appropriate and is based on a widely shared understanding across disciplines and professions. (Drisko, 2016)

Denis Kuanyshevich Davletkaliev, Natalia Konstantinovna Zueva1 *et al.* (2015) the goal of their work is to study the psychological-pedagogical approaches to the understanding of the idea of professional competence of social work specialists as well as the role of study in the system of additional educations in professional-personal development of the listeners. Professional competence of a social work specialist is a wide concept which includes theoretical knowledge and its practical application, axiological orientations and integral indices of its culture (speech, way of communication etc.). Special competence includes professional skills, understanding of the essence of purpose of the work of social work specialist, mastering norms of professional activity and high effectiveness. Special competencies are Communicative competence, Organizational competence, Analytical competence, Reflexive competence, Motivational-personal competence and Social competence. (Davletkaliev1, 2015).

Mulder. M. (2014). This chapter goes into the roots of the competence movement, and evaluates the contributions of these to the field of professional and practice-based learning. The question is whether conceptions of professional competence have helped the practice of professional learning. In this chapter it is argued that this is indeed the case. Although various attempts to implement competence-based professional learning programmes were heavily criticized, later developments in competence theory and research gave new insights which emphasized the integrative meaning of competence.

Ying (2013) examined the potential contribution of self-compassion to perceived competence and mental health in master's of Social Work students (N=65). It was hypothesized that the components of self-compassion (i.e., mindfulness, common humanity, self-kindness, over identification, isolation, and self-judgment) would impact perceived competence (sense of coherence), which in turn would mediate mental health (depressive symptom level). Students completed the Self-Compassion Scale, the Sense of Coherence Questionnaire, and the California Psychological Inventory–Depression Scale. Results showed that over identification directly and indirectly (as mediated by decreased coherence) affected depressive symptom level. Implications for Social Work education are discussed. (ying, 2013)

Canadian Council of Social Work Regulators (2012) developed a common profile of entry level competencies for social work profession across Canada. Social Work entry level competencies profile describes the core professional competencies that the beginning social workers across Canada required regardless of the context in which they are employed. The profile consists of six competency blocks that represent six primary areas of practice with 152 items. The six competency blocks are 1) applying ethical standards, 2) conducting assessment, 3) planning interventions, 4) delivering services, 5) improving policies and practices, 6) engaging in reflective practice and professional development. (Regulators, 2012)

Harvey Bosma *et al.* (2009) "Creating social work competencies for practice in hospice palliative care" Social workers play an important role in the delivery of Hospice Palliative Care in many diverse settings. Despite the prominent and longstanding position of social work in this area, the role and functions of social workers had not been clearly defined. A Canadian task group of social work practitioners and educators have developed a set of core competencies for practice in hospice palliative care. These competencies are relevant for social workers at different experience levels across care settings. They can be used to inform social work practice, as well as professional development and educational curricula. (School of Social Work, University of British Columbia, Vancouver, BC, Canada 2009)

CSWE (2008), The Council on Social Work Education has established core competencies for social work education that span the classroom and field in the 2008 Educational Policy and Accreditation Standards (EPAS). Competency 1: Professional Identity Competency 2: Values & Ethical Competency 3: Critical Thinking Competency 4: Engage diversity & Difference Competency 5: Social & Economic Justice Competency 6: Research Competency 7: Human Behavior & the Social Environment Competency 8: Social Policy Competency 9: Context Competency 10A: Engagement Competency 10B: Assessment Competency 10C: Intervention Competency 10D: Evaluation. (education, 2015)

Bogo, M., Regehr, C., Hughes, J., Power, R., and Globerman, J. (2002) they found from their study indicate that there is some theoretical and practice coherence in the factors and associated skills that comprise the Competency Based Evaluation Tool (CBE). It is recommended that all social work programs test and report the reliability and validity of the tools they use to evaluate students' performance in Field Practicum. (Bogo, 2002).

David McClelland (1973) argued that neither tests nor school grades "seem to have much power to predict real competence in many real-life outcomes, aside from the advantages that credentials convey on the individuals concerned". To test competence, McClelland (1973) argued, five points must be considered.

First, "tests should assess clusters of competencies involved in life outcomes rather than single aspects of competencies". Second, he argued that testers must go into the field and test for the actual result or criterion sought. Third, he argued that tests of competency must include what he called "operant" or spontaneous behaviors of individuals in the absence of a clearly delimited stimulus. Fourth, he argued that how to improve on a competency should be made public and explicit. Fifth "tests of competency should be designed to reflect changes in what the individual has learned". These five criteria have become key parts of competency assessment in today's higher education. real-world practice. Multiple measures and multiple methods of assessment are encouraged to build validity through triangulation of results across tasks and settings. (Drisko., 17th July 2014).

Prof. P.K. Shajahan, Prof. Lina Kashyap and Prof. John Menachery, created a module in order to meet the emerging demands and the engage diversity in practice, contemporary social work practitioners, will need to add to their repertoire of generic social work knowledge and skills, certain specific knowledge and skills needed to achieve competencies in social work practice in family studies. The add on core social work competencies are,

- Identify yourself as a family studies social worker and conduct yourself accordingly.
- Apply social work ethical principles to guide professional practice.
- Have developed self-awareness and support structures for effective practice.

- Apply Critical thinking to inform and communicate professional judgments.
- Engage diversity and difference in practice.
- Advocate for human rights and social and economic justice by engaging in practice that advance social and economic justice.
- Apply knowledge of human Behavior and the social environment.
- Integrate theory and practice.
- Demonstrate your ability to engage, assess, intervene and evaluate with individuals, families, groups, organizations and communities by the following processes. (Prof. P.K. Shajahan)

CHAPTER 3

Theoretical Frame Work

Core Competencies for Social Work

The accrediting body of social work education programs in the United States is the CSWE Commission on Accreditation (COA). Educational policy for Social Work is given by CSWE and accreditation by COA. In United States, educational policy and accreditation of social work education guides the baccalaureate and master's level social work educational programs. Council of Social Work Education established the nine professional competencies based on the knowledge, values, skills of the profession.

- *Competency 1:* Demonstrate Ethical and Professional Behavior.
- *Competency 2:* Engage diversity and Difference in Practice.
- *Competency 3:* Advance Human Rights and Social, Economic, and Environmental Justice.
- *Competency 4:* Engage in Practice-Informed Research and Research-Informed Practice.
- *Competency 5:* Engage in Policy Practice.
- *Competency 6:* Engage with Individuals, Families, Groups, Organizations, and Communities.
- *Competency 7:* Assess Individuals, Families, Groups, Organizations, and Communities.
- *Competency 8:* Intervene with Individuals, Families, Groups, Organizations, and Communities.
- *Competency 9:* Evaluate Practice with Individuals, Families, Groups, Organizations, and Communities.

According to the Council on Social Work Education Social workers understand the value base of the profession and its ethical standards, as well as relevant laws and regulations that may impact practice at the micro, mezzo, and macro levels. Social workers are aware of ethical decision-making frameworks and how to apply critical thinking concepts to such frameworks in practise, research, and policy. Personal values and the contrast between personal and professional values are recognised by social workers. They are vital to the construction of the human experience because they comprehend how engage diversity and distinction characterise and shape the profession. (Boston University school of social work 2015).

Education policy accreditation Standard (2015). Social work competency is the ability to integrate and apply social work knowledge, values, and skills to practice situations in a purposeful, intentional, and professional manner to promote human and community well-being. Social work competence rests upon a shared view of the nature of competence in professional practice. Competency-based education aims to identify and assess students' ability to demonstrate the competencies identified in the educational policy. (2008 CSWE, EPAS 2015)

Holistic Competency

McKnigt (2013) proposes that competence is an "ongoing ability" to "integrate knowledge, skills, judgment, and professional attributes in order to practice safely and ethically" within one's professional scope. The CSWE defines holistic competence as the "demonstration of knowledge, values, skills, and cognitive and affective processes that include the social worker's critical thinking, affective reactions, and exercise of judgment in regard to unique practice situations. (Poulin, 2019)

Knowledge

Knowledge dimension of social work curricula are constructed to provide students with coursework that provides readings, assignments, and discussions that educate students on the current knowledge related to each competency.

Values

Understanding the values and Ethical associated with the application of the different social work competencies in unique practice situations is the fundamental aspect of ethical decision-making and professional social work competence.

Skills

The skill dimension refers to your ability to apply social work knowledge and values in your social work practice. There are numerous skills associated with each professional competency. (Poulin, 2019)

Canadian Council of Social Work Regulators (2012) developed a common profile of entry level competencies for social work profession across Canada. The profile is organized as six competency blocks,

1. Applying ethical standards
2. Conducting assessments
3. Planning interventions
4. Delivering services
5. Improving policies and practices
6. Engage in reflective practices and Professional Development

National Social Work Competency framework (2013), developed core competencies into three 1) knowledge 2) skills and 3) behavioural. Further the three competencies are categorized into direct practice and indirect practice in different levels. Knowledge and skill competencies in direct practices involves case work, group work, community work, environmental systems and social policies, Ethical, values and legislation, system linkage, analysis and development, social work/clinical supervision, professional leadership and research and program evaluation. Behavioural competencies are common for both direct and indirect practices involves ten competencies categorized into five clusters as follows, envision, empower, enable, elevate, evaluate and energize self.

National Association of Social Work

A lack of cultural humility and a lack of interest and knowledge in different cultures are both unacceptable, says Dr. Jodie O'Neill. Cultural humility involves having a non-paternalistic attitude towards clients from different socioeconomic groups, and towards marginalized and oppressed groups. It requires clinicians to learn from culturally diverse clients and to empower clients and let them be experts on their own culture. (NASW)

Competency Model of Social Work Practice

Poulin *et al.* (2019) proposed a competency-based model for social work practice. The nine professional competencies are interconnected in the delivery of social work practice with clients and constituencies. For example, a social worker's ability to engage with an individual client is influenced by his or her ethical and professional behaviour competency; engage diversity and difference competency; social, economic, and environmental justice competency; and possibly his or her policy practice and research competencies. In short, most social work practice situations require the use of all or most of the nine professional competencies. Thus, to be a competent social work practitioner, you must develop knowledge, values, skill, cognitive process, and affective reaction competencies for each professional competency and be able to apply multiple competencies in a variety of practice situations. (Poulin, 2019).

Competency Model

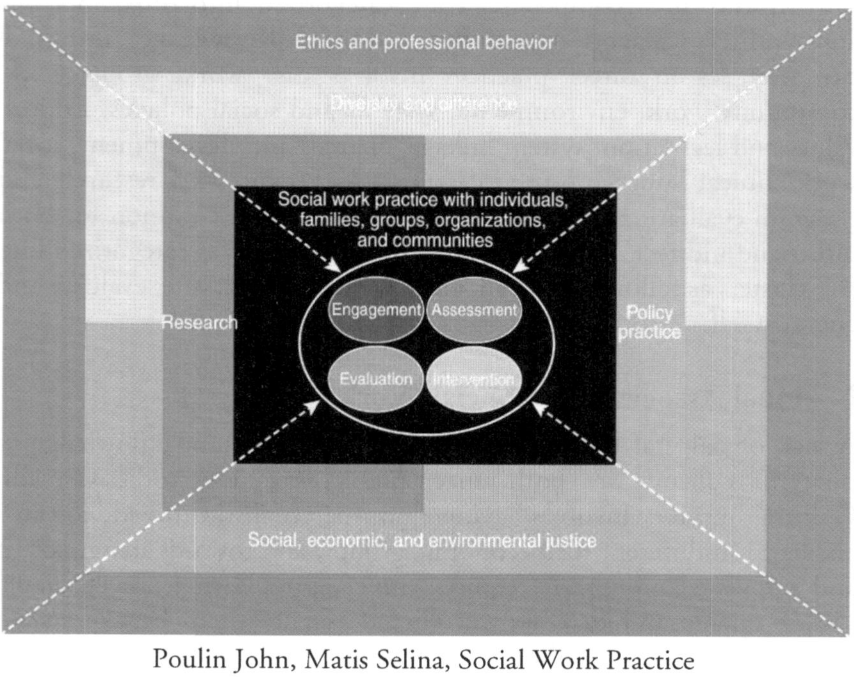

Poulin John, Matis Selina, Social Work Practice (2019)

Higher education is the key to "competency building" of an economy that desires to excel in innovation, cultivating a capable workforce equipped with essential skills and knowledge (Mok, 2013), with the goal of increasing employability and productivity. (Yu Guo, 2018). Canada Revenue Agency describes a competency as any measurable or observable knowledge, skill, ability or behavioural characteristics that contributes to successful job performance. Similarly Canadian centre on substance abuse (2007) defines competencies as measurable specific knowledge and skills required to effectively perform a particular job function or role. (Regulators, 2012)

Across profession competency plays a major role in the curriculum. There is a slow transition of curriculum from knowledge based to competent based learning. In any profession before becoming proficient in their area of practice, they need to develop strong theoretical knowledge of the field as well as demonstrate appropriate skills. Competency are viewed as more than an individual skills and knowledge, it intended to represent the combination of knowledge, values and skills. Competence is measurable as defined by educational policy and accreditation standards for social work education, USA. It can be measured in the form of broad statements.

First person to talk about competence in social work education was David McClelland (1973). Heargued that neither tests nor school grades "seem to have much power to predict real competence in many real-life outcomes, aside from the advantages that credentials convey on the individuals concerned". He also suggested five reasons to incorporate the competency testing among social workers. (Drisko., 17th July 2014)

Second remarkable development in the field of social work education was the development of ten core competencies by the council of social work education, USA. This as base many countries were trying to define their own competencies of their region. One among is China they developed the competency-based approach to social work education an empirical study through scale development. Russia also conducted a study and developed the professional competence of the social work specialist. Canadian council of social work regulators established an entry level social work competencies profile consisting of six core competencies.

In Singapore with a joint initiative of the Ministry of Social and Family Development and the Ministry of Health developed the National Social Work Competency Framework (NSWCF), which provides clear articulation of social work roles across the profession with the corresponding knowledge and skills required for effective delivery of interventions, in the areas of casework, group work or community work. The competencies are categorized into three as knowledge, skills and behavioral in both direct and indirect practices. (Ms Chee Liee Chin, 2013).

Professional competency was given a new nomenclature in England as professional capabilities. It is the profession owned backbone for the social work education and professional development. British association for social workers, the professional association for social work and social workers in England, categorized nine competencies under three super domains namely, purpose, practice and impact. It was first devised in 2012 and reviewed latest by 2018. Each domain descriptors are defined and the level or proficiency are measurable with appropriate statements. The nine capabilities are:

1. *Professionalism:* Identify and behave as a professional social worker, committed to professional development.
2. *Values and Ethical:* Apply social work ethical principles and values to guide professional practice.
3. *Engage Diversity:* Recognise engage diversity and apply anti-discriminatory and anti—oppressive principles in practice.
4. *Rights, Justice and Economic Wellbeing:* Advance human rights and promote social justice and economic wellbeing.
5. *Knowledge:* Apply knowledge of social sciences, law and social work practice theory.
6. *Critical Thinking and Analysis:* Apply critical thinking and analysis to inform and provide a rationale for professional decision-making.
7. *Intervention and Skills:* Use judgement and authority to intervene with individuals, families and communities to promote independence, provide support and prevent harm, neglect and abuse.
8. *Contexts and Organisations:* Engage with, inform, and adapt to changing contexts that shape practice. Operate effectively within

own organisational frameworks and contribute to the development of services and organisations. Operate effectively within multi-agency and inter-professional settings.

9. *Professional Leadership:* Take responsibility for the professional learning and development of others through supervision, mentoring, assessing, research, teaching, leadership and management. (Workers, 2018).

In Indian scenario only one study throwed the light on the core competencies of social workers. Jasmine Sarah (2017), established the core competencies as core knowledge, core, values, core skills and core intervention and special emphasis on the intervention aspects. (Alexander, 2017). This book attempts to assess the professional competencies of social workers at the intermediate level, consisting of II and III years under graduate and II year post graduate students of Tamilnadu. Hence based on the literature nine competencies and descriptors are as follows.

PROFESSIONALISM	As social workers, they must have the understanding about their profession and act accordingly. They have to maintain the professional roles and boundary in any difficult circumstances. One should respect his/her own profession, and should raise against any violation of practice either through organization or independently. Professional identity should be reflected in their behaviour, appearance and communication.
VALUES & ETHICS	Social workers must apply the values and follow the ethical principles for effective professional practice. They must aware that code of Ethical is underpinned in the process of problem solving and decision making.
ENGAGE DIVERSITY & EQUALITY	Recognize diversity among human being based on caste, creed, race, religion, economy and explore ways to promote equality. Maintain the diversity in practice with conscious elimination of personal biases and pre-judice.
RIGHTS, JUSTICE & ECONOMIC WELLBEING	Knowledge about human rights, social and economic justice is essential for social worker. Recognize and address the different forms of oppression and social injustice in accordance with the law. Enhance the condition of economically backward and enable them to access the basic requirements. (Food, housing, education, health and other welfare measures).

KNOWLEDGE ABOUT HUMAN BEHAVIOUR	Understanding a person with problem is an inevitable task in social work. In the process of helping, worker must recognize the persons behaviour within the context of social environment since human being and environment are in separable. Social work knowledge includes psychology, law, environmental studies etc.
CRITICAL THINKING & ANALYSIS	Critical thinking, curiosity, and creativity enable the process of making professional decisions in complex cases and situation. Social workers must evaluate the impact and benefit to service users.
INTERVENTION & SKILLS	Intervention in social work involves complete assessment of the needs and problems of individual, group and community. Social worker employs different skills like communication, purposeful relationship, listening, observation for a desired outcome. Social worker drives knowledge from theory, research, practice experience to select appropriate intervention strategies.
CONTEXT & ORGANIZATION	Social work is a human based profession it is essential to update the knowledge continuously and constantly to render quality service. Social worker must be aware of the emerging trend, technology developments, and policy changes that shape practice. It is necessary to inform and collaborate with other social workers, other professionals in the helping process of an individual, group and community.
PROFESSIONAL LEADERSHIP	Social workers must involve in ongoing professional development by participating in knowledge enhancement programs and efforts to evaluate new and existing approaches. Professional leadership can be achieved through advance practice, educating others, actively involving in professional bodies and networks.

CHAPTER 4

Psycho Metric Assessment of Professional Competencies for Social Work

In Indian scenario, the core competencies of social workers by Jasmine Sarah (2017), established the core competencies as core knowledge, core, values, core skills and core intervention and special emphasis on the intervention aspects. (Alexander, 2017).

This book attempts to assess the professional competencies of social workers at the intermediate level, consisting of II and III year under graduate and II year post graduate students of Tamilnadu. The term professional competencies of social worker were operationally defined based on the professional capabilities frame work of British association for social workers. Based on the literature, nine competencies were categorized as follows:

1. Professionalism
2. Values and Ethical
3. Engage diversity and Equality
4. Right, Justice and Economic Wellbeing
5. Knowledge about Human Behaviour
6. Critical thinking and Analysis
7. Intervention and Skills
8. Context and Organization
9. Professional Leadership.

The authors reviewed the literature to find an effective tool to measure the professional competencies of social workers. The available tools talk about the competencies in general and field work competencies. Considering the uniqueness of the profession and its importance, the authors constructed and validated a scale to measure the professional competencies of social workers.

The authors carried out the process of item selection, content validity, consultation with experts and reliability in the process of construction of the Professional Competencies of Social Worker scale. This scale was based on the Likert summated rating scale method of five-point rating.

Item Selection

After reviewing many literatures, the authors found that competency measurement is carried in various levels. Since this study focuses on the competencies of social work graduates, the item selection was done based on the professional capabilities' framework for social workers at training level. Based on this the Professional Competencies of Social Workers scale with nine domains are constructed. The following are the authors domain descriptors.

Professionalism Competency this involves the understanding about the profession and act accordingly. Social workers have to maintain the professional roles and boundary in any difficult circumstances. One should respect his/her own profession, and should raise against any violation of practice either through organization or independently. Professional identity should be reflected in their behaviour, appearance and communication.

Values and Ethical Competency involves application of values and follow the ethical principles for effective professional practice. Social Workers must aware that code of Ethical is underpinned in the process of problem solving and decision making.

Engage in engage diversity and equality competency, this involves the recognition of engage diversity among human being based on caste, creed, race, religion, economy and explore ways to promote equality. Maintaining engage diversity in practice with conscious elimination of personal biases and pre-judice.

Rights, Justice and economic wellbeing competency is an essential requirement for social worker. Recognize and address the different forms of oppression and social injustice in accordance with the law. Enhance the condition of economically backward and enable them to access the basic requirements. (Food, housing, education, health and other welfare measures).

Knowledge about human behaviour and social environment competency, includes an understanding of a person with problem is an inevitable task in social work. In the process of helping, worker must recognize the persons behaviour within the context of social environment since human being and environment are in separable. Social work knowledge includes psychology, law, environmental studies etc.

Critical thinking and analysis competency, thisinvolves enabling the process of making professional decisions in complex cases and situation. Social workers must evaluate the impact and benefit to service users.

Intervention and Skills competency, in social work involves complete assessment of the needs and problems of individual, group and community. Social worker employs different skills like communication, purposeful relationship, listening, observation for a desired outcome. Social worker drives knowledge from theory, research, practice experience to select appropriate intervention strategies.

Context and Organization competency: Social work is a human based profession it is essential to update the knowledge continuously and constantly to render quality service. Social worker must be aware of the emerging trend, technology developments, and policy changes that shape practice. It is necessary to inform and collaborate with other social workers, other professionals in the helping process of an individual, group and community.

Professional Leadership competency: Social workers must involve in ongoing professional development by participating in knowledge enhancement programmes and efforts to evaluate new and existing approaches. Professional leadership can be achieved through advance practice, educating others, actively involving in professional bodies and networks.

Based on the domains and descriptors the item selection was carried out.

Content Validity

After the items were selected and constructed it was subjected to validity testing. The authors framed 133 items comprising of all the nine domains. In-order to test the validity the authors used content validity method. At first level the items are validated on the grounds of logical inference and the relevance to the domains descriptors. Based on which few items were eliminated. Then the statements were subjected to grammatical, and meaning check, those statements that could be modified are retained and few are eliminated. In order to avoid the systematic bias, few statements are formulated as negative. Thus, the statements were formulated with at most care to retain the meaning and intensity of the words with reference to the subject matter.

Consultation with Expert

In the above process the items were reduced to 129 with both positively and negatively scored. Five experts in social work with relevant knowledge in the topic and experience were identified and the 129 items were given to them for content validity check. The experts were asked to review the statements, whether it reflects and measure the professional competencies of social workers. The experts gave suggestions over some items to be modified and removed. The authors removed 7 items based on the agreement among the five experts and modified 2 items. Thereby this process helps the authors to remove the poor items and finally 122 items were retained with content validity.

Reliability

The next step in the process of scale construction is checking the reliability of the items. There are many methods available to check the reliability of the items in the scale, one among is the item total correlation method. The authors using SPSS (Statistical package for Social Sciences) tested and found the reliability score. It was found that 4 items are having low item valve indicating the inefficiency in measuring the subject matter, hence those items were discarded. Finally, the Professional Competencies of Social Worker scale was constructed with 118 items both positive and negative scoring. The Cronbach alpha value of the final scale is presented below:

Table 4.1: Validity Score—Professional Competencies Scale

Professional Competencies Domain	*Frequency*	*Items*	*Cronbach Alpha*
Professionalism	304	18	0.896
Values and Ethical	304	17	0.917
Engage in Diversity and Equality	304	7	0.883
Rights, Justice and Economic Well being	304	11	0.880
Knowledge about Human Behaviour and Social Environment	304	14	0.885
Critical thinking and Analysis	304	5	0.858
Intervention and Skills	304	29	0.939
Contexts and Organizations	304	7	0.848
Professional Leadership	304	10	0.902
Total	**304**	**118**	**0.939**

Thus, the scale "Professional Competencies of Social Worker" was developed ensuring the validity and reliability using content validity method and item total correlation method respectively. The tool with overall reliability score 0.939, will measure the Professional Competencies and the nine domains of it.

CHAPTER 5

Demographic Profile

This chapter contains the analysed data with its interpretation. After the data collection the data were edited, coded and entered in the computer using SPSS – Ver 16.0 spread sheet. Then using this software data was analysed and presented in the form of tables and diagrams as follows, In Part – along with demographic variables, reason for choosing social work, perception, career ambition, aspiration, criticism faced and the professional competencies are analysed and presented in the form of tables and figures.

Table 5.1: Demographic Profile of the Respondents

Sl. No.	*Demographic Profile of the Respondents*		*Frequency*	*Percent*
1.	Age of the respondents (Years)	Below 22	152	50.0
		22–25	139	45.7
		25–29	13	4.3
2.	Gender of the respondents	Male	105	34.5
		Female	198	65.1
		Prefer not to say	1	0.3
3.	Educational Qualification of the respondents	II-year UG	76	25
		III-year UG	76	25
		II-year PG	152	50
4.	Respondents Under Graduate degree	BSW	69	22.7
		Other Degree	83	27.3
		NA (UG)	152	50
5.	Domicile of the respondents	Tamilnadu	257	84.5
		Outside Tamilnadu	47	15.5

Sl. No.	*Demographic Profile of the Respondents*		*Frequency*	*Percent*
6.	Major subject studied in 12th standard	Bio-Maths	59	19.4
		Computer Science	52	17.1
		Commerce	154	50.7
		Humanities	39	12.8
Total			**304**	**100**

The above table shows the age of the respondents. Half (50%) of the respondents are below the age of 22 years. Nearly half (45.7%) of the respondents are between the age of 22 and 25 years. Very few (4.3%) respondents are belonging the age category of 25 to 29 years. The study is conducted among the under graduate and post graduate students pursing social work. On an average students will be passing out from under graduate programme between 20 and 21 years and post-graduation will be completed between 23 and 24 years. However, this may vary for post-graduation depending on the factors like economic and family circumstances, and for few professional courses work experience is an added advantage.

Above two third (65.1%) of the respondents are female and more than one third (34.1%) of the respondents are male. One respondent was not preferred to say the gender. It is evident that at present girls are more interested to choose social work course rather than male.

The authors chosen the sample based on proportionate stratified random sampling. One fourth (25%) of the respondents pursuing II year under graduate social work and one fourth (25%) of the respondents pursuing III year under graduate social work, which constitute the half. The remaining half (50%) of the respondents are chosen who pursues their II-year post graduation social work.

The percentage of students under graduate degree those who are pursuing social work as their post-graduation is depicted in the table. Hence this is not applicable for half (50%) of the participants pursuing under graduate social work. Among the other half (50%) of the respondents 22.7% of the respondents completed social work in their under graduation and 27.3% of the respondents completed some other degree other than social work. The colleges offering under graduation is limited than post-graduate social work, the students pursed social work as their UG (22.7%) would prefer to pursue post-graduation in the same. On the other hand, those pursed UG other than social work (27.3%) is equally interested to pursue social work as their post-graduation. This shows evidently the increased demand for social work course.

As the study focused within Tamilnadu, majority (84.5%) participants are from Tamilnadu. Whereas 15.5% participants are from outside Tamilnadu. This shows the awareness about social work course and its importance especially in Tamilnadu.

Half (50%) of the respondents are from commerce subject background. 19.4% of the respondents are studied mathematics with biology as the major subjects in their 12th standard. 17.1% of the students are from computer science subject background and 12.8% of the respondents studied humanities subjects including history, economics, social sciences, etc.,

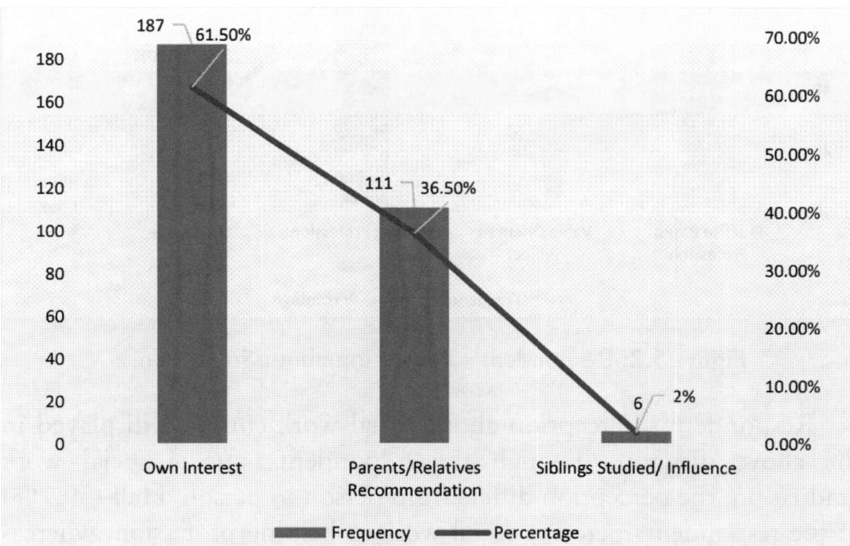

Figure 5.1: Respondent's Reason for Choosing Social Work

The above diagram shows the respondents reason for choosing social work as their graduation. Two third (61.5%) of the respondents chosen social work on their own interest, this interprets that many are aware about social work course and interested to study. In Indian scenario the decisions regarding higher studies and even career is chosen by parents, hence for one third (36.5%) of the respondents the parents and relatives recommended social work. On the other hand, it is evident that social work is recognized by parents too. Only 2% of the respondents recorded that their siblings studied or suggested to take social work as their career.

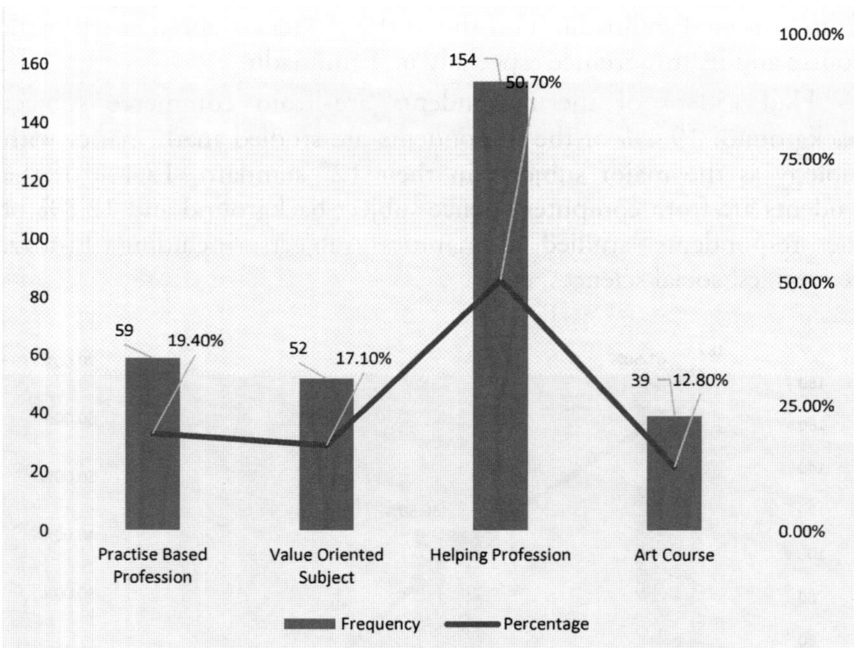

Figure 5.2: Respondent's Perception about Social Work

Respondent's perception about social work course is displayed in the above diagram. Though the respondents pursue social work graduation, the perception differs from person to person. Half (50.7%) of the respondents perceive social work as helping profession, whereas 19.4% of the respondents perceive social work as practice-based profession. Few (17.1%) respondents perceive social work as value-oriented subject and 12.8% of the respondents perceive social work as an art course. Thus, the respondents pursing social work have different perception about profession, hence it is not recognized widely.

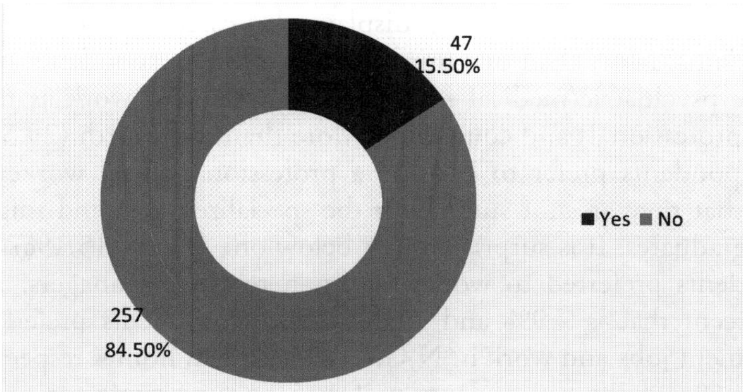

Figure 5.3: Family Members of the Respondents Studied Social Work

The above diagram shows the family members of the respondents studied social work. Majority (84.5%) of the respondent's family members didn't study social work, whereas 15.5% of the respondent's family member pursued social work. This shows that social work is slowly gaining momentum at present.

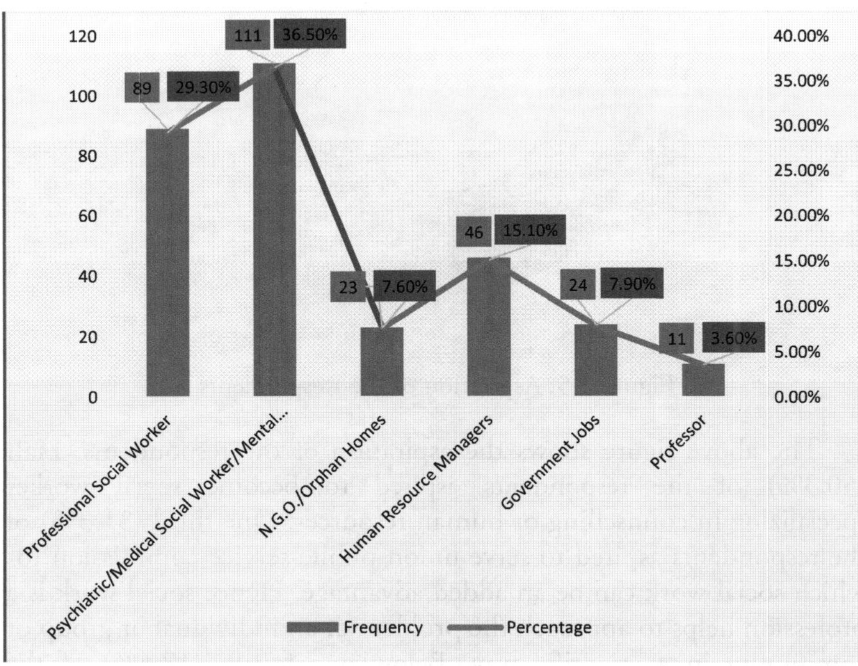

Figure 5.4: Career Ambition of the Respondents

The diagram (Figure 5.4) displays the career ambition of the respondents. More than one third (36.5%) of the respondents aims to become psychiatric/medical social worker, prefer to work as mental health professionals and counsellor. More than one fourth (29.3%) of the respondents prefer to become a professional social worker, this shows that they are not sure about the specialized area and might be under graduates. It is surprising that below one fourth (15.1%) of the respondents preferred to work as human resource managers. Below ten percent that is 7.9% and 7.6% of the respondents prefer to do government jobs and work in N.G. O's or orphan homes respectively. Only 3.6% of the respondents prefer to become professor to teach social work. This can be interpreted that most of the respondents are prefer to practice social work rather than teaching.

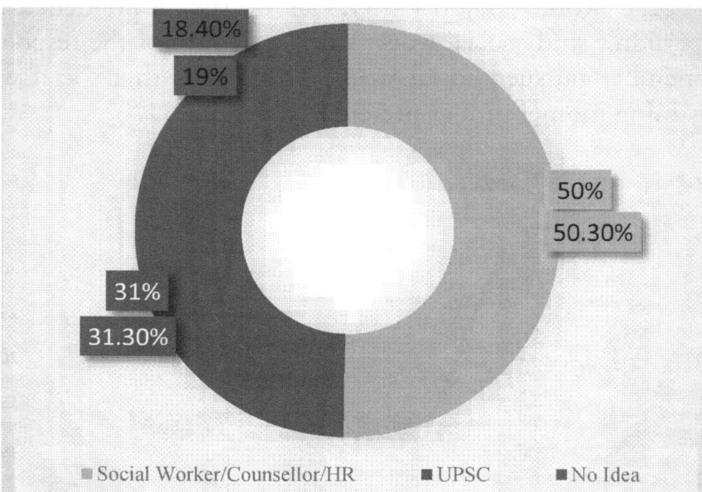

Figure 5.5: Aspiration of the Respondents

The above figure shows the aspiration of the respondents. Half (50.3%) of the respondents aspired to become social worker specializing in counselling or human resources. One third (31.3%) of the respondents aspired to serve union public service commission for which social work can be an added advantage. Hence social work is a profession helps to approach the problem of an individual or group or community in a scientific way. Below one fourth (18.4%) of the respondents are not having any idea.

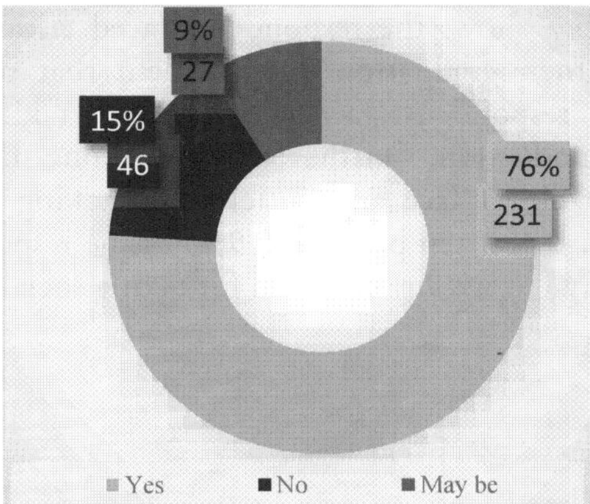

Figure 5.6: Respondent's Awareness about Social Work as a Professional Course

The above figure shows the respondent's awareness about social work as a professional course. This question was asked since many are not aware that social work is a professional course. More than two third (76%) of the respondents are aware that social work is a professional course, whereas below one fourth (15.1%) of the respondents are not aware that social work is a professional course. Below ten percent (8.9%) are in-between, whether social work is a professional course or not.

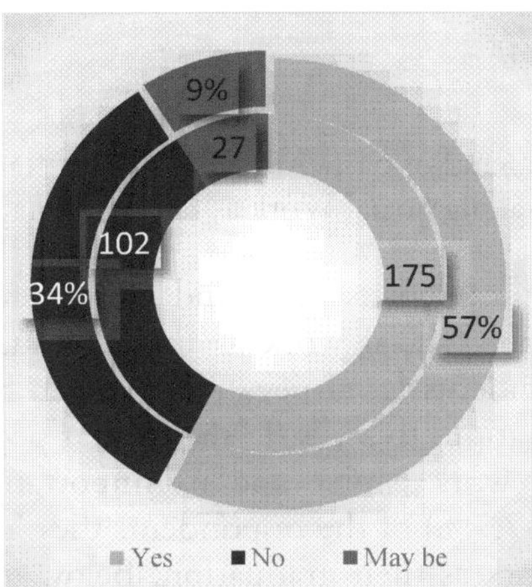

Figure 5.7: Respondents Faced Criticism for Taking Social Work as Their Graduation

The figure 5.7 shows the respondents faced criticism for taking social work as their graduation. It is evident that more than half (57.6%) of the respondents faced criticism for taking social work course as their graduation. On the other hand, one third (33.6%) of the respondents didn't face any criticism for taking social work as their graduation. Below ten percent (8.9%) of the respondents are not sure whether they receive any criticism for taking social work course.

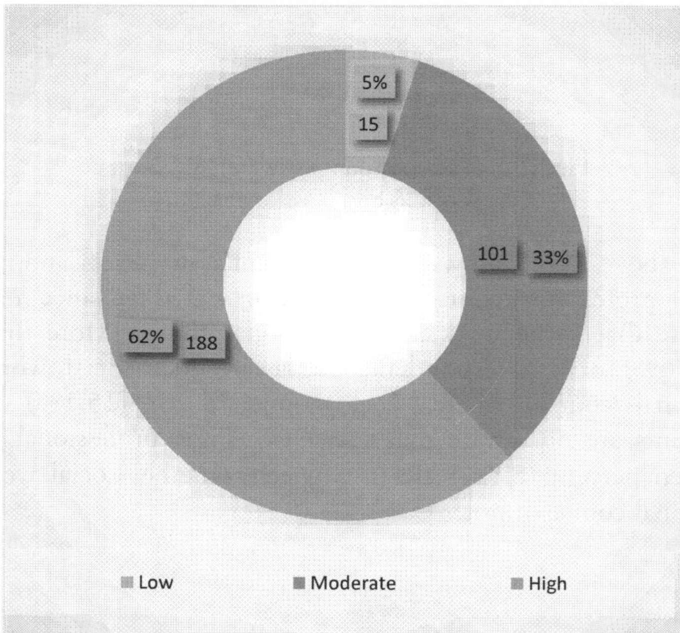

Figure 5.8: Kind of Criticism Faced by the Respondents for Taking Social Work as their Graduation

The above figure depicts the kind of criticism faced by the respondents for taking social work as their graduation. Nearly half (47%) of the respondents faced negative criticism for choosing social work as their graduation, this clearly shows that people are not much aware about social work course and its importance. On the other hand, nearly half (47.7%) of the respondents didn't face any criticism for taking social work as their graduation. Below ten percent (5.3%) of the respondents only had positive criticism for taking up social work career.

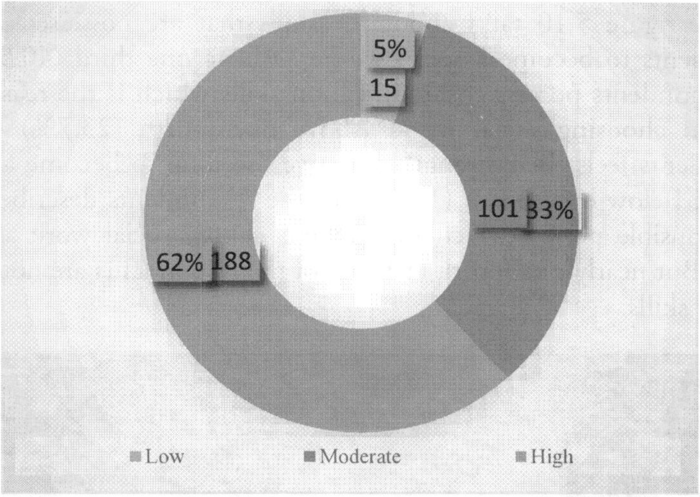

Figure 5.9: Respondents Feeling of Competent with Regard to Social Work

The respondents are pursuing social work; hence the authors would like to know whether the respondents feel competent. The above figure shows the respondents feeling of competent with regard to social work. Nearly half (48.4%) of the respondents feel that they are competent social worker. Whereas nearly half (49.7%) of the respondents are not confident to record that they are competent social work. Two percent of the respondents agrees that they are not competent social worker, this shows that they might need some support.

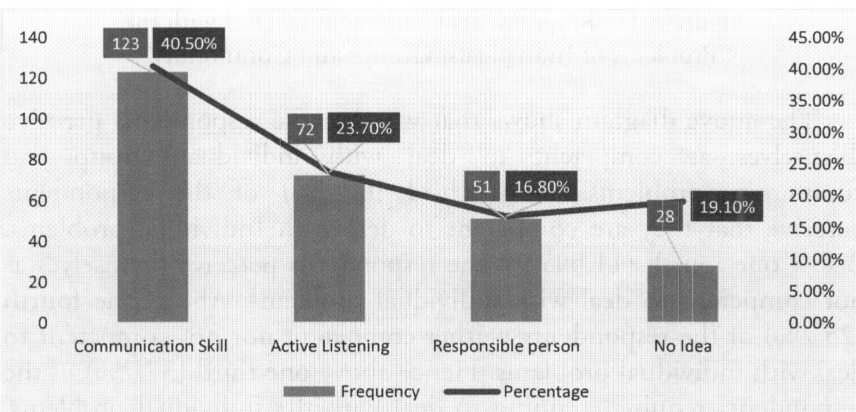

Figure 5.10: Respondent's Possession of Skills to Become a Social Worker

The figure 5.10 talks about the skills that are possessed by the respondents to become a social worker. Above one third (40.5%) of the respondents possess communication skills which is the reason for them in choosing social work. Above one fourth (23.7%) of the respondents feels their strength as active listening to become a social worker. Below one fourth (16.8%) of the respondents describe them as responsible person which made them choose social work as their career. But nearly one fourth (19.1%) of the respondents are not aware of their skills.

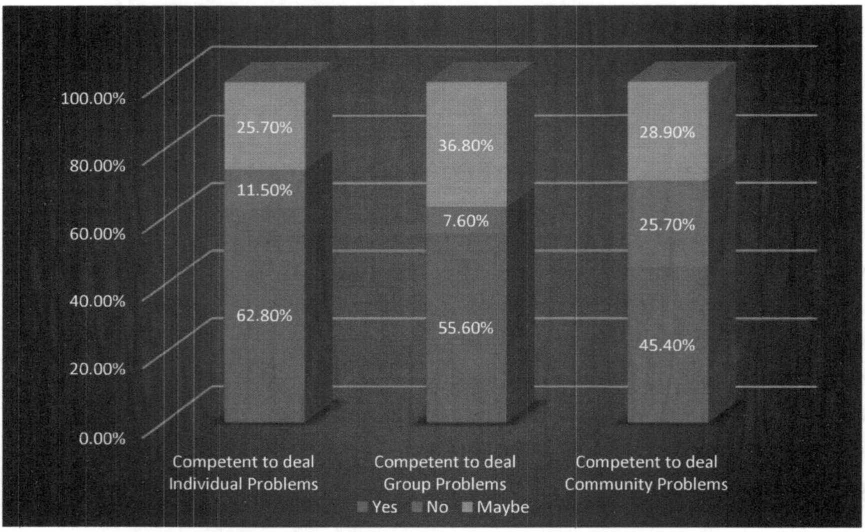

Figure 5.11: Respondents Competent to Deal with the Problems of Individuals, Groups and Community

The above diagram shows that whether the respondents perceive themselves as competent to deal with individual, group and community problems. Two Third (62.8%) of the respondents perceive that they are competent to deal with Individual problems. Below one fourth (11.5%) of the respondents perceive themselves as not competent to deal with individual problems. Above one fourth (25.7%) of the respondents neither competent nor not competent to deal with individual problems. Hence above one third (37.2%) of the respondents required training to deal with the individual problems. More than half (55.6%) of the respondents perceive that they are competent to deal with group problems. Above one third (36.8%) of the respondents perceive themselves neither competent nor not competent to deal with group problems. Below ten percent (7.6%) of the respondents perceive that they are not competent to deal with group problems. Hence nearly half (44.4%) of the respondents required training to deal with the group problems. Nearly half (45.4%) of the respondents perceive that they are competent to deal with community problems. Above one fourth (28.9%) of the respondents perceive themselves neither competent nor not competent to deal with community problems. Above one fourth (25.7%) of the respondents perceive that they are not competent to deal with community problems. Hence more than half (55%) of the respondents required training to deal with the community problems.

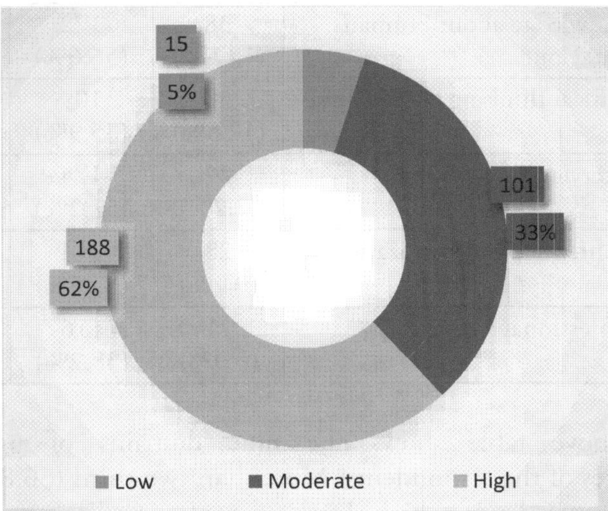

Figure 5.12: Level of Professional Competencies of Social Work Students

The above figure shows the level of professional competencies of the respondents. Two third (61.8%) of the respondents have high level of professional competencies, whereas more than one third (33.2%) of the respondents have moderate level of professional competencies. Only five percent (5%) of the respondents have low level of professional competencies.

Table 5.2: Domain Wise Level of Professional Competencies of the Respondents

Sl. No.	*Professional Competencies Domains*	*Level of Professional Competencies*		
		Low	*Moderate*	*High*
1.	Professionalism	10 (3.3%)	91 (29.9%)	203 (66.8%)
2.	Values and Ethical	19 (6.3%)	97 (31.9%)	188 (61.8%)
3.	Engage diversity and Equality	40 (13.2%)	160 (52.6%)	104 (34.2%)
4.	Rights, Justice and Economic Well being	30 (9.9%)	106 (34.9%)	168 (55.3%)
5.	Knowledge about Human Behaviour	38 (12.5%)	172 (56.6%)	94 (30.9%)
6.	Critical thinking and Analysis	38 (12.5%)	109 (35.9%)	157 (51.6%)
7.	Intervention and Skills	22 (7.2%)	174 (57.2%)	108 (35.5%)
8.	Contexts and Organization	28 (9.2%)	114 (37.5%)	162 (53.3%)
9.	Professional Leadership	21 (6.9%)	116 (38.2%)	167 (54.9%)

The above table shows the nine domains of professional competencies of the respondents. More than two third (66.8%) of the respondents are having high level of professionalism competency, whereas nearly one third (29.9%) of the respondents possess moderate level of professionalism competency. Three percent (3.3%) of the respondents are possessing low level of professionalism competency.

Two third (61.8%) of the respondents are having high level of values and Ethical competency, where as one third (31.9%) of the respondents possess moderate level of values and Ethical competency. Below ten percent (6.3%) of the respondents are possessing low level of values and Ethical competency.

Half (52.6%) of the respondents are having moderate level of engage diversity and equality competency, whereas more than one third (34.2%) of the respondents possess high level of engage diversity and equality of the competency. Below one fourth (13.2%) of the respondents possess low level of engage diversity and equality competency.

More than half (55.3%) of the respondents are having high level of competency with regard to rights, justice and economic well-being, whereas more than one third (34.9%) of the respondents possess moderate level of competency with regard to rights, justice and economic well-being. Nearly ten percent (9.9%) of the respondents possess low level of competency with regard to rights, justice and economic well-being.

More than half (56.6%) of the respondents are having moderate level of knowledge about human behaviour competency, whereas one third (30.9%) of the respondents possess high level of knowledge about human behaviour. Below one fourth (12.5%) of the respondents possess low level of knowledge competency about human behaviour.

Half (51.6%) of the respondents are having high level of competency with regard to critical thinking and analysis, whereas more than one fourth (35.9%) of the respondents possess moderate level of competency with regard to critical thinking and analysis. Below one fourth (12.5%) of the respondents possess low level of competency with regard to critical thinking and analysis.

More than half (57.2%) of the respondents are having moderate level of competency with regard to knowledge about intervention and skills, whereas more than one third (35.5%) of the respondents possess high level of competency with regard to knowledge about intervention and skills. Only seven percent (7.2%) of the respondents possess low of competency with regard to intervention and skills.

More than half (53.3%) of the respondents are having high level of competency about contexts and organization, whereas more than one third (37.5%) of the respondents possess moderate level of competency with regard to contexts and organization. Nearly ten percent (9.2%) of the respondents possess low level of competency with regard to contexts and organizations.

More than half (54.9%) of the respondents possess high level of professional leadership competency, whereas more than one third (38.2%) of the respondents possess moderate level of professional leadership competency. Nearly seven percent (6.9%) of the respondents possess low level of professional leadership competency.

CHAPTER 6

Demographic Variables of the Respondents...

In this chapter the demographic variables of the respondents are analyzed along with the career ambition, aspiration, criticism and their competency to deal with individual, group and community problems and presented in the form of tables.

Table 6.1: Age and Career Ambition of the Respondents

Age of the Respondents	*Career Ambition of the Respondents*						
	Professional Social Worker	*Psychiatry/ Medical Social Worker/Mental Health/Counsellor*	*N.G.O/Orphan Homes*	*Human Resource Manager*	*Govt. Jobs*	*Professor*	*Total*
Below 21	40 (13.2%)	61 (20.1%)	10 (3.3%)	25 (8.2%)	10 (3.3%)	6 (2.0%)	152 (50.0%)
21–25	47 (15.5%)	43 (14.1%)	12 (3.9%)	20 (6.6%)	13 (4.3%)	4 (1.3%)	139 (45.7%)
25–29	2 (0.7%)	7 (2.3%)	1 (0.3%)	1 (0.3%)	1 (0.3%)	1 (0.3%)	13 (4.3%)
Total	**89 (29.3%)**	**111 (36.5%)**	**23 (7.6%)**	**46 (15.1%)**	**24 (7.9%)**	**11 (3.6%)**	**304 (100%)**

The above cross table shows the age and career ambition of the respondents. Half (50.0%) of the respondents are below the age category of 21 years, among which one fourth (20.1%) of the respondents prefer to become psychiatry/medical social worker or mental health professionals or counsellors and below one fourth (13.2%) of the respondent's career ambition is to become a professional social worker. Eight percent (8.2%) of the respondents are prefer to become human resource managers, whereas three percent (3.3%) of the respondents would like to enter Government jobs or work with N.G.O/orphan homes. Only two percent (2%) of the respondents are aimed to become professor.

Between the age category of 21 and 25 years (45.7%), below one fourth (15.5%) of the respondents are prefer to become professional social worker and the remaining are distributed as 14.1% of the respondents prefer to become psychiatry/medical social worker or mental health professionals or counsellors, 6.6% of the respondents would prefer to become human resource manager, 4.3% of the respondents aim to enter Government jobs, 3.9% of the respondents prefer to work in N.G.O/orphan homes and only one percent (1.3%) of the respondents are aimed to become professor. Each of the respondents aspire to become professor, entering into Government jobs, human resource manager and to serve in an orphan home or N.G.O respectively, among the age category of 25 to 29 years (4.3%), and the remaining 2.3% of the respondents aspire to become psychiatry/medical social worker or mental health professionals or counsellors. From the table it is inferred that most preferred career by the respondents in all the age category is the medical/psychiatry/mental health professional/counsellor, followed by that is professional social worker and human resource managers and the least preferred is professor.

Table 6.2: Age and Aspiration of the Respondents

Aspiration of the Respondents				
Age of the Respondents	*Social Worker/ Counsellor/HR*	*UPSC*	*No Idea*	*Total*
Below 21	77 (25.3%)	49 (16.1%)	26 (8.6%)	152 (50.0%)
21–25	68 (22.4%)	43 (14.1%)	28 (9.2%)	139 (45.7%)
25–29	8 (2.6%)	3 (1.0%)	2 (0.7%)	13 (4.3%)
Total	**153 (50.3%)**	**95 (31.2%)**	**56 (18.4%)**	**304 (100%)**

The table 6.2 shows the age and aspiration of the respondents. Half (50%) of the respondents belong to the age category of below 21 years, among it one fourth (25.3%) of the respondents aspired to become a social worker/counsellor/HR, 16.1% of the respondents aspired to be civil servant and the remaining 8.6% of the respondents don't have any idea. Nearly half (45.7%) of the respondents belong to the age category of 21–25 years among which above one fourth (22.4%) of the respondents aspired to become a social worker/counsellor/HR, 14.1% of the respondents aspired to do civil service and the remaining 9.2% of the respondents not yet decided. Four percent (4.3%) of the respondents between the age category 25 and 29 years among which 2.6% of the respondents aspire to become a social worker/counsellor/HR, one percent aspire to be civil servant. It is inferred that among the three-age category majority of the respondents aspired to become a social worker/counsellor/HR, followed by that one third (31.2%) of the respondents aspired to become civil servants. But still below one fourth (18.4%) of the respondents are not having any idea.

Table 6.3: Age of the Respondents and their Competency to Deal with the Problems of Individuals

Competent to Deal with the Problems of Individuals				
Age of the Respondents	*Yes*	*No*	*May be*	*Total*
Below 21	91 (29.9%)	21 (6.9%)	40 (13.2%)	152 (50.0%)
21–25	88 (28.9%)	13 (4.3%)	38 (12.5%)	139 (45.7%)
25–29	12 (3.9%)	1 (0.3%)	0 (0.0%)	13 (4.3%)
Total	**191 (62.8%)**	**35 (11.5%)**	**78 (25.7%)**	**304 (100%)**

From the above table the age and their competency to deal with the problems of individuals is displayed. Among half (50%) of the respondents below the age category of 21 years, nearly one third (29.9%) of the respondents feel competent to deal with the problems of individuals, whereas 7% of the respondents doesn't feel competent to deal with individual problems. Between the age category of 21 and 25 years, above one fourth (28.9%) of the respondents feel competent to deal with individual problems, where as 4.3% of the respondents don't feel competent to deal with individual problems. Among 4.3% of the respondents between the age category 25 and 29 years, 3.9% of the respondents feel that they are competent to deal with individual problems and one respondent alone feel that not competent to deal with individual problems. From the table it is inferred that in all the three-age category above two third of the respondents feels competent to deal with individual problems, whereas above one fourth (25.7%) of the respondents are not confident about their competency in dealing with individual problems and 11.5% of the respondents are not feeling competent to deal the problems of individuals.

Table 6.4: Age of the Respondents and Their Competency to Deal with the Group Problems

Respondents Competent to Deal with the Group Problems				
Age of the Respondents	*Yes*	*No*	*May be*	*Total*
Below 21	90 (29.6%)	14 (4.6%)	48 (15.8%)	152 (50.0%)
21–25	69 (22.7%)	8 (2.6%)	62 (20.4%)	139 (45.7%)
25–29	10 (3.3%)	1 (0.3%)	2 (0.7%)	13 (4.3%)
Total	**169 (55.6%)**	**23 (7.6%)**	**112 (36.8%)**	**304 (100%)**

From the above table the age and their competency to deal with the group problems is displayed. Among half (50%) of the respondents below the age category of 21 years, nearly one third (29.6%) of the respondents feel competent to deal with the group problems, whereas nearly 5% of the respondents doesn't feel competent to deal with group problems and 15.8% of the respondents are not sure about their competency to deal with group problems. Between the age category of 21 and 25 years, above one fourth (22.7%) of the respondents feel competent to deal with individual problems, whereas 2.6% of the respondents don't feel competent to deal with group problems and one fourth (20.4%) of the respondents are not sure about their competency to deal with group problems. Among 4.3% of the respondents between the age category 25 and 29 years, 3.3% of the respondents feel that they are competent to deal with group problems and one respondent alone feel not competent to deal with group problems. From the table it is inferred that in all the three-age category above half (55.6%) of the respondents feels competent to deal group problems, whereas above one third (36.8%) of the respondents are not confident about their competency in dealing with group problems and 7.6% of the respondents are not feeling competent to deal with group problems.

Table 6.5: Gender and Career Ambition of the Respondents

	Career Ambition of the Respondents						
Gender of the Respondents	*Professional Social Worker*	*Psychiatry/Medical Social Worker/Mental Health/Counsellor*	*N.G.O/Orphan Homes*	*Human Resource Manager*	*Government Jobs*	*Professor*	*Total*
Prefer not to say	0 (0.0%)	0 (0.0%)	1 (0.3%)	0 (0.0%)	0 (0.0%)	0 (0.0%)	1 (0.3%)
Female	68 (22.4%)	68 (22.4%)	17 (5.6%)	21 (6.9%)	16 (5.3%)	8 (2.6%)	198 (65.1%)
Male	21 (6.9%)	43 (14.1%)	5 (1.6%)	25 (8.2%)	8 (2.6%)	3 (1.0%)	105 (34.5%)
Total	**89 29.3%)**	**111 36.5%)**	**23 (7.6%)**	**46 (15.1%)**	**24 (7.9%)**	**11 (3.6%)**	**304 (100%)**

The above cross table shows the gender and career ambition of the respondents. Among two third (65.1%) of the female respondents, equally one fourth (22.4%) of the respondent's career ambition is to become a professional social worker and medical/psychiatry/ mental health/counsellor, 6.9% of the respondent's career ambition is to become human resource manager, 5.6% and 5.3% of the respondent's career ambition is to work with an orphan home/non-governmental organization and Government Jobs respectively, and 2.6% of the respondent's career ambition is to become professor. Among one third of the male respondents' below one fourth (14.1%) of the respondents career ambition is to become a medical/psychiatry/mental health/counsellor, 8.2% of the respondents career ambition is to become a human resource manager, 6.9% of the respondents would like to become a professional social worker, 2.6% of the respondents career ambition is to become Government employees, 1.6% and 1% of the respondents career ambition is to work with an orphan home/non-governmental organization and professor respectively. 0.3% of the respondents, who prefer not to say would like to work with non-governmental organization/orphan homes. It is inferred from the table that most of the male and female respondents career ambition is to become psychiatry/medical social worker/mental health/counsellor and second preference is to become a professional social worker and the least preferred is to become professor.

Table 6.6: Gender and Aspiration of the Respondents

	Aspiration of the Respondents			
Gender of the Respondents	*Social Worker/ Counsellor/HR*	*UPSC*	*No Idea*	*Total*
Prefer not to say	0 (0.0%)	1 (0.3%)	0 (0.0%)	1 (0.3%)
Female	107 (35.2%)	59 (19.4%)	32 (10.5%)	198 (65.1%)
Male	46 (15.1%)	35 (11.5%)	24 (7.9%)	105 (34.5%)
Total	**153 (50.3%)**	**95 (31.2%)**	**56 (18.4%)**	**304 (100%)**

The above table shows the gender and aspiration of the respondents. Among two third (65.1%) of the female respondents, above one third (35.2%) of the respondents aspire to become social worker/counsellor/HR, nearly one fourth (19.4%) of the respondents aspire to enter union public service commission and 10.5% of the respondents doesn't have any idea. Among 34.5% of the male respondents 15.1% of the respondents aspire to become social worker/counsellor/HR, 11.5% of the respondents aspire to become civil servant and 7.9% of the respondents do not have any idea. 0.3% of the respondents who prefer not to say would aspire to write union public service commission exams. From the above table it is inferred that both male and female highly aspired to become a social worker/ counsellor/HR, secondly aspire to enter union public service commission and still 18.4% of the respondents doesn't aspire.

Table 6.7: Gender and Competency of the Respondents to Deal with Individual Problems

Respondents Competent to deal with the problems of Individuals				
Gender of the Respondents	***Yes***	***No***	***May be***	***Total***
Female	129 (42.4%)	26 (8.6%)	43 (14.1%)	198 (65.1%)
Male	61 (20.1%)	9 (3.0%)	35 (11.5%)	105 (34.5%)
Prefer not to say	1 (0.3%)	0 (0.0%)	0 (0.0%)	1 (0.3%)
Total	**191 (62.8%)**	**35 (11.5%)**	**78 (25.7%)**	**304 (100.0%)**

The above table shows the gender and competency of the respondents to deal with the problems of individuals. Among two third (65.1%) of the female respondents, 42.4% of the respondents feels competent to deal with the problems of individuals, 14.1% of the respondents are not confident in dealing with the problems of individuals and 8.6% of the respondents are not feeling competent to deal with the problems of an individual. Above one third (34.5%) of the male respondents, one fourth (20.1%) of the respondent feels competent to deal with the problems of individuals, 11.5% of the respondents are not confident in dealing with the problems of the individuals, whereas 3.0% of the respondents are not feeling competent to deal with the problems of individuals. One respondent who prefer not to say the gender, feels competent to deal with the problems of individuals. It is evident that two third (62.8%) of the respondents invariable of gender feels competent to deal with problems of individuals, whereas above one fourth of the respondents are not confident to deal with the problems of individuals and 11.5% of the respondents are not feeling confident to deal with individual problems.

Table 6.8: Gender and Respondents Competency to Deal with Group Problems

Respondents Competent to deal with the Group Problems				
Gender of the Respondents	*Yes*	*No*	*May be*	*Total*
Female	114 (37.5%)	18 (5.9%)	66 (21.7%)	198 (65.1%)
Male	54 (17.8%)	5 (1.6%)	46 (15.1%)	105 (34.5%)
Prefer not to say	1 (0.3%)	0 (0.0%)	0 (0.0%)	1 (0.3%)
Total	**169 (55.6%)**	**23 (7.6%)**	**112 (36.8%)**	**304 (100.0%)**

The above table shows the respondents gender and their competency to deal with the problems of groups. Among two third (65.1%) of the female respondents, 37.5% of the respondents feels competent to deal with the group problems, one fourth (21.7%) of the respondents are not confident to deal with the group problems, whereas 5.9% of the respondents feels that they are not competent to deal with group problems. Above one third (34.5%) of the male respondents, 17.8% of the respondents feels competent to deal with group problems, 15.1% of the respondents feels not confident to deal with group problems and 1.6% of the respondents feels not competent to deal with group problems. One respondent who prefer not to say the gender, feels competent to deal with the group problems. It is clear that above half (55.6%) of the respondents invariable of gender are competent to deal with the group problems, 36.8% of the respondents are not feeling confident in dealing with group problems and 7.6% of the respondents feels that they are not competent to deal with the problems of group.

Table 6.9: Educational Qualification and Career Ambition of the Respondents

Educational Qualification of the Respondents	*Career Ambition of the Respondents*						
	Professional Social Worker	*Psychiatry/Medical Social Worker/Mental Health/Counsellor*	*N.G.O/Orphan Homes*	*H.R.*	*Government Jobs*	*Professor*	*Total*
II & III BSW	43 (14.1%)	55 (18.1%)	11 (3.6%)	26 (8.6%)	12 (3.9%)	5 (1.6%)	152 (50%)
II MSW	46 (15.1%)	56 (18.4%)	12 (3.9%)	20 (6.6%)	12 (3.9%)	6 (2.0%)	152 (50%)
Total	**89 (29.3%)**	**111 (36.5%)**	**23 (7.6%)**	**46 (15.1%)**	**24 (7.9%)**	**11 (3.6%)**	**304 (100%)**

The above table shows the educational qualification and career ambition of the respondents. Among half (50.0%) of the under graduate II and III year respondents 18.1% of the respondents wants to become psychiatry/medical social worker/mental health/counsellor, 14.1% of the respondents career ambition is to become professional social worker, 8.6% of the respondents wants to become human resource managers, 3.9% and 3.6% of the respondents career ambition is to get government jobs and to enter non-governmental organization or orphan homes respectively, and 1.6% of the respondents career ambition is to become professor. Among half (50.0%) of the II year post graduate respondents, 18.4% of the respondents wants to become psychiatry/medical social worker/mental health/counsellor, 15.1% of the respondents career ambition is to become professional social worker, 6.6% of the respondents wants to become human resource managers, 3.9% of the respondents career ambition is to get government jobs and to enter non-governmental organization or orphan homes respectively and 2.0% of the respondents career ambition is to become professor. Form the table it is inferred that both under graduate and post graduate are equally thought of the career as psychiatry/medical social worker/mental health/counsellor, followed by that as professional social worker and least preferred career ambition is to become professor.

Table 6.10: Educational Qualification and Aspiration of the Respondents

Aspiration of the Respondents				
Educational Qualification of the Respondents	*Social Worker/ Counsellor/HR*	*UPSC*	*No Idea*	*Total*
II & III BSW	76 (25.0%)	47 (15.5%)	29 (9.5%)	152 (50.0%)
II MSW	77 (25.3%)	48 (15.8%)	27 (8.9%)	152 (50.0%)
Total	**153 (50.3%)**	**95 (31.2%)**	**56 (18.4%)**	**304 (100.0%)**

The above table shows the respondents educational qualification and their aspiration. Among the II and III years (50%) under graduate respondents 25% of the respondents aspire to become social worker/counsellor/HR,15.5% of the respondents aspire to become civil servant and 9.5% of the respondents do not have any idea. Among the II-year (50%) post graduate respondents, 25.3% of the respondents aspire to become social worker/counsellor/HR, 15.8% of the respondents aspire to become civil servant and 8.9% of the respondents doesn't have any idea with regard to their aspiration. It is evident that half (50%) of the under graduate and post graduate respondents aspire to become social worker/counsellor/H.R. and opted it as their career, whereas one third (31.2%) of the under graduate and post graduate respondents aspire to become civil servant and chosen social work and 18.4% of the under graduate and post graduate respondents without any idea chosen social work.

Table 6.11: Educational Qualification and Competency to Deal with Individual Problems

Respondents Competent to Deal with the Problems of Individuals				
Educational Qualification of the Respondents	*Yes*	*No*	*May be*	*Total*
II & III BSW	93 (30.6%)	17 (5.6%)	42 (13.8%)	152 (50.0%)
II MSW	98 (32.2%)	18 (5.9%)	36 (11.8%)	152 (50.0%)
Total	**191 (62.8%)**	**35 (11.5%)**	**78 (25.7%)**	**304 (100.0%)**

The above table shows the educational qualification of the respondents and their competency to deal with individual problems. Among the half (50%) of II and III years under graduate respondents one third (30.6%) of the respondents feels competent to deal with individual problems, 13.8% of the respondents are not confident in their competency to deal with individual problems and 5.6% of the respondents are not competent to deal with individual problems. Among the half (50%) of II year post graduate students, 32.2% of the respondents feels competent to deal with individual problems, 11.8% of the respondents are not confident in their competency to deal with individual problems and 5.9% of the respondents are not competent to deal with individual problems. It is evident from the above table that above two third (62.8%) of the respondents both under graduate and post graduate feels competent to deal with the problems of individuals, 25.7% of the respondents are not confident in their competency to deal with individual problems and 11.5% of the both under graduate and post graduate respondents are not competent to deal with individual problems.

Table 6.12: Educational Qualification and Competency to deal with Group Problems

Respondents Competent to Deal with the Group Problems				
Educational Qualification of the Respondents	*Yes*	*No*	*May be*	*Total*
II & III BSW	84 (27.6%)	12 (3.9%)	56 (18.4%)	152 (50.0%)
II MSW	85 (28.0%)	11 (3.6%)	56 (18.4%)	152 (50.0%)
Total	**169 (55.6%)**	**23 (7.6%)**	**112 (36.8%)**	**304 (100.0%)**

The above table depicts the educational qualification and respondent's competency to deal with group problems. Among the half (50%) of the II and III years under graduate respondents, above one fourth (27.6%) of the respondents feels competent to deal with group problems, 18.4% of the respondents are not confident in their competency to deal with group problems and 3.9% of the respondents are not competent to deal with the group problems. Among the half (50%) of the II years post graduates, more than one fourth (28%) of the respondents feels competent to deal with group problems, 18.4% of the respondents are not confident in their competency to deal with group problems and 3.6% of the respondents are not competent to deal with the group problems. It is evident that more than half (55.6%) of the both under graduate and post graduate are competent to deal with the group problems, whereas more than one third (36.8%) of the respondents belong to under graduate and post graduate are not confident in their competency to deal with the group problems and 7.6% are not competent to deal with the group problems.

Table 6.13: Post Graduate Respondents under Graduate Degree and their Career Ambition

	Career Ambition of the Respondents						
Post Graduate Respondent's UG Degree	*Professional Social Worker*	*Psychiatry/Medical Social Worker/Mental Health/Counsellor*	*N.G.O/Orphan Homes*	*H.R.*	*Government Jobs*	*Professor*	*Total*
BSW	21 (6.9%)	25 (8.2%)	4 (1.3%)	10 (3.3%)	7 (2.3%)	2 (0.7%)	69 (22.7%)
Other Degree	2 (8.2%)	31 (10.2%)	8 (2.6%)	10 (3.3%)	5 (1.6%)	4 (1.3%)	83 (27.3%)
NA (Pursuing Social Work UG)	43 (14.1%)	55 (18.1%)	11 (3.6%)	26 (8.6%)	12 (3.9%)	5 (1.6%)	152 (50.0%)
Total	**89 (29.3%)**	**111 (36.5%)**	**23 (7.6%)**	**46 (15.1%)**	**24 (7.9%)**	**11 (3.6%)**	**304 (100%)**

The above table shows the under graduate degree of post graduate respondents and their career ambition. Among the post graduate respondents who studied social work 8.2% of the respondents career ambition is to become psychiatry/medical social worker/mental health/ counsellor, 6.9% of the respondents career ambition is to become professional social worker, 3.3% of the respondents would like to become human resource managers, 2.3% of the respondents aimed to get government jobs, 1.3% of the respondents aimed to work in non-governmental organization/orphan homes and very least percent (0.7%) preferred to become professor. Among the post graduate respondents those who studied other than social work, 10.2% of the respondents career ambition is to become psychiatry/medical social worker/mental health/counsellor, 8.2% of the respondents career ambition is to become professional social worker, 3.3% of the respondents would like to become human resource managers,2.6% of the respondents aimed to work in non-governmental organization/ orphan homes, 1.6% and 1.3% of the respondents aimed to get government jobs and preferred to become professor respectively. It is understood from the above table that those who have not studied social work in their under graduation had social work career ambition equally with those who done social work in their under graduation.

Table 6.14: Post Graduate Respondents under Graduate Degree and their Aspiration

Aspiration of the Respondents				
Post Graduate Respondent's UG Degree	*Social Worker/ Counsellor/HR*	*UPSC*	*No Idea*	*Total*
BSW	31 (10.2%)	26 (8.6%)	12 (3.9%)	69 (22.7%)
Other Degree	46 (15.1%)	22 (7.2%)	15 (4.9%)	83 (27.3%)
NA (Pursuing Social Work UG)	76 (25.0%)	47 (15.5%)	29 (9.5%)	152 (50.0%)
Total	**153 (50.3%)**	**95 (31.2%)**	**56 (18.4%)**	**304 (100.0%)**

The above table depicts the post graduate respondents under graduate degree and their aspiration. Among the post graduate respondents who studied social work, 10.2% of the respondents aspire to become social worker/counsellor/HR, whereas 8.6% of the respondents aspire to do civil service and 3.9% of the respondents without any aspiration, chosen social work. Among the post graduate respondents those who studied other than social work, 15.1% of the respondents aspire to become social worker/counsellor/HR, 7.2% of the respondents aspire to become civil servant and 4.9% of the respondents chosen social work without any aspiration. It can be inferred from the above table that the respondents from other than social work background aspire to become social workers.

Table 6.15: Post Graduate Respondents under Graduate Degree and Their Competency to Deal with the Individual Problems

Respondents Competent to deal with the problems of Individuals				
Post Graduate Respondents Under Graduate Degree	***Yes***	***No***	***May be***	***Total***
BSW	42 (13.8%)	5 (1.6%)	22 (7.2%)	69 (22.7%)
Other Degree	56 (18.4%)	13 (4.3%)	14 (4.6%)	83 (27.3%)
NA (Pursuing Social Work UG)	93 (30.6%)	17 (5.6%)	42 (13.8%)	152 (50.0%)
Total	**191 (62.8%)**	**35 (11.5%)**	**78 (25.7%)**	**304 (100.0%)**

The above table shows the post graduate respondents under graduate degree and their competency to deal with the individual problems. Among the post graduate respondents who studied social work, 13.8% of the respondents feels competent to deal with individual problems whereas 7.2% of the respondents feels that they are not confident to deal with individual problems and least percent (1.6%) of the respondents feels not competent to deal with individual problems. Among the post graduate respondents those who studied other than social work, 18.4% of the respondents feels competent to deal with individual problems, whereas 4.6% of the respondents are not confident to deal with individual problems and 4.3% of the respondents feels not competent to deal with individual problems. It can be inferred that the more number respondents from other background feels competent to deal with individual problems than compared with respondents from social work background.

Table 6.16: Post Graduate Respondents under Graduate Degree and their Competency to Deal with the Group Problems

Respondents Competent to deal with the Group Problems				
Post Graduate Respondents Under Graduate Degree	***Yes***	***No***	***May be***	***Total***
BSW	34 (11.2%)	6 (2.0%)	29 (9.5%)	69 (22.7%)
Other Degree	51 (16.8%)	5 (1.6%)	27 (8.9%)	83 (27.3%)
NA (Pursuing Social Work UG)	84 (27.6%)	12 (3.9%)	56 (18.4%)	152 (50.0%)
Total	**169 (55.6%)**	**23 (7.6%)**	**112 (36.8%)**	**304 (100%)**

The above table depicts the post graduate respondents under graduate degree and their competency to deal with group problems. Among the post graduate respondents who studied social work, 11.2% of the respondents feels competent to deal with the group problems, 9.5% of the respondents are not confident in their competency to deal with group problems and least percent (2.0%) of the respondents feels they are not competent to deal with the group problems. Among the post graduate respondents those who studied other than social work,16.8% of the respondents feels competent to deal the group problems, whereas 8.9% of the respondents are not confident in their competency and least percent (1.6%) of the respondents feels not competent to deal with group problems. It can be inferred that the more numbers respondents from other background feels competent to deal with group problems than compared with respondents from social work background.

Table 6.17: Domicile and Career Ambition of the Respondents

Career Ambition of the Respondents							
Domicile of the Respondents	*Professional Social Worker*	*Psychiatry/Medical Social Worker/Mental Health/Counsellor*	*N.G.O/Orphan Homes*	*H.R.*	*Government Jobs*	*Professor*	*Total*
Tamil Nadu	73 (24.0%)	97 (31.9%)	19 (6.2%)	39 (12.8%)	20 (6.6%)	9 (3.0%)	257 (84.5%)
Outside Tamil Nadu	16 (5.3%)	14 (4.6%)	4 (1.3%)	7 (2.3%)	4 (1.3%)	2 (0.7%)	47 (15.5%)
Total	**89 (29.3%)**	**111 (36.5%)**	**23 (7.6%)**	**46 (15.1%)**	**24 (7.9%)**	**11 (3.6%)**	**304 (100%)**

The above table depicts the domicile and career ambition of the respondents. Majority (84.5%) of the respondents are within Tamilnadu, among them, one third (31.9%) of the respondents career ambition is to become psychiatry/medical social worker, mental health/counsellor, 24% of the respondents ambition is to become professional social worker, 12.8% of the respondents ambition is to become human resource manager, 6.6% and 6.2% of the respondents aimed to get government jobs and work in nongovernmental organization respectively, and least percent (3%) of the respondents aimed to become professor. Less number of respondents (15.5%) are from outside Tamilnadu among which 5.3% of the respondent's career respondents is to become professional social worker, followed by that 4.6% of the respondent's ambition is to become psychiatry/medical social worker/mental health/counsellor. 2.3% of the respondents from outside Tamilnadu would aim to become human resource managers whereas 1.3% of the respondents equally aimed to work in non-governmental/orphan homes and to get government jobs respectively. Very least percent (0.7%) of the respondents from outside Tamilnadu prefer become professor.

Table 6.18: Domicile and Aspiration of the Respondents

Aspiration of the Respondents				
Domicile of the Respondents	*Social Worker/ Counsellor/HR*	*UPSC*	*No Idea*	*Total*
Tamil Nadu	123 (40.5%)	86 (28.3%)	48 (15.8%)	257 (84.5%)
Outside Tamil Nadu	30 (9.9%)	9 (3.0%)	8 (2.6%)	47 (15.5%)
Total	**153 (50.3%)**	**95 (31.2%)**	**56 (18.4%)**	**304 (100.0%)**

The above table shows the domicile and aspiration of the respondents. Above one third (40.5%) of the respondents from Tamilnadu aspire to become social worker/counsellor/HR, whereas 28.3% of the respondents aspire to become civil servants and 15.8% of the respondents didn't have any aspiration. Among 15.5% of the respondents from outside Tamilnadu, 9.9% of the respondents aspire to become social worker/counsellor/HR, 3% of the respondents aspire to become civil servant and 2.6% of the respondents without any aspiration chosen social work. From the above table it can be inferred that majority of the respondents from Tamilnadu had aspiration to become social worker and chosen social work.

Table 6.19: Domicile and Competency of the Respondents to Deal with Individual Problems

Respondents Competency to deal with the problems of Individuals				
Domicile of the Respondents	*Yes*	*No*	*May be*	*Total*
Tamil Nadu	160 (52.6%)	28 (9.2%)	69 (22.7%)	257 (84.5%)
Outside Tamil Nadu	31 (10.2%)	7 (2.3%)	9 (3.0%)	47 (15.5%)
Total	**191 (62.8%)**	**35 (11.5%)**	**78 (25.7%)**	**304 (100.0%)**

The above table depicts the domicile of the respondents and their competency to deal with individual problems. More than half

(52.6%) of the respondents from Tamilnadu feels competent to deal with problems of individual, whereas 22.7% of the respondents are not confident in their competency to deal with individual problems and 9.2% of the respondents feels that they are not competent to deal with individual problems. Among the respondents form outside Tamilnadu (15.5%) below one fourth (10.2%) of the respondents feels competent to deal with individual problems, whereas 3% and 2.3% of the respondents are not confident and not competent to deal with individual problems respectively. It can be inferred that two third (62.8%) of the respondents invariable of their domicile feels competent to deal with individual problems.

Table 6.20: Domicile and Competency of the Respondents to Deal with Group Problems

Respondents Competent to Deal with the Group Problems				
Domicile of the Respondents	*Yes*	*No*	*May be*	*Total*
Tamil Nadu	139 (45.7%)	17 (5.6%)	101 (33.2%)	257 (84.5%)
Outside Tamil Nadu	30 (9.9%)	6 (2.0%)	11 (3.6%)	47 (15.5%)
Total	**169 (55.6%)**	**23 (7.6%)**	**112 (36.8%)**	**304 (100.0%)**

The above table depicts the domicile of the respondents and their competency to deal with group problems. Below half (45.7%) of the respondents from Tamilnadu feels competent to deal with group problems, whereas 33.2% of the respondents are not confident in their competency to deal with group problems and 5.6% of the respondents are not feeling competent. Among the respondents from outside Tamilnadu, 9.9% of the respondents feels competent to deal with group problems, 3.6% are not confident in their competency, whereas 2% of the respondents feels not competent to deal with group problems. It can be inferred that more than half (55.6%) of the respondents invariable of their domicile feels competent to deal with group problems.

Table 6.21: Major Subjects Studied During 12th Standard and Career Ambition of the Respondents

	Career Ambition of the Respondents						
Major subjects studied by the Respondents during 12th Standard	*Professional Social Worker*	*Psychiatry/Medical Social Worker/Mental Health/ Counsellor*	*N.G.O/Orphan Homes*	*H.R.*	*Government Jobs*	*Professor*	*Total*
Bio-Maths	23 (7.6%)	29 (9.5%)	1 (0.3%)	6 (2.0%)	0 (0.0%)	0 (0.0%)	59 (19.4%)
Computer Sciences	11 (3.6%)	17 (5.6%)	0 (0.0%)	18 (5.9%)	1 (0.3%)	5 (1.6%)	52 (17.1%)
Commerce	45 (14.8%)	48 (15.8%)	16 (5.3%)	22 (7.2%)	17 (5.6%)	6 (2.0%)	154 (50.7%)
Humanities	10 (3.3%)	17 (5.6%)	6 (2.0%)	0 (0.0%)	6 (2.0%)	0 (0.0%)	39 (12.8%)
Total	**89 (29.3%)**	**111 (36.5%)**	**23 (7.6%)**	**46 (15.1%)**	**24 (7.9%)**	**11 (3.6%)**	**304 (100.0%)**

The above table shows the major subjects studied during 12th standard by the respondents and their career ambition. Below ten percent (9.5%) of the respondents studied bio-maths during 12th standard wish to become psychiatry/medical social worker/mental health/counsellor, whereas 7.6% of the respondent's career ambition is to become professional social worker, 2% of the respondent's ambition to become human resource manager and very least percent (0.3%) respondents aimed to work with non-governmental organization/orphan homes. 5.9% and 5.6% of the respondents who pursued computer science during 12th standard aimed to become human resource manager and psychiatry/medical social worker/mental health/counsellor respectively, whereas 3.6% of the respondents aimed to become professional social worker, 1.6% of the respondents wants to become professor and one respondent aimed for government job. Half (50%) of the respondents pursuing social work are from commerce background, among them 15.8% of the respondents career ambition is to become psychiatry/medical social worker/mental health/ counsellor, 14.8% of the respondents wants to become professional social worker, 7.2% of the respondents aimed to become human resource manager, 5.6% and 5.3% of the respondents aimed to become government employee and to work with non-governmental organization respectively and 2% percent of the respondents wants to become professor. 5.6% of the respondents, who pursued humanities aimed to become psychiatry/medical social worker/mental health/ counsellor, 3.3% of the respondents wants to become professional social worker and 2% of the respondents wants to become professor and government employee respectively.

Table 6.22: Major Subjects Studied During 12th Standard and Aspiration of the Respondents

	Aspiration of the Respondents			
Major Subjects Studied by the Respondents during 12th Standard	*Social Worker/ Counsellor/HR*	*UPSC*	*No Idea*	*Total*
Bio-Maths	18 (5.9%)	35 (11.5%)	6 (2.0%)	59 (19.4%)
Computer Sciences	40 (13.2%)	6 (2.0%)	6 (2.0%)	52 (17.1%)
Commerce	62 (20.4%)	48 (15.8%)	44 (14.5%)	154 (50.7%)
Humanities	33 (10.9%)	6 (2.0%)	0 (0.0%)	39 (12.8%)
Total	**153 (50.3%)**	**95 (31.2%)**	**56 (18.4%)**	**304 (100.0%)**

The above table depicts the major subjects studied during 12th standard by the respondents and their aspiration. 11.5% of the respondents who studied bio-maths subject in their 12th standard aspire to become civil servant, whereas 5.9% of the respondents aspire to become social worker/counsellor/HR and 2% of the respondents without any aspiration chosen social work. Among the respondents who studied computer science in their 12th standard 13.2% of the respondents aspire to become social worker/counsellor/HR, whereas 2% of the respondents aspire to become civil servant and 2% of the respondents without any aspiration chosen social work. Half (50%) of the respondents pursuing social work are from commerce background, among them one fourth (20.4%) of the respondents aspire to become social worker/counsellor/HR, whereas 15.8% of the respondents aspire to become civil servants and 14.5% of the respondents without any aspiration chosen social work. Among the respondents who studied humanities in their 12th standard, 10.9% of the respondents aspire to become social worker/counsellor/HR, and 2% of the respondents aspire to become civil servants. From the table it can inferred that most of the respondents had aspire to become social worker and chosen social work

Table 6.23: Major Subjects Studied during 12th Standard and Competency of the Respondents to Deal with Individual Problems

Respondents Competent to deal with the problems of Individuals				
Major subjects studied by the Respondents during 12th Standard	*Yes*	*No*	*May be*	*Total*
Bio-Maths	47 (15.5%)	6 (2.0%)	6 (2.0%)	59 (19.4%)
Computer Sciences	29 (9.5%)	12 (3.9%)	11 (3.6%)	52 (17.1%)
Commerce	99 (32.6%)	11 (3.6%)	44 (14.5%)	154 (50.7%)
Humanities	16 (5.3%)	6 (2.0%)	17 (5.6%)	39 (12.8%)
Total	**191 (62.8%)**	**35 (11.5%)**	**78 (25.7%)**	**304 (100.0%)**

The above table shows the respondents major subjects studied during 12th standard and their competency to deal with the individual problems. Among the respondents pursued bio-maths during 12th standard, 15.5% of the respondents feels competent to deal with individual problems, whereas 2% of the respondents are not confident in their competency and 2% of the respondents feels not competent to deal with individual problems. Among 17% of the respondents pursued computer science during 12th standard, 9.5% of the respondents feels competent to deal with individual problems, 3.9% of the respondents are not feeling competent whereas 3.6% of the respondents are not confident in their competency to deal with individual problems. Half (50%) of the respondents pursuing social work are from commerce background, among them above one third (32.6%) of the respondents feels competent to deal with individual problems, 14.5% of the respondents are not confident in their competency and 3.6% of the respondents are feeling not competent to deal with individual problems. Among the respondents who pursued humanities during 12th standard, 5.3% of the respondents feels competent to deal with individual problems, 5.6% of the respondents are not confident in their competency and 2% of the respondents are feeling not competent to deal with individual problems. It can be inferred that most of the respondents feels competent to deal with individual problems invariable of the subjects studied during 12th standard but yet one fourth of the respondents are not confident in their competency.

Table 6.24: Major Subjects Studied During 12th Standard and Competency of the Respondents to Deal with Group Problems

Respondents Competent to Deal with the Group Problems				
Major Subjects Studied by the Respondents during 12th Standard	Yes	*No*	*May be*	*Total*
Bio-Maths	47 (15.5%)	6 (2.0%)	6 (2.0%)	59 (19.4%)
Computer Sciences	29 (9.5%)	0 (0.0%)	23 (7.6%)	52 (17.1%)
Commerce	76 (25.0%)	6 (2.0%)	72 (23.7%)	154 (50.7%)
Humanities	17 (5.6%)	11 (3.6%)	11 (3.6%)	39 (12.8%)
Total	**169 (55.6%)**	**23 (7.6%)**	**112 (36.8%)**	**304 (100.0%)**

The table 6.24 shows the respondents major subjects studied during 12th standard and their competency to deal with group problems. Among the respondents pursued bio-maths during 12th standard, 15.5% of the respondents feels competent to deal with group problems, whereas 2% of the respondents feeling not competent and 2% of the respondents are not confident in their competency to deal with group problems. Among 17% of the respondents pursued computer science during 12th standard, 9.5% of the respondents feels competent to deal with group problems and 7.6% of the respondents are not confident in their competency to deal with group problems. Half (50%) of the respondents pursuing social work are from commerce background, among them 25% of the respondents feels competent to deal with group problems, whereas 23.7% of the respondents are not confident in their competency and 2% of the respondents are feeling not competent to deal with group problems. Among the respondents who pursued humanities during 12th standard, 5.6% of the respondents feels competent to deals with group problems, whereas 3.6% are not feeling competent and 3.6% are not confident in their competency to deal with group problems. It can be inferred that most of the respondents feels competent to deal with group problems invariable of the subjects studied during 12th standard but yet more than one third of the respondents are not confident in their competency.

CHAPTER 7

Level of Professionalism Competency

This chapter involves the analysis and interpretation of level of professionalism competency and demographic variable, reason for choosing social work, perception, career ambition, aspiration, criticism faced and social worker skills.

Table 7.1: Age of the Respondents and the Level of Professionalism Competency

Age of the Respondents	*Level of Professionalism Competency*			*Total*
	Low	*Moderate*	*High*	
Below 21	7 (70.0%)	44 (48.4%)	101 (49.8%)	152 (50.0%)
21–25	3 (30.0%)	42 (46.2%)	94 (46.3%)	139 (45.7%)
25-29	0 (0.0%)	5 (5.5%)	8 (3.9%)	13 (4.3%)
Total	**10 (100%)**	**91 (100%)**	**203 (100%)**	**304 (100%)**

The above table represents the level of professionalism based on the age of the respondents. Among the respondents below the age of 21 years, 70% of the respondents possess low level, 49.8% possess high level and 48.4% possess moderate level of professionalism competency. Among the respondents between the age of 21 and 25 years, 46.3% possess high level, 46.2% possess moderate level and 30% of the respondents possess low level of professionalism competency. Among the respondents between the age 25 and 29 years, 5.5% of the respondents possess moderate level and 3.9% of the respondents possess high level of professionalism competency.

Table 7.2: Gender of the Respondents and the Level of Professionalism Competency

Gender of the Respondents	*Level of Professionalism Competency*			*Total*
	Low	*Moderate*	*High*	
Prefer not to say	0 (0.0%)	0 (0.0%)	1 (0.5%)	1 (0.3%)
Female	4 (40.0%)	58 (63.7%)	136 (67.0%)	198 (65.1%)
Male	6 (60.0%)	33 (36.3%)	66 (32.5%)	105 (34.5%)
Total	**10 (100%)**	**91 (100%)**	**203 (100%)**	**304 (100%)**

The above table represents the level of professionalism competency based on respondent's gender. The level of professionalism competency among the female are high for 67% respondents, it is moderate for 63.7% respondents, low for 40.0% respondents. The level of professionalism competency among the male gender are low for 60% respondents, moderate for 36.3% respondents and high for 32.5% of the respondents. .5% of the respondent who prefer not to say the gender, possess high level of professionalism competency.

Table 7.3: Educational Qualification of the Respondents and the Level of Professionalism Competency

Educational Qualification of the Respondents	*Level of Professionalism*			*Total*
	Low	*Moderate*	*High*	
II & III BSW	7 (70.0%)	52 (57.1%)	93 (45.8%)	152 (50.0%)
II MSW	3 (30.0%)	39 (42.9%)	110 (54.2%)	152 (50.0%)
Total	**10 (100.0%)**	**91 (100.0%)**	**203 (100.0%)**	**304 (100.0%)**

The above table represents the level of professionalism competency based on respondent's educational qualification. The level of professionalism competency among the respondents pursuing II- & III-year BSW is low for 70.0% respondents, moderate for 57.1% respondents, and high for 45.8% respondents. The level of professionalism competency among the respondents pursuing II-year MSW, high for 54.2% respondents, moderate for 42.9% respondents and low for 30% respondents.

Table 7.4: Post Graduate Respondents Under-graduation and the Level of Professionalism Competency

Post Graduate Respondents Under-graduation	*Level of Professionalism Competency*			*Total*
	Low	*Moderate*	*High*	
BSW	1 (10.0%)	14 (15.4%)	54 (26.6%)	69 (22.7%)
Other Degree	2 (20.0%)	25 (27.5%)	56 (27.6%)	83 (27.3%)
Not Applicable (Respondents pursuing Under-Graduation)	7 (70.0%)	52 (57.1%)	93 (45.8%)	152 (50.0%)
Total	**10 (100.0%)**	**91 (100.0%)**	**203 (100.0%)**	**304 (100.0%)**

The above table represents the level of professionalism competency based on post graduate respondents Under-graduation. Among the post graduate respondents, who pursued social work in their under graduate, 26.6% of the respondents possess high level of professionalism competency, 15.4% possess moderate level and 10% possess low level of professionalism competency. Among the respondents, who pursued subjects other than social work during their under graduation, 27.6% of the respondents possess high level, 27.5% of the respondents possess moderate level and 20% possess low level of professionalism competency.

Table 7.5: Domicile of the Respondents and the Level of Professionalism Competency

Domicile of the Respondents	*Level of Professionalism Competency*			*Total*
	Low	*Moderate*	*High*	
Tamil Nadu	10 (100.0%)	75 (82.4%)	172 (84.7%)	257 (84.5%)
Outside Tamil Nadu	0 (0.0%)	16 (17.6%)	31 (15.3%)	47 (15.5%)
Total	**10 (100.0%)**	**91 (100.0%)**	**203 (100.0%)**	**304 (100.0%)**

The above table represents the level of professionalism competency based on respondent's domicile. Among the respondents from Tamilnadu, 100% possess low level, 84.7% possess high level and 82.4% of the respondents possess moderate level of professionalism competency. Among the respondents from outside Tamilnadu, 17.6% of the respondents possess moderate level and 15.3% of the respondents possess high level of professionalism competency.

Table 7.6: Major Subjects Studied by the Respondents during 12th Standard and the Level of Professionalism Competency

Major Subjects Studied by the Respondents during 12th	*Level of Professionalism Competency*			*Total*
	Low	*Moderate*	*High*	
Bio Maths	1 (10.0%)	18 (19.8%)	40 (19.7%)	59 (19.4%)
Computer Sciences	2 (20.0%)	16 (17.6%)	34 (16.7%)	52 (17.1%)
Commerce	4 (40.0%)	46 (50.5%)	104 (51.2%)	154 (50.7%)
Humanities	3 (30.0%)	11 (12.1%)	25 (12.3%)	39 (12.8%)
Total	**10 (100.0%)**	**91 (100.0%)**	**203 (100.0%)**	**304 (100.0%)**

The table 7.6 represents the level of professionalism competency based on respondent's major subject studied during 12th standard. Among the respondents who pursued Bio-maths during 12th standard, 19.8% possess moderate level, 19.7% possess high level and 10% possess low level of professionalism competency. Among the respondents who pursued computer sciences during 12th standard, 20% possess low level, 17.6% possess moderate level and 16.7% possess high level of professionalism competency. Among the respondents who pursued commerce, during 12th standard, 51.2% of the respondents possess high level, 50.5% possess moderate level and 40% possess low level of professionalism competency. Among the respondents who pursued humanities during 12th standard, 30% possess low level, 12.3% possess high level and 12.1% possess moderate level of professionalism competency.

Table 7.7: Respondents Reasons for Choosing Social Work and the Level of Professionalism Competency

Respondent's Reasons for Choosing Social Work	*Level of Professionalism Competency*			*Total*
	Low	*Moderate*	*High*	
Own Interest	7 (70.0%)	57 (62.6%)	123 (60.6%)	187 (61.5%)
Parents/Relatives Recommendation	3 (30.0%)	32 (35.2%)	76 (37.4%)	111 (36.5%)
Siblings Studied/Influence	0 (0.0%)	2 (2.2%)	4 (2.0%)	6 (2.0%)
Total	**10 (100.0%)**	**91 (100.0%)**	**203 (100.0%)**	**304 (100.0%)**

The above table represents the level of professionalism competency based on respondent's reasons for choosing social work. Among the respondents who chose social work on their own interest, 70% of the respondents possess low level, 62.6% of the respondents possess moderate level and 60.6% of the respondents possess high level of professionalism competency. Among the respondents who chose social work because of the parents/relative recommendation, 37.4% possess high level, 35.2% possess moderate level and 30% possess low level of professionalism competency. Among the respondents who chose social work because of the siblings studied social work/influenced, 2.2% of the respondents possess moderate level and 2% possess high level of professionalism competency.

Table 7.8: Respondents Perception about Social Work and the Level of Professionalism Competency

Respondents Perception about Social Work	*Level of Professionalism Competency*			*Total*
	Low	*Moderate*	*High*	
Practise Based Profession	1 (10.0%)	18 (19.8%)	40 (19.7%)	59 (19.4%)
Value Oriented Subject	2 (20.0%)	16 (17.6%)	34 (16.7%)	52 (17.1%)
Helping Profession	4 (40.0%)	46 (50.5%)	104 (51.2%)	154 (50.7%)
Art Course	3 (30.0%)	11 (12.1%)	25 (12.3%)	39 (12.8%)
Total	**10 (100.0%)**	**91 (100.0%)**	**203 (100.0%)**	**304 (100%)**

The above table represents the level of professionalism competency based on respondent's perception about social work. Among the respondents who perceive social work as practice-based profession, 19.8% possess moderate level, 19.7% possess high level and 10% possess low level of professionalism competency. Among the respondents who perceive social work as value-oriented subject, 20% possess low level, 17.6% possess moderate level and 16.7% of the respondents possess high level of professionalism competency. Among the respondents who perceive social work as helping profession, 51.2% possess high level, 50.5% possess moderate level and 40% possess low level of professionalism competency. Among the respondents who perceive social work as art course, 30% possess low level, 12.3% possess high level and 12.1% possess moderate level of professionalism competency.

Table 7.9: Family Members of the Respondents studied Social Work and the Level of Professionalism Competency

Family Members of the Respondents Studied Social Work	*Level of Professionalism Competency*			*Total*
	Low	*Moderate*	*High*	
Yes	1 (10.0%)	13 (14.3%)	33 (16.3%)	47 (15.5%)
No	9 (90.0%)	78 (85.7%)	170 (83.7%)	257 (84.5%)
Total	**10 (100.0%)**	**91 (100.0%)**	**203 (100.0%)**	**304 (100.0%)**

The above table represents the level of professionalism competency based on respondent's family members studied social work. Among the respondent's family members who pursued social work, 16.3% of the respondents possess high level, 14.3% possess moderate level and 10% possess low level of professionalism competency. Among the respondent's family members who haven't studied social work subject, 90% possess low level, 85.7% possess moderate level and 83.7% possess high level of professionalism competency.

Table 7.10: Career Ambition of the Respondents and the Level of Professionalism Competency

Career Ambition of the Respondents	*Level of Professionalism Competency*			*Total*
	Low	*Moderate*	*High*	
Professional Social Worker	2 (20.0%)	24 (26.4%)	63 (31.0%)	89 (29.3%)
Psychiatric/Medical Social Worker/Mental Health/Counsellor	5 (50.0%)	34 (37.4%)	72 (35.5%)	111 (36.5)
N.G.O/Orphan Homes	0 (0.0%)	9 (9.9%)	14 (16.9%)	23 (7.6%)
Human Resource Mangers	1 (10.0%)	13 (14.3%)	32 (15.8%)	46 (15.1%)

Career Ambition of the Respondents	*Level of Professionalism Competency*			*Total*
	Low	*Moderate*	*High*	
Government Jobs	1 (10.0%)	6 (6.6%)	17 (8.4%)	24 (7.9%)
Professor	1 (10.0%)	5 (5.5%)	5 (2.5%)	11 (3.6%)
Total	**10 (100.0%)**	**91 (100.0%)**	**203 (100.0%)**	**304 (100.0%)**

The above table represents the level of professionalism competency based on respondent's career ambition. Among the respondents whose ambition is to become professional social worker, 31% possess high level, 26.4% possess moderate level and 20% possess low level of professionalism competency. Among the respondents whose ambition is to become psychiatric social worker/medical social worker/mental health/counsellor, 50% possess low level, 37.4% possess moderate level and 35.5% possess high level of professionalism competency. Among the respondents whose ambition is to work in a non-governmental organization/orphan home, 16.9% possess high level and 9.9% possess moderate level of professionalism competency. Among the respondents whose ambition is to become human resource managers, 15.8% possess high level, 14.3% possess moderate level and 10% possess low level of the professionalism competency. Among the respondents whose ambition is get Government Jobs, 10% possess low level, 8.4% possess high level and 6.6% possess moderate level of professionalism competency. Among the respondents whose ambition is to become professor, 10% of the respondents possess low level, 5.5% of the respondents possess moderate level and 2.5% possess high level of professionalism competency.

Table 7.11: Aspiration of the Respondents and the Level of Professionalism Competency

Aspiration of the Respondents	*Level of Professionalism Competency*			*Total*
	Low	*Moderate*	*High*	
Social Worker/ Counsellor/HR	8 (80.0%)	49 (53.8%)	96 (47.3%)	153 (50.3%)

Aspiration of the Respondents	*Level of Professionalism Competency*			*Total*
	Low	*Moderate*	*High*	
UPSC	1 (10.0%)	28 (30.8%)	66 (32.5%)	95 (31.2%)
No Idea	1 (10.0%)	14 (15.4%)	41 (20.2%)	56 (18.4%)
Total	**10 (100.0%)**	**91 (100.0%)**	**203 (100.0%)**	**304 (100.0%)**

The above table represents the level of professionalism competency based on respondent's aspiration. Among the respondents who aspire to become social worker/counsellor/human resource managers, 80% of the respondents possess low level, 53.8% of the respondents possess moderate level and 47.3% of the respondents possess high level of professionalism competency. Among the respondents who aspire to write union public service commission, 32.5% of the respondents possess high level, 30.8% possess moderate level and 10% possess low level of professionalism competency. Among the respondents who doesn't have any idea, 20.2% possess high level, 15.4% possess moderate level and 10% possess low level of professionalism competency.

Table 7.12: Respondent's Awareness about Social Work as a Professional Course and the Level of Professionalism Competency

Respondent's Awareness about Social Work as a Professional Course	*Level of Professionalism Competency*			*Total*
	Low	*Moderate*	*High*	
Yes	7 (70.0%)	74 (81.3%)	150 (73.9%)	231 (76.0%)
No	2 (20.0%)	11 (12.1%)	33 (16.3%)	46 (15.1%)
May be	1 (10.0%)	6 (6.6%)	20 (9.9%)	27 (8.9%)
Total	**10 (100.0%)**	**91 (100.0%)**	**203 (100.0%)**	**304 (100.00%)**

The table 7.12 represents the level of professionalism competency based on respondent's awareness about Social Work as a Professional Course. Among the respondents who are aware that social work is a professional course, 81.3% of the respondents possess moderate level, 73.9% of the respondents possess high level and 70% of the respondents possess low level of professionalism competency. Among the respondents who are not aware that social work is a professional course, 20% possess low level, 16.3% possess high level and 12.1% of the respondents possess moderate level of professionalism competency. Among the respondents who may or may not aware that social work is a professional course, 10% possess low level, 9.9% of the respondents possess high level and 6.6% of the respondents possess moderate level of professionalism competency.

Table 7.13: Respondents Faced Criticism for Taking Social Work as their Graduation and the Level of Professionalism Competency

Respondents Faced Criticism for Taking Social Work as their Graduation	*Level of Professionalism Competency*			*Total*
	Low	*Moderate*	*High*	
Yes	5 (50.0%)	51 (56.0%)	119 (58.6%)	175 (57.6%)
No	5 (50.0%)	32 (35.2%)	65 (32.0%)	102 (33.6%)
May be	0 (0.0%)	8 (8.8%)	19 (9.4%)	27 (8.9%)
Total	**10 (100.0%)**	**91 (100.0%)**	**203 (100.0%)**	**304 (100.0%)**

The above table represents the level of professionalism competency based on the criticism faced by the respondents for taking Social Work as their graduation. Among the respondents who faced criticism for taking social work as their graduation, 58.6% possess high level, 56% possess moderate level and 50% possess low level of professionalism competency. Among the respondents who doesn't face criticism for taking social work as their graduation, 50% possess low level, 35.2% possess moderate level and 32% possess high level of professionalism competency. Among the respondents who may or may not faced criticism, 9.4% possess high level and 8.8% of the respondents possess moderate level of professionalism competency.

Table 7.14: Kind of Criticism Faced by the Respondents for Taking Social Work as Their Graduation and the Level of Professionalism Competency

Kind of Criticism Faced by the Respondents for Taking Social Work as their Graduation	*Level of Professionalism Competency*			*Total*
	Low	*Moderate*	*High*	
No	6 (60.0%)	41 (45.1%)	98 (48.3%)	145 (47.7%)
Positive Criticism	1 (10.0%)	6 (6.6%)	9 (4.4%)	16 (5.3%)
Negative Criticism	3 (30.0%)	44 (48.4%)	96 (47.3%)	143 (47.0%)
Total	**10 (100.0%)**	**91 (100.0%)**	**203 (100.0%)**	**304 (100.0%)**

The above table represents the level of professionalism competency based on respondents kind of criticism faced for taking social work as their graduation. Among the respondents who doesn't face any kind of criticism for taking social work as their graduation, 60% possess low level, 48.3% possess high level and 45.1% possess moderate level of professionalism competency. Among the respondents who faced positive criticism, 10% possess low level, 6.6% of the respondents possess moderate level and 4.4% of the respondents possess high level of professionalism competency. Among the respondents who faced negative criticism, 48.4% possess moderate level, 47.3% possess high level and 30% of the respondents possess low level of professionalism competency.

Table 7.15: Respondents Feeling of Competent with Regard to Social Work Profession and the Level of Professionalism Competency

Respondents Feeling of Competent with Regard to Social Work Profession	*Level of Professionalism*			*Total*
	Low	*Moderate*	*High*	
Yes	4 (40.0%)	45 (49.5%)	98 (48.3%)	147 (48.4%)
No	0 (0.0%)	2 (2.2%)	4 (2.0%)	6 (2.0%)
May be	6 (6.0%)	44 (48.4%)	101 (49.8%)	151 (49.7%)
Total	**10 (100.0%)**	**91 (100.0%)**	**203 (100.0%)**	**304 (100.0%)**

The above table represents the level of professionalism competency based on respondents feeling of Competent with regard to Social Work Profession. Among the respondents who feel competent with regard to social work profession, 49.5% of the respondents possess moderate level, 48.3% possess high level and 40% possess low level of professionalism competency. Among the respondents who doesn't feel competent, 2.2% possess moderate level and 2% possess high level of professionalism competency. Among the respondents who may or may not be competent with regard to social work, 49.8% possess high level, 48.4% possess moderate level and 6% possess low level of professionalism competency.

Table 7.16: List of Skills and the Level of Professionalism Competency

List of Skills	*Level of Professionalism Competency*			*Total*
	Low	*Moderate*	*High*	
Communication Skill	4 (40.0%)	30 (33.0%)	89 (43.8%)	123 (40.5%)
Active Listening	2 (20.0%)	26 (28.6%)	44 (21.7%)	72 (23.7%)
Responsible	1 (10.0%)	16 (17.6%)	34 (16.7%)	51 (16.8%)

List of Skills	*Level of Professionalism Competency*			*Total*
	Low	*Moderate*	*High*	
No Idea	3 (30.0%)	19 (20.9%)	36 (17.7%)	58 (19.1%)
Total	**10 (100.0%)**	**91 (100.0%)**	**203 (100.0%)**	**304 (100.0%)**

The above table represents the level of professionalism competency based on respondents list of skills. Among the respondents who possess communication skill, 43.8% possess high level, 40% possess low level and 33% possess moderate level of professionalism competency. Among the respondents who possess active listening skill, 28.6% possess moderate level, 21.7% possess high level and 20% possess low level of professionalism competency. Among the respondents who feel that being responsible is their skill, 17.6% possess moderate level, 16.7% possess high level and 10% possess low level of professionalism competency. Among the respondents who doesn't have any idea about their skills, 30% possess low level, 20.9% possess moderate level and 17.7% possess high level of professionalism competency.

Table 7.17: Respondents Competent to Deal with the Problems of Individuals and the Level of Professionalism Competency

Respondents Competent to Deal with the Problems of Individuals	*Level of Professionalism Competency*			*Total*
	Low	*Moderate*	*High*	
Yes	8 (80.0%)	59 (64.8%)	124 (61.1%)	191 (62.8%)
No	0 (0.0%)	12 (13.2%)	23 (11.3%)	35 (11.5%)
May be	2 (2.0%)	20 (22.0%)	56 (27.6%)	78 (25.7%)
Total	**10 (100.0%)**	**91 (100.0%)**	**203 (100%)**	**304 (100.0%)**

The above table represents the level of professionalism competency based on respondents competent to deal with the problems of individuals. Among the respondents who feel competent to deal with individual's problems, 80% possess low level, 64.8% possess moderate level and 61.1% possess high level of professionalism. Among the respondents who doesn't feel competent to deal with individual problems, 13.2% possess moderate level and 11.3% possess high level of professionalism competency. Among the respondents who may or may not be competent to deal with individual problems, 27.6% possess high level, 22% of the respondents possess moderate level and 2% of the respondents possess low level of professionalism competency.

Table 7.18: Respondents Competent to Deal with the Group Problems and the Level of Professionalism Competency

Respondents Competent to deal with the Group Problems	*Level of Professionalism Competency*			*Total*
	Low	*Moderate*	*High*	
Yes	5 (50.0%)	57 (62.6%)	107 (52.7%)	169 (55.6%)
No	1 (10.0%)	5 (5.5%)	17 (8.4%)	23 (7.6%)
May be	4 (40.0%)	29 (31.9%)	79 (38.9%)	112 (36.8%)
Total	**10 (100.0%)**	**91 (100.0%)**	**203 (100.0%)**	**304 (100.0%)**

The above table represents the level of professionalism competency based on respondents competent to deal with the group problems. Among the respondents who feel competent to deal with group problems, 62.6% of the respondents possess moderate level, 52.7% of the respondents possess high level and 50% possess low level of professionalism competency. Among the respondents who doesn't feel competent to deal with group problems, 10% possess low level, 8.4% of the respondents possess high level and 5.5% possess moderate level of professionalism competency. Among the respondents who may or may not feel competent to deal with group problems, 40% possess low level, 38.9% of the respondents possess high level and 31.9% possess moderate level of professionalism competency.

Table 7.19: Respondents Competent to Deal with the Community Problems and the Level of Professionalism Competency

Respondents Competent to Deal with the Community Problems	*Level of Professionalism Competency*			*Total*
	Low	*Moderate*	*High*	
Yes	5 (50.0%)	44 (48.4%)	89 (43.8%)	138 (45.4%)
No	2 (20.0%)	25 (27.5%)	51 (25.1%)	78 (25.7%)
May be	3 (30.0%)	22 (24.2%)	63 (31.0%)	88 (28.9%)
Total	**10 (100.0%)**	**91 (100.0%)**	**203 (100.0%)**	**304 (100.0%)**

The above table represents the level of professionalism based on respondents competent to deal with the community problems. Among the respondents who feel competent to deal with community problems, 50% possess low level, 48.4% possess moderate level and 43.8% possess high level of professionalism competency. Among the respondents who doesn't feel competent to deal with community problems, 27.5% possess moderate level, 25.1% possess high level and 20% possess low level of professionalism competency. Among the respondents who may or may not feel competent to deal with community problems, 31% possess high level, 30% possess low level and 24.2% possess moderate level of professionalism competency.

CHAPTER 8

Level of Values and Ethical Competency

This chapter involves the analysis and interpretation of level of values and ethical competency and demographic variable, reason for choosing social work, perception, career ambition, aspiration, criticism faced and social worker skills.

Table 8.1: Age of the Respondents and the Level of Values and Ethical Competency

Age of the Respondents	*Level of Values and Ethical Competency*			*Total*
	Low	*Moderate*	*High*	
Below 21	9 (47.4%)	46 (47.4%)	97 (51.6%)	152 (50.0%)
21–25	9 (47.4%)	48 (49.5%)	82 (43.6%)	139 (45.7%)
25–29	1 (5.3%)	3 (3.1%)	9 (4.8%)	13 (4.3%)
Total	**19 (100.0%)**	**97 (100.0%)**	**188 (100.0%)**	**304 (100.0%)**

The above table shows the level of values and Ethical competency with regard to the respondent's age. Among the respondents below the age of 21 years, 51.6% of the respondents possess high level, 47.4% of the respondents possess low and moderate level of values and Ethical competency respectively. Among the respondents between the age of 21 and 25 years, 49.5% of the respondents possess moderate level, 47.4% of the respondents possess low level and 43.6% of the respondents possess high level of values and Ethical competency. Among the respondents between the age of 25 and 29 years, 5.3% of the respondents possess low level, 4.8% of the respondents possess high level and 3.1% of the respondents possess moderate level of values and Ethical competency.

Table 8.2: Gender of the Respondents and the Level of Values and Ethical Competency

Gender of the Respondents	*Level of Values and Ethical Competency*			*Total*
	Low	*Moderate*	*High*	
Prefer not to say	0 (0.0%)	0 (0.0%)	1 (0.5%)	1 (0.3%)
Female	8 (42.1%)	61 (62.9%)	129 (68.6%)	198 (65.1%)
Male	11 (57.9%)	36 (37.1%)	58 (30.9%)	105 (34.5%)
Total	**19 (100.0%)**	**97 (100.0%)**	**188 (100.0%)**	**304 (100.0%)**

This table depicts the level of values and Ethical competency based on the gender. Among the women respondents, 68.6% respondents possess high level, 62.9% of the respondents possess moderate level and 42.1% of the respondents possess low level of values and Ethical competency. Among the male respondents 57.9% of the respondents possess low level, 37.1% of the respondents possess moderate level and 30.9% of the respondents possess high level of values and Ethical competency. 0.5% of the respondent who prefer not to say the gender possess high level of values and Ethical competency.

Table 8.3: Educational Qualification of the Respondents and the Level of Values and Ethical Competency

Educational Qualification of the Respondents	*Level of Values and Ethical Competency*			*Total*
	Low	*Moderate*	*High*	
II & III BSW	12 (63.2%)	48 (49.5%)	92 (48.9%)	152 (50.0%)
II MSW	7 (36.8%)	49 (50.5%)	96 (51.1%)	152 (50.0%)
Total	**19 (100.0%)**	**97 (100.0%)**	**188 (100.0%)**	**304 (100.0%)**

This table depicts the level of values and Ethical competency based on the educational qualification. Among the respondents pursuing II-

and III-year BSW, 63.2% of the respondents possess low level, 49.5% of the respondents possess moderate level and 48.9% of the respondents possess high level of values and Ethical competency. Among the respondents pursuing II-year MSW, 51.1% of the respondents possess high level, 50.5% of the respondents possess moderate level and 36.8% of the respondents possess low level of values and Ethical competency.

Table 8.4: Post Graduate Respondents Under-graduation and the Level of Values and Ethical Competency

Post Graduate Respondents Under-graduation	*Level of Values and Ethical Competency*			*Total*
	Low	*Moderate*	*High*	
BSW	1 (5.3%)	19 (19.6%)	49 (26.1%)	69 (22.7%)
Other Degree	6 (31.6%)	30 (30.9%)	47 (25.0%)	83 (27.3%)
Not Applicable (U.G. Respondents)	12 (63.2%)	48 (49.5%)	92 (48.9%)	152 (50.0%)
Total	**19 (100.0%)**	**97 (100.0%)**	**188 (100.0%)**	**304 (100.0%)**

The above table represents the level of values and Ethical competency in accordance with the respondent's under-graduation. Among the respondents pursued social work in their under-graduation, 26.1% of the respondents possess high level, 19.6% of the respondents possess moderate level and 5.3% of the respondents possess low level of values and Ethical competency. Among the respondents pursued other than social work in their under-graduation, 31.6% of the respondents possess low level, 30.9% of the respondents possess moderate level and 25% of the respondents possess high level of values and Ethical competency.

Table 8.5: Domicile of the Respondents and the Level of Values and Ethical Competency

Domicile of the Respondents	*Level of Values and Ethical Competency*			*Total*
	Low	*Moderate*	*High*	
Tamil Nadu	16 (84.2%)	84 (86.6%)	157 (83.5%)	257 (84.5%)
Outside Tamil Nadu	3 (15.8%)	13 (13.4%)	31 (16.5%)	47 (15.5%)
Total	**19 (100.0%)**	**97 (100.0%)**	**188 (100.0%)**	**304 (100.0%)**

This table shows the level of values and Ethical competency based on the domicile of the respondents. Among the respondents from Taminadu, 86.6% of the respondents possess moderate level, 84.2% of the respondents possess low level and 83.5% of the respondents possess high level of values and Ethical competency. Among the respondents from outside Tamilnadu, 16.5% of the respondents possess high level, 15.8% of the respondents possess low level and 13.4% of the respondents possess moderate level of values and Ethical competency.

Table 8.6: Major Subjects Studied by the Respondents during 12th Standard and the Level of Values and Ethical Competency

Major Subjects Studied by the Respondents During 12th Standard	*Level of Values and Ethical Competency*			*Total*
	Low	*Moderate*	*High*	
Bio maths	3 (15.8%)	15 (15.5%)	41 (21.8%)	59 (19.4%)
Computer science	3 (15.8%)	20 (20.6%)	29 (15.4%)	52 (17.1%)
Commerce	10 (52.6%)	49 (50.5%)	95 (50.5%)	154 (50.7%)
Humanities	3 (15.8%)	13 (13.4%)	23 (12.2%)	39 (12.8%)
Total	**19 (100.0%)**	**97 (100.0%)**	**188 (100.0%)**	**304 (100.0%)**

The table 8.6 shows the level of values and Ethical based on the major subjects studied by the respondents during 12th standard. Among the respondents who studied Bio-Maths during 12th standard, 21.8% respondents possess high level, 15.8% respondents possess low level and 15.5% respondents possess moderate level of values and Ethical competency. Among the respondents who pursued Computer science during 12th standard, 20.6% of the respondents possess moderate level, 15.8% respondents possess low level and 15.4% of the respondents possess high level of values and Ethical competency. Among the respondents who studied Commerce during 12th standard, 52.6% of the respondents possess low level, 50.5% of the respondents possess moderate and high level of values and Ethical competency respectively. Among the respondents who studied Humanities during 12th standard, 15.8% of the respondents possess low level, 13.4% of the respondents possess moderate level and 12.2% of the respondents possess high level of values and Ethical competency.

Table 8.7: Respondents Reasons for Choosing Social Work and the Level of Values and Ethical Competency

Respondent's Reasons for Choosing Social Work	*Level of Values and Ethical Competency*			*Total*
	Low	*Moderate*	*High*	
Own interest	12 (63.2%)	58 (59.8%)	117 (62.2%)	187 (61.5%)
Parents/relatives recommendation	7 (36.8%)	38 (39.2%)	66 (35.1%)	111 (36.5%)
Sibling studied/influence	0 (0.0%)	1 (1.0%)	5 (2.7%)	6 (2.0%)
Total	**19 (100.0%)**	**97 (100.0%)**	**188 (100.0%)**	**304 (100.0%)**

This table depicts the level of values and Ethical competency based on the reason for choosing social work as their undergraduate discipline. 63.2% respondents chose social work with their own interest possess low level of values and Ethical competency. 62.2% respondents chose social work with their own interest possess high level of values and Ethical competency. 59.8% respondents chose social work with their own interest possess moderate level of values and Ethical competency.39.2% of the respondents chose social work because of their parents/relatives recommendation possess moderate level of values and Ethical competency. 36.8% of the respondents chose social work because of their parents/relatives recommendation possess low level of values and Ethical competency. 35.1% of the respondents chose social work because of their parents/relatives recommendation possess high level of values and Ethical competency. 2.7% respondents chose social work since their sibling studied/influenced possess high level knowledge of values and Ethical competency. 1% respondents chose social work since their sibling studied/influenced who possess moderate level knowledge of values and Ethical competency.

Table 8.8: Respondents Perception about Social Work and the Level of Values and Ethical Competency

Respondents Perception about Social Work	*Level of Values and Ethical Competency*			*Total*
	Low	*Moderate*	*High*	
Practise Based Profession	3 (15.8%)	15 (15.5%)	41 (21.8%)	59 (19.4%)
Value Oriented Subject	3 (15.8%)	20 (20.6%)	29 (15.4%)	52 (17.1%)
Helping Profession	10 (52.6%)	49 (50.5%)	95 (50.5%)	154 (50.7%)
Art Course	3 (15.8%)	13 (13.4%)	23 (12.2%)	39 (12.8%)
Total	**19 (100.0%)**	**97 (100.0%)**	**188 (100.0%)**	**304 (100.0%)**

The table states the level of values and Ethical competency based on the perception about social work. Among the respondents who perceive social work as practice-based profession, 21.8% of the respondents possess high level, 15.8% of the respondents possess low level and 15.5% respondents possess moderate level of values and Ethical competency. Among the respondents who perceive social work as value oriented subject 20.6% of the respondents possess moderate level, 15.8% respondents possess low level and 15.4% of the respondents possess high level of the values and Ethical competency. Among the respondents who perceive social work as helping profession, 52.6% of the respondents possess low level, 50.5% of the respondents possess moderate and high level of values and Ethical competency respectively. Among the respondents who perceive social work as art course, 15.8% of the respondents possess low level, 13.4% respondents possess moderate level and 12.2% of the respondents possess high level of values and Ethical competency.

Table 8.9: Family Members of the Respondents Studied Social Work and the Level of Values and Ethical Competency

Family Members of the Respondents Studied Social Work	*Level of Values and Ethical Competency*			*Total*
	Low	*Moderate*	*High*	
Yes	1 (5.3%)	17 (17.5%)	29 (15.4%)	47 (15.5%)
No	18 (94.7%)	80 (82.5%)	159 (84.6%)	257 (84.5%)
Total	**19 (100.0%)**	**97 (100.0%)**	**188 (100.0%)**	**304 (100.0%)**

This table represents the level of values and Ethical competency with respect to the family members of the respondents studied social work. 17.5% respondents whose family members studied social work possess moderate.,. level of values and Ethical competency. 15.4% respondents whose family members studied social work possess high level of values and Ethical competency. 5.3% respondents whose family members studied social work possess low level of values and Ethical competency. Among the respondents whose family members not pursued social work, 94.7% respondents possess low level, 84.6% respondents possess high level and 82.5% of the respondents possess moderate level of values and Ethical competency.

Table 8.10: Career Ambition of the Respondents and the Level of Values and Ethical Competency

Career Ambition of the Respondents	*Level of Values and Ethical Competency*			*Total*
	Low	*Moderate*	*High*	
Professional Social Worker	4 (21.1%)	30 (30.9%)	55 (29.3%)	89 (29.3%)
Psychiatric/Medical Social Worker/ Mental Health/ Counsellor	7 (36.8%)	35 (36.1%)	69 (36.7%)	111 (36.5%)
N.G.O/Orphan homes	2 (10.5%)	8 (8.2%)	13 (6.9%)	23 (7.6%)
H.R	2 (10.5%)	13 (13.4%)	31 (16.5%)	46 (15.1%)
Government Jobs	3 (15.8%)	17 (7.2%)	14 (7.4%)	24 (7.9%)
Professor	1 (5.3%)	4 (4.1%)	16 (3.2%)	11 (3.6%)
Total	**19 (100.0%)**	**97 (100.0%)**	**188 (100.0%)**	**304 (100.0%)**

The above table represents the level of values and Ethical competency based on the career ambition of the respondents. Among the respondents whose ambition is to become professional social worker, 30.9% respondents possess moderate level, 29.3% respondents possess high level and 21.1% respondents possess low level of values and Ethical competency. Among the respondents whose ambition is to become Psychiatric/Medical Social Worker/Mental Health/ Counsellor, 36.8% respondents possess low level, 36.7% respondents possess high level and 36.1% of the respondents possess moderate level of values and Ethical competency. Among the respondents whose ambition is to work in non-governmental organization/orphan homes, 10.5% of the respondents possess low level, 8.2% of the respondents possess moderate and 6.9% of the respondents possess high level of values and Ethical competency. Among the respondents whose ambition is to become human resource professional, 16.5% of the respondents possess high level, 13.4% of the respondents possess moderate level and 10.5% of the respondents possess low level of the values and Ethical competency. Among the respondents whose ambition is to get government jobs, 15.8% of the respondents possess low level, 7.4% of the respondents possess high level and 7.2% of the respondents possess moderate level of values and Ethical competency. Among the respondents whose ambition is to become professor, 5.3% of the respondents possess low level, 4.1% of the respondents possess moderate level and 3.2% of the respondents possess high level of values and Ethical competency.

Table 8.11: Aspiration of the Respondents and the Level of Values and Ethical Competency

Aspiration of the Respondents	*Level of Values and Ethical Competency*			*Total*
	Low	*Moderate*	*High*	
Social Worker/ Counsellor/HR	13 (68.4%)	46 (47.4%)	94 (50.0%)	153 (50.3%)
UPSC	4 (21.1%)	33 (34.0%)	58 (30.9%)	95 (31.2%)
No idea	2 (10.5%)	18 (18.6%)	36 (19.1%)	56 (18.4%)
Total	**19 (100.0%)**	**97 (100.0%)**	**188 (100.0%)**	**304 (100.0%)**

This table shows the level of values and Ethical competency in accordance with the aspiration of the respondents. Among the respondents who aspire to become Social Worker/HR/Counsellor, 68.4% respondents possess low level, 50% of the respondents possess high level and 47.4% respondents possess moderate level of values and Ethical competency. Among the respondents who aspire to serve union public service commission (UPSC), 34% of the respondents possess moderate level, 30.9% respondents possess high level and 21.1% possess low level of values and Ethical competency. Among the respondents who doesn't have any idea, 19.1% of the respondents possess high level, 18.6% of the respondents possess moderate level and 10.5% of the respondents possess low level of values and Ethical competency.

Table 8.12: Respondent's Awareness about Social Work as a Professional Course and the Level of Values and Ethical Competency

Respondent's Awareness about Social Work as a Professional Course	*Level of Values and Ethical Competency*			*Total*
	Low	*Moderate*	*High*	
Yes	15 (78.9%)	69 (71.1%)	147 (78.2%)	23176.0%)
No	2 (10.5%)	18 (18.6%)	26 (13.8%)	46 (15.1%)
May be	2 (10.5%)	10 (10.3%)	15 (8.0%)	27 (8.9%)
Total	**19 (100.0%)**	**97 (100.0%)**	**188 (100.0%)**	**304 (100.0%)**

The above table shows the level of values and Ethical competency based on the respondent's awareness about social work as a professional course. Among the respondents who are aware that social work is a professional course, 78.9% respondents possess low level, 78.2% respondents possess high level and 71.1% of the respondents possess moderate level of values and Ethical competency. Among the respondents who were not aware that social work is a professional course, 18.6% of the respondents possess moderate level, 13.8% of the respondents possess high level and 10.5% of the respondents possess low level of values and Ethical competency. Among the respondents who may or may not aware that social work is a professional course, 10.5% of the respondents possess low level, 10.3% of the respondents possess moderate level and 8% respondents possess high level of values and Ethical competency.

Table 8.13: Respondents Faced Criticism for Taking Social Work as their Graduation and the Level of Values and Ethical Competency

Respondents Faced Criticism for Taking Social Work as their Graduation	*Level of Values and Ethical Competency*			*Total*
	Low	*Moderate*	*High*	
Yes	10 (52.6%)	58 (59.8%)	107 (56.9%)	175 (57.6%)

Respondents Faced Criticism for Taking Social Work as their Graduation	*Level of Values and Ethical Competency*			*Total*
	Low	*Moderate*	*High*	
No	8 (42.1%)	28 (28.9%)	66 (35.1%)	102 (33.6%)
May be	1 (5.3%)	11 (11.3%)	15 (8.0%)	27 (8.9%)
Total	**19** **(100.0%)**	**97** **(100.0%)**	**188** **(100.0%)**	**304** **(100.0%)**

The above table depicts the level of values and Ethical competency with regard to the criticism faced by the respondents for taking social work as their graduation. Among the respondents who faced criticism for taking up social work as their graduation, 59.8% of the respondents possess moderate level, 56.9% of the respondent possess high level and 52.6% of the respondents possess low level of values and Ethical competency. Among the respondents who didn't face any criticism for taking up social work as their graduation, 42.1% of the respondents possess low level, 35.1% of the respondents possess high level and 28.9% of the respondents possess moderate level of values and Ethical competency. Among the respondents who may or may be faced criticism, 11.3% possess moderate level, 8% respondents possess high level and 5.3% of the respondents possess low level of values and Ethical competency.

Table 8.14: Kind of Criticism Faced by the Respondents for Taking Social Work as their Graduation and the Level of Values and Ethical Competency

Kind of Criticism Faced by the Respondents for Taking Social Work as their Graduation	*Level of Values and Ethical Competency*			*Total*
	Low	*Moderate*	*High*	
No	8 (42.1%)	50 (51.5%)	87 (46.3%)	145 (47.7%)
Positive Criticism	2 (10.5%)	4 (4.1%)	10 (5.3%)	16 (5.3%)

Kind of Criticism Faced by the Respondents for Taking Social Work as their Graduation	*Level of Values and Ethical Competency*			*Total*
	Low	*Moderate*	*High*	
Negative Criticism	9 (47.4%)	43 (44.3%)	91 (48.4%)	143 (47.0%)
Total	**19 (100.0%)**	**97 (100.0%)**	**188 (100.0%)**	**304 (100.0%)**

This table represents the level of values and Ethical competency based on the kind of criticism faced by the respondents for taking social work as their graduation. Among the respondents who doesn't face any criticism, 51.5% of the respondents possess moderate level, 46.3% of the respondents possess high level and 42.1% of the respondents possess low level of values and Ethical competency. Among the respondents who faced positive criticism, 10.5% of the respondents possess low level, 5.3% of the respondents possess high level and 4.1% of the respondents possess moderate level of values and Ethical competency. Among the respondents who faced negative criticism, 48.4% of the respondents possess high level, 47.4% of the respondents possess low level and 44.3% of the respondents possess moderate level of values and Ethical competency.

Table 8.15: Respondents Feeling of Competent with Regard to Social Work Profession and the Level of Values and Ethical Competency

Respondents Feeling of Competent with Regard to Social Work Profession	*Level of Values and Ethical Competency*			*Total*
	Low	*Moderate*	*High*	
Yes	10 (52.6%)	46 (47.4%)	91 (48.4%)	147 (48.4%)
No	0 (0.0%)	1 (1.0%)	5 (2.7%)	6 (2.0%)
May be	9 (47.4%)	50 (51.5%)	92 (48.9%)	151 (49.7%)
Total	**19 (100.0%)**	**97 (100.0%)**	**188 (100.0%)**	**304 (100.0%)**

The table 8.15 depicts the level of values and Ethical competency based on the respondents feeling of competent with regard to social work profession. Among the respondents who feels competent with regard to social work profession, 52.6% of the respondents possess low level, 48.4% of the respondents possess high level and 47.4% of the respondents possess moderate level values and Ethical competency. Among the respondents who doesn't feel competent with regard to social work profession, 2.7% of the respondents possess high level and 1% of the respondent possess moderate level of values and Ethical competency. Among the respondents who may or may not be competent with regard to social work profession, 51.5% of the respondents possess moderate level, 48.9% of the respondents possess high level and 47.4% of the respondents possess low level of values and Ethical competency.

Table 8.16: List of Skills and the Level of Values and Ethical Competency

List of Skills	*Level of Values and Ethical Competency*			*Total*
	Low	*Moderate*	*High*	
Communication Skill	6 (31.6%)	41 (42.3%)	76 (40.4%)	123 (40.5%)
Active Listening	6 (31.6%)	21 (21.6%)	45 (23.9%)	72 (23.7%)
Responsible	1 (5.3%)	18 (18.6%)	32 (17.0%)	51 (16.8%)
No idea	6 (31.6%)	17 (17.5%)	35 (18.6%)	58 (19.1%)
Total	**19 (100.0%)**	**97 (100.0%)**	**188 (100.0%)**	**304 (100.0%)**

This table shows the level of values and Ethical competency based on the skills of the respondents. Among the respondents who possess communication skills, 42.3% of the respondents have moderate level, 40.4% respondents have high level and 31.6% of the respondents have low level of values and Ethical competency. Among the respondents who possess active listening skills, 31.6% of the respondents have low level, 23.9% of the respondents have high level and 21.6% of the respondents have moderate level of values and

Ethical competency. Among the respondents who feels responsible as their skill, 18.6% of the respondents possess moderate level, 17% of the respondents possess high level and 5.3% of the respondents possess low level of values and Ethical competency. Among the respondents who doesn't have any idea about their skills, 31.6% of the respondents possess low level, 18.6% of the respondents possess high level and 17.5% of the respondents possess moderate level of values and Ethical competency.

Table 8.17: Respondents Competent to Deal with the Problems of Individuals and the Level of Values and Ethical Competency

Respondents Competent to Deal with the Problems of Individuals	*Level of Values and Ethical Competency*			*Total*
	Low	*Moderate*	*High*	
Yes	15 (78.9%)	51 (58.8%)	119 (63.3%)	191 (62.8%)
No	2 (10.5%)	10 (10.3%)	23 (12.2%)	35 (11.5%)
Maybe	2 (10.5%)	30 (30.9%)	46 (24.5%)	78 (25.7%)
Total	**19 (100.0%)**	**97 (100.0%)**	**188 (100.0%)**	**304 (100.0%)**

The above table represents the level of values and Ethical competency with regard to the respondents competent to deal with the individuals' problems. Among the respondents who are competent to deal with individual problems, 78.9% of the respondents possess low level, 63.3% of the respondents possess high level and 58.8% of the respondents possess moderate level of values and Ethical competency. Among the respondents who are not competent to deal with individual problems, 12.2% of the respondents possess high level, 10.5% of the respondents possess low level and 10.3% respondents possess moderate level of values and Ethical competency. Among the respondents who are may or may not be competent to deal with individual problems, 30.9% of the respondents possess moderate level, 24.5% of the respondents possess high level and 10.5% of the respondents possess low level of values and Ethical competency.

Table 8.18: Respondents Competent to Deal with the Group Problems and the Level of Values and Ethical Competency

Respondents Competent to deal with the Group Problems	*Level of Values and Ethical Competency*			*Total*
	Low	*Moderate*	*High*	
Yes	10 (52.6%)	54 (55.7%)	105 (55.9%)	169 (55.6%)
No	0 (0.0%)	6 (6.2%)	17 (9.0%)	23 (7.6%)
May be	9 (47.4%)	37 (38.1%)	66 (35.1%)	112 (36.8%)
Total	**19 (100.0%)**	**97 (100.0%)**	**188 (100.0%)**	**304 (100.0%)**

The above table represents the level of values and Ethical competency with regard to the respondents competent to deal with the group problems. Among the respondents who are competent to deal with group problems, 55.9% of the respondents possess high level, 55.7% of the respondents possess moderate level and 52.6% of the respondents possess low level of values and Ethical competency. Among the respondents who doesn't feel competent to deal with group problems, 9% of the respondents possess high level and 6.2% possess moderate level of values and Ethical competency. Among the respondents who may or may not feel competent to deal with group problems, 47.4% of the respondents possess low level, 38.1% of the respondents possess moderate level and 35.1% of the respondents possess high level of values and Ethical competency.

Table 8.19: Respondents Competent to Deal with the Community Problems and the Level of Values and Ethical Competency

Respondents Competent to Deal with the Community Problems	*Level of Values and Ethical Competency*			*Total*
	Low	*Moderate*	*High*	
Yes	9 (47.4%)	45 (46.4%)	84 (44.7%)	138 (45.4%)
No	5 (26.3%)	26 (26.8%)	47 (25.0%)	78 (25.7%)
May be	5 (26.3%)	26 (26.8%)	57 (30.3%)	88 (28.9%)
Total	**19 (100.0%)**	**97 (100.0%)**	**188 (100.0%)**	**304 (100.0%)**

This table depicts the level of values and Ethical competency based on the respondents competent to deal with community problems. Among the respondents who are competent to deal with community problems, 47.4% of the respondents possess low level, 46.4% of the respondents possess moderate level and 44.7% of the respondents possess high level of values and Ethical competency. Among the respondents who doesn't feel competent to deal with community problems, 26.8% of the respondents possess moderate level, 26.3% possess low level and 25% of the respondents possess high level of values and Ethical competency. Among the respondents who may or may not feel competent to deal with community problems, 30.3% of the respondents possess high level, 26.8% of the respondents possess moderate level and 26.3% of the respondents possess low level of values and Ethical competency.

CHAPTER 9

Level of Engage Diversity and Equality Competency

This chapter involves the analysis and interpretation of level of engage diversity and equality competency and demographic variable, reason for choosing social work, perception, career ambition, aspiration, criticism faced and social worker skills.

Table 9.1: Age of the Respondents and their Level of Engage Diversity and Equality Competency

Age of the Respondents	*Level of Engage Diversity and Equality Competency*			*Total*
	Low	*Moderate*	*High*	
Below 21	22 (55.0%)	77 (48.1%)	53 (51.0%)	152 (50.0%)
21–25	16 (40.0%)	75 (46.9%)	48 (46.2%)	139 (45.7%)
25-29	2 (5.0%)	8 (5.0%)	3 (2.9%)	13 (4.3%)
Total	**40 (100.0%)**	**160 (100.0%)**	**104 (100.0%)**	**304 (100.0%)**

The above table shows the age of the respondents and level of engage diversity and equality competency. The respondents below 21, 55% possess low level of engage diversity and equality competency, 51% possess high level of engage diversity and equality competency and 48.1% possess moderate level of engage diversity and equality competency. Between the age of 21 and 25 years 46.9% possess moderate level of engage diversity and equality competency, 46.2% possess high level of engage diversity and equality competency and 40% possess low level of engage diversity and equality competency.

Between 25 and 29 years, 5% possess low and moderate level of engage diversity and equality competency each and 2.9% possess high level of engage diversity and equality competency. From the table it can be inferred that invariable of the age, the respondents possess moderate level of engage diversity and equality competency.

Table 9.2: Gender of the Respondents and their Level of Engage Diversity and Equality Competency

Gender of the Respondents	*Level of Engage diversity and Equality Competency*			*Total*
	Low	*Moderate*	*High*	
Prefer not to say	0 (0.0%)	0 (0.0%)	1 (1.0%)	1 (0.3%)
Female	25 (62.5%)	95 (59.4%)	78 (75.0%)	198 (65.1%)
Male	15 (37.5%)	65 (40.6%)	25 (24.0%)	105 (34.5%)
Total	**40 (100.0%)**	**160 (100.0%)**	**104 (100.0%)**	**304 (100.0%)**

The above table shows the gender of respondents and level of engage diversity and equality competency. Of the respondents who prefer not to say, 1% possesses high level of engage diversity and equality competency. Of the female respondents, 75% possess high level of engage diversity and equality competency, 62.5% possess low level of engage diversity and equality competency and 59.4% possess moderate level of engage diversity and equality competency. Of the male respondents, 40.6% possess moderate level of engage diversity and equality competency, 37.5% possess low level of engage diversity and equality competency and 24% possess high level of engage diversity and equality competency. From the table it can be inferred that irrespective of gender, the respondents possess moderate level of engage diversity and equality competency. And equally there are respondents who possess low level of engage diversity and equality competency.

Table 9.3: Educational Qualification of the Respondents and their Level of Engage Diversity and Equality Competency

Educational Qualification of the Respondents	*Level of Engage Diversity and Equality Competency*			*Total*
	Low	*Moderate*	*High*	
II & III BSW	23 (57.5%)	86 (53.8%)	43 (41.3%)	152 (50.0%)
II MSW	17 (42.5%)	74 (46.2%)	61 (58.7%)	152 (50.0%)
Total	**40 (100.0%)**	**160 (100.0%)**	**104 (100.0%)**	**304 (100.0%)**

The above table shows the educational qualification of the respondents and level of engage diversity and equality competency. Of the respondents with II & III BSW qualification, 57.5% possess low level of engage diversity and equality competency 53.8% possess moderate level of engage diversity and equality competency and 41.3% possess high level of engage diversity and equality competency. Of the respondents with II MSW qualification, 58.7% possess high level of engage diversity and equality competency, 46.2% possess moderate level of engage diversity and equality competency and 42.5% possess low level of engage diversity and equality competency. From the above table it can be inferred that irrespective of the qualification of the respondents, the respondents majorly possess moderate level of engage diversity and equality competency.

Table 9.4: Post Graduate Respondents Under-graduation and their Level of Engage Diversity and Equality Competency

Post Graduate Respondents Under-graduation	*Level of Engage Diversity and Equality Competency*			*Total*
	Low	*Moderate*	*High*	
BSW	5 (12.5%)	32 (20.0%)	32 (30.8%)	69 (22.7%)
Other Degree	12 (30.0%)	42 (26.2%)	29 (27.9%)	83 (27.3%)

Post Graduate Respondents Under-graduation	*Level of Engage Diversity and Equality Competency*			*Total*
	Low	*Moderate*	*High*	
Not Applicable (Under Graduate Respondents)	23 (57.5%)	86 (53.8%)	43 (41.3%)	152 (50.0%)
Total	**40 (100.0%)**	**160 100.0%)**	**104 (100.0%)**	**304 (100.0%)**

The above table shows the respondents' under-graduation and level of engage diversity and equality competency. Of the respondents with BSW as under graduation, 30.8% of the respondents possess high level of engage diversity and equality competency, 20% possess moderate level of engage diversity and equality competency and 12.5% possess low level of engage diversity and equality competency. Of the respondents with other degree, 30% possess low level of engage diversity and equality competency 27.9% and 26.2% possess high level and moderate level of engage diversity and equality competency respectively. About half of the respondents (50%) have not completed their under graduation. From the above table it can be inferred that invariable of the under-graduation of the respondents, majorly the respondents possess moderate level of engage diversity and equality competency followed by high level and low level of engage diversity and equality competency.

Table 9.5: Domicile of the Respondents and their Level of Engage Diversity and Equality Competency

Domicile of the Respondents	*Level of Engage Diversity and Equality Competency*			*Total*
	Low	*Moderate*	*High*	
Tamil Nadu	35 (87.5%)	136 (85.0%)	86 (82.7%)	257 (84.5%)
Outside Tamil Nadu	5 (12.5%)	24 (15.0%)	18 (17.3%)	47 (15.5%)
Total	**40 (100.0%)**	**160 (100.0%)**	**104 (100.0%)**	**304 (100.0%)**

The table 9.5 shows the domicile of the respondents and level of engage diversity and equality competency. Of the respondents within TN, 87.5% possess low level of engage diversity and equality competency, 85% moderate level and 82.7% possess high level of engage diversity and equality competency. Of the respondents with domicile outside TN, 17.3% possess high level of engage diversity and equality competency, 15% possess moderate level and 12.5% possess low level of engage diversity and equality competency. From the above table it can be inferred that invariable of the domicile of the respondents, they possess moderate level of engage diversity and equality competency to a major extent followed by high and low level of engage diversity and equality competency.

Table 9.6: Major Subjects Studied by the Respondents during 12th Standard and their Level of Engage Diversity and Equality Competency

Major Subjects Studied by the Respondents During 12th Standard	*Level of Engage Diversity and Equality Competency*			*Total*
	Low	*Moderate*	*High*	
Bio-Maths	8 (20.0%)	31 (19.4%)	20 (19.2%)	59 (19.4%)
Computer Sciences	8 (20.0%)	29 (18.1%)	15 (14.4%)	52 (17.1%)
Commerce	19 (47.5%)	79 (49.4%)	56 (53.8%)	154 (50.7%)
Humanities	5 (12.5%)	21 (13.1%)	13 (12.5%)	39 (12.8%)
Total	**40 (100.0%)**	**160 (100.0%)**	**104 (100.0%)**	**304 (100.0%)**

The above table shows the major subjects studied by the respondents during 12th standard and level of engage diversity and equality competency. Of the respondents with Bio-Maths as their major subject, 20% possess low level of engage diversity and equality competency, 19.4% and 19.2% possess moderate and high level of engage diversity and equality competency respectively. Of the respondents with computer science as their major subject, 20% possess low level of engage diversity and equality competency, 18.1%

moderate level and 14.4% possess high level of engage diversity and equality competency. Of the respondents with commerce as their major subject, 53.8% possess high level of engage diversity and equality competency, 49.4% possess moderate level of engage diversity and equality competency and 47.5% possess low level of engage diversity and equality competency. Of the respondents with humanities as major subjects, 13.1% possess moderate level of engage diversity and equality competency and 12.5% possess low level and high level of engage diversity and equality competency each. From the above table it is inferred that irrespective of the major subjects chosen in 12th standard, the respondents possess moderate level of engage diversity and equality competency majorly. The respondents equally possess high level of engage diversity and equality competency.

Table 9.7: Respondents Reasons for Choosing Social Work and Their Level of Engage Diversity and Equality Competency

Respondents' Reasons for Choosing Social Work	*Level of Engage Diversity and Equality Competency*			*Total*
	Low	*Moderate*	*High*	
Own Interest	26 (65.0%)	98 (61.2%)	63 (60.6%)	187 (61.5%)
Parents/Relatives Recommendation	14 (35.0%)	60 (37.5%)	37 (35.6%)	111 (36.5%)
Siblings Studied/Influence	0 (0.0%)	2 (1.2%)	4 (3.8%)	6 (2.0%)
Total	**40 (100.0%)**	**160 (100.0%)**	**104 (100.0%)**	**304 (100.0%)**

The above table shows the respondents' reason for choosing social work and level of engage diversity and equality competency. Of the respondents choosing social work by their own interest, 65% possess low level of engage diversity and equality competency, 61.2% possess moderate and 60.6% possess high level of engage diversity and equality competency. Of the respondents choosing social work with parents or relative's recommendation, 37.5% possess moderate level of engage diversity and equality competency, 35.6% and 35% possess high level and low level of engage diversity and equality competency respectively. Of the respondents choosing social work with sibling's influence, 3.8% possess high level of engage diversity and equality competency and 1.2% possesses moderate level of engage diversity and equality competency. From the above table it can be inferred that invariable of the reasons for choosing social work, the respondents majorly possess moderate level of engage diversity and equality competency.

Table 9.8: Respondents Perception about Social Work and their Level of Engage Diversity and Equality Competency

Respondents' Perception About Social Work	*Level of Engage Diversity And Equality Competency*			*Total*
	Low	*Moderate*	*High*	
Practise Based Profession	8 (20.0%)	31 (19.4%)	20 (19.2%)	59 (19.4%)
Value Oriented Subject	8 (20.0%)	29 (18.1%)	15 (14.4%)	52 (17.1%)
Helping Profession	19 (47.5%)	79 (49.4%)	56 (53.8%)	154 (50.7%)
Art Course	5 (12.5%)	21 (13.1%)	13 (12.5%)	39 (12.8%)
Total	**40 (100.0%)**	**160 (100.0%)**	**104 (100.0%)**	**304 (100.0%)**

The above table shows the respondents perception about social work and level of engage diversity and equality competency. Of the respondents perceiving social work as practise-based profession, 20% possess low level of engage diversity and equality competency, 19.4% and 19.2% possess moderate and high level of engage diversity and equality competency respectively. Of the respondents perceiving social work as value-oriented subject, 20% possess low level of engage diversity and equality competency, 18.1% possess moderate level of engage diversity and equality competency and 14.4% possess high level of engage diversity and equality competency. Of the respondents perceiving social work as a helping profession, 53.8% possess high level of engage diversity and equality competency 49.4% possesses moderate level and 47.5% possess low level of engage diversity and equality competency. Of the respondents perceiving social work as an art course, 13.1% possess moderate level of engage diversity and equality competency and 12.5% possess high and low level of engage diversity and equality competency each. From the above table it can be inferred that irrespective of the perception on social work, the respondents majorly possess moderate level of engage diversity and equality competency followed by high level of engage diversity and equality competency.

Table 9.9: Family Members of the Respondents Studied Social Work and the Level of Engage Diversity and Equality Competency

Family Members of the Respondents Studied Social Work	*Level of Engage Diversity and Equality Competency*			*Total*
	Low	*Moderate*	*High*	
Yes	3 (7.5%)	31 (19.4%)	13 (12.5%)	47 (15.5%)
No	37 (92.5%)	129 (80.6%)	91 (87.5%)	257 (84.5%)
Total	**40 (100.0%)**	**160 (100.0%)**	**104 (100.0%)**	**304 (100.0%)**

The table shows the family members of the respondents studied social work and level of engage diversity and equality competency. Of the respondents whose family members have studied social work, 19.4% possess moderate level of engage diversity and equality competency, 12.5% possess high level of engage diversity and equality competency and 7.5% possess low level of engage diversity and equality competency. Of the respondents whose family members has not studied social work, 92.5% possess low level of engage diversity and equality competency 87.5% possess high level of engage diversity and equality competency and 80.6% possess moderate level of engage diversity and equality competency. From the above table it can be inferred that invariable of the respondent's family members studying social work, the respondents majorly possess moderate level of engage diversity and equality competency. The respondents equally possess high level of engage diversity and equality competency followed by low level of engage diversity and equality competency.

Table 9.10: Career Ambition of the Respondents and Their Level of Engage Diversity and Equality Competency

Career Ambition of Respondents	*Level of Engage Diversity and Equality Competency*			*Total*
	Low	*Moderate*	*High*	
Professional Social Worker	12 (30.0%)	50 (31.2%)	27 (26.0%)	89 (29.3%)
Psychiatric/Medical Social Worker/Mental Health/Counsellor	16 (40.0%)	57 (35.6%)	38 (36.5%)	111 (36.5%)
N.G.O/Orphanage	3 (7.5%)	8 (5.0%)	12 (11.5%)	23 (7.6%)
H.R.	4 (10.0%)	25 (15.6%)	17 (16.3%)	46 (15.1%)
Government Jobs	3 (7.5%)	13 (8.1%)	8 (7.7%)	24 (7.9%)
Professor	2 (5.0%)	7 (4.4%)	2 (1.9%)	11 (3.6%)
Total	**40 (100.0%)**	**160 (100.0%)**	**104 (100.0%)**	**304 (100.0%)**

The above table shows the career ambitions of respondents and level of engage diversity and equality competency. Of the respondents with career ambition of professional social worker 31.2% possess moderate level of engage diversity and equality competency, 30% low level and 26% possess high level of engage diversity and equality competency. Of the respondents with career ambition of Counsellor, 40% possess low level of engage diversity and equality competency, 36.5% and 35.6% possess high level and moderate level of engage diversity and equality competency respectively. Of the respondents with career ambition NGO/Orphanage, 11.5% possess high level of engage diversity and equality competency, 7.5% low level and 5% moderate level of engage diversity and equality competency. Of respondents with career ambition of HR 16.3% possess high level, 15.6% moderate level and 10% possess low level of engage diversity and equality competency. Of respondents with career ambition of government job 8.1% possess moderate level, 7.7% and 7.5% possess high and low level of engage diversity and equality competency. Of respondents with career ambition of professor 5% possess low level of engage diversity and equality competency, 4.4% possess moderate level, 1.9% possess high level of engage diversity and equality competency. From the above table it can be inferred invariable of the career ambition of the respondents, they majorly possess moderate level of engage diversity and equality competency.

Table 9.11: Aspiration of the Respondents and their Level of Engage Diversity and Equality Competency

Aspiration of the Respondents	*Level of Engage Diversity and Equality Competency*			*Total*
	Low	*Moderate*	*High*	
Social Worker/Counsellor/HR	25 (62.5%)	74 (46.2%)	54 (51.9%)	153 (50.3%)
UPSC	9 (22.5%)	55 (34.4%)	31 (29.8%)	95 (31.2%)
No Idea	6 (15.0%)	31 (19.4%)	19 (18.3%)	56 (18.4%)
Total	**40 (100.0%)**	**160 (100.0%)**	**104 (100.0%)**	**304 (100.0%)**

The above table shows the aspiration of the respondents and level of engage diversity and equality competency. Of the respondents with aspiration of becoming social worker, counsellor or HR, 62.5% possess low level of engage diversity and equality competency and 46.2% & 51.9% possess moderate and high level of engage diversity and equality competency. Of the respondents aspiring to become UPSC, 34.4% possess moderate level of engage diversity and equality competency, 29.8% & 22.5% possess high and low level of engage diversity and equality competency. Of the respondents who have no idea regarding their aspiration, 19.4% of the respondents possess moderate level of engage diversity and equality competency, 18.3% possess high level of engage diversity and equality competency and 15% possess low level of engage diversity and equality competency. From the above table it can be inferred that irrespective of the aspirations of the respondents majorly respondents possess moderate level of engage diversity and equality competency. The respondents equally possess high level of engage diversity and equality competency.

Table 9.12: Respondent's Awareness about Social Work as a Professional Course and their Level of Engage Diversity and Equality Competency

Respondents' Awareness about Social Work as a Professional Course	***Level of Engage Diversity and Equality Competency***			***Total***
	Low	***Moderate***	***High***	
Yes	34 (85.0%)	120 (75.0%)	77 (74.0%)	231 (76.0%)
No	3 (7.5%)	28 (17.5%)	15 (14.4%)	46 (15.1%)
May be	3 (7.5%)	12 (7.5%)	12 (11.5%)	27 (8.9%)
Total	**40 (100.0%)**	**160 (100.0%)**	**104 (100.0%)**	**304 (100.0%)**

The table shows the respondents' awareness about social work as a professional course and level of engage diversity and equality competency. Of the respondents who have awareness about social work as a profession 85% of the respondents possess low level of engage diversity and equality competency, 75% and 74% possess moderate and high level of engage diversity and equality competency respectively. Of the respondents who don't have awareness on social work as professional course, 17.5% possess moderate level of engage diversity and equality competency, 14.4% possess high level and 7.5% possess low level of engage diversity and equality competency. Of the respondents who have neutral awareness 11.5% possess high level and 7.5% possess moderate and low level of engage diversity and equality competency each. It can be inferred from the table that irrespective of the awareness of professional course on social work, the respondents majorly possess moderate level of engage diversity and equality competency.

Table 9.13: Respondents Faced Criticism for Taking Social Work as Their Graduation and their Level of Engage Diversity and Equality Competency

Respondents Faced Criticism for Taking Social Work as Their Graduation	*Level of Engage Diversity and Equality Competency*			*Total*
	Low	*Moderate*	*High*	
Yes	24 (60.0%)	92 (57.5%)	59 (56.7%)	175 (57.6%)
No	14 (35.0%)	54 (33.8%)	34 (32.7%)	102 (33.6%)
May be	2 (5.0%)	14 (8.8%)	11 (10.6%)	27 (8.9%)
Total	**40 (100.0%)**	**160 (100.0%)**	**104 (100.0%)**	**304 (100.0%)**

The above table shows the respondents faced criticism for taking social work as their graduation and level of engage diversity and equality competency. Of the respondents faced criticism, 60% possess low level, 57.5% possess moderate level and 56.7% possess high level of engage diversity and equality competency. Of the respondents who have not faced criticism 35% possess low level, 33.8% possess moderate and 32.7% possess high level of engage diversity and equality competency. Of the respondents who are neutral regarding the criticism, 10.6% possess high level, 8.8% possess moderate and 5% possess low level of engage diversity and equality competency. It can be inferred from the table that invariable of the criticism faced by respondents, they majorly possess moderate level of engage diversity and equality competency followed by high and low level of engage diversity and equality competency.

Table 9.14: Kind of Criticism Faced by the Respondents for Taking Social Work as their Graduation and their Level of Engage Diversity and Equality Competency

Kind of Criticism Faced by Respondents for Taking Social Work as Their Graduation	*Level of Engage Diversity and Equality Competency*			*Total*
	Low	*Moderate*	*High*	
No	19 (47.5%)	74 (46.2%)	52 (50.0%)	145 (47.7%)

Kind of Criticism Faced by Respondents for Taking Social Work as Their Graduation	*Level of Engage Diversity and Equality Competency*			*Total*
	Low	*Moderate*	*High*	
Positive Criticism	3 (7.5%)	9 (5.6%)	4 (3.8%)	16 (5.3%)
Negative Criticism	18 (45.0%)	77 (48.1%)	48 (46.2%)	143 (47.0%)
Total	**40 (100.0%)**	**160 (100.0%)**	**104 (100.0%)**	**304 (100.0%)**

The table shows the kind of criticism faced by respondents for taking social work as their graduation and level of engage diversity and equality competency. Of the respondents who have not faced criticism, 50% possess high level of engage diversity and equality competency, 47.5% possess low level and 46.2% possess moderate level of engage diversity and equality competency. Of the respondents who faced positive criticism, 7.5% possess low level, 5.6% and 3.8% possess moderate and low level of engage diversity and equality competency respectively. Of the respondents faced negative criticism, 48.1% possess moderate level of engage diversity and equality competency, 46.2% and 45% possess high and low level of engage diversity and equality competency respectively. From the above table it can be inferred that invariable of the kind of criticism faced, the respondents majorly possessed moderate level of engage diversity and equality competency.

Table 9.15: Respondents Feeling of Competent with Regard to Social Work Profession and the Level of Engage Diversity and Equality Competency

Respondents Feeling of Competent with Regard to Social Work Profession	*Level of Engage Diversity and Equality Competency*			*Total*
	Low	*Moderate*	*High*	
Yes	24 (60.0%)	75 (46.9%)	48 (46.2%)	147 (48.4%)
No	0 (0.0%)	2 (1.2%)	4 (3.8%)	6 (2.0%)

Respondents Feeling of Competent with Regard to Social Work Profession	*Level of Engage Diversity and Equality Competency*			*Total*
	Low	*Moderate*	*High*	
No Idea	16 (40.0%)	83 (51.9%)	52 (50.0%)	151 (49.7%)
Total	**40 (100.0%)**	**160 (100.0%)**	**104 (100.0%)**	**304 (100.0%)**

The table shows the respondents feeling of competent with regard to social work profession and level of engage diversity and equality competency. Of the respondents feeling competent, 60% possess low level of engage diversity and equality competency 46.9% and 46.2% possess moderate and low level of engage diversity and equality competency respectively. Of the respondents who don't feel competent 3.8% possess high level and 1.2% possess moderate level of engage diversity and equality competency. Of the respondents who feel neutral, 51.9% possess moderate level, 50% possess high level and 40% possess low level of engage diversity and equality competency. From the above table it can be inferred that irrespective of the feeling of competency of respondents, they majorly possess moderate level of engage diversity and equality competency.

Table 9.16: Respondents List of Skills and the Level of Engage Diversity and Equality Competency

List of Skills	*Level of Engage Diversity and Equality Competency*			*Total*
	Low	*Moderate*	*High*	
Communication Skill	14 (35.0%)	64 (40.0%)	45 (43.3%)	123 (40.5%)
Active Listening	14 (35.0%)	31 (19.4%)	27 (26.0%)	72 (23.7%)
Responsible	3 (7.5%)	38 (23.8%)	10 (9.6%)	51 (16.8%)
No Idea	9 (22.5%)	27 (16.9%)	22 (21.2%)	58 (19.1%)
Total	**40 (100.0%)**	**160 (100.0%)**	**104 (100.0%)**	**304 (100.0%)**

The table 9.16 shows the list of competencies and level of engage diversity and equality competency. Of the respondents with communication skill 43.3% and 40% possess high and moderate level of engage diversity and equality competency respectively and 35% possess low level of engage diversity and equality competency. Of the respondents with active listening skill, 35% possess low level, 26% and 19.4% possess high and moderate level of engage diversity and equality competency respectively. Of the respondents being responsible as their skill, 23.8% possess moderate level of engage diversity and equality competency, 9.6% and 7.5% possess high and low level of engage diversity and equality competency respectively. Of the respondents with no idea on their skills, 22.5% possess low level, 21.2% possess high level and 16.9% possess moderate level of engage diversity and equality competency. From the above table it can be inferred that invariable of the list of skills, the respondents possess moderate level of engage diversity and equality competency.

Table 9.17: Respondents Competent to Deal with the Problems of Individuals and the Level of Engage Diversity and Equality Competency

Respondents Competent to Deal with the Problems of Individual	*Level of Engage Diversity and Equality Competency*			*Total*
	Low	*Moderate*	*High*	
Yes	25 (62.5%)	103 (64.4%)	63 (60.6%)	191 (62.8%)
No	7 (17.5%)	13 (8.1%)	15 (14.4%)	35 (11.5%)
May be	8 (20.0%)	44 (27.5%)	26 (25.0%)	78 (25.7%)
Total	**40 (100.0%)**	**160 (100.0%)**	**104 (100.0%)**	**304 (100.0%)**

The above table shows the respondents competent to deal with the problems of the individual and level of engage diversity and equality competency. Of the respondents who are competent to deal with problems of individual, 64.4% possess moderate level, 62.5% possess low level, 60.6% possess high level of engage diversity and equality competency. Of the respondents who are not competent to deal with problems of individual, 17.5% possess low level, 14.4% possess high level and 8.1% possess moderate level of engage diversity and equality competency. Of the respondents who might be competent to deal with problems of individual, 27.5% possess moderate level, 25% possess high level and 20% possess low level of engage diversity and equality competency. From the above table it can be inferred that irrespective of the respondent's competency to deal with the problem of the individual, the respondents majorly possess moderate level of engage diversity and equality competency.

Table 9.18: Respondents Competent to Deal with the Group Problems and the Level of Engage Diversity and Equality Competency

Respondent's Competent to Deal with the Group Problems	*Level of Engage Diversity and Equality Competency*			*Total*
	Low	*Moderate*	*High*	
Yes	25 (62.5%)	95 (59.4%)	49 (47.1%)	169 (55.6%)
No	3 (7.5%)	12 (7.5%)	8 (7.7%)	23 (7.6%)
May be	12 (30.0%)	53 (33.1%)	47 (45.2%)	112 (36.8%)
Total	**40 (100.0%)**	**160 (100.0%)**	**104 (100.0%)**	**304 (100.0%)**

The above table shows the respondents' competency to deal with the group problems and level of engage diversity and equality competency. Of the respondents who are competent to deal with problems of group, 62.5% possess low level of engage diversity and equality competency, 59.4% and 47.1% possess moderate and high level of engage diversity and equality competency respectively. Of the respondents who are not competent to deal with group problems, 7.7% possess high level and 7.5% possess low and moderate level of engage diversity and equality competency each. Of the respondents who might be competent to deal with group problems, 45.2% possess high level of engage diversity and equality competency, 33.1% possess moderate level and 30% possess low level of engage diversity and equality competency. It can be inferred from the above table that irrespective of the competency to deal with the problems of the group, the respondents majorly possess moderate level of engage diversity and equality competency followed by high level of engage diversity and equality competency.

Table 9.19: Respondents Competent to Deal with the Community Problems and the Level of Engage Diversity and Equality Competency

Respondent's Competent to Deal with the Community Problems	*Level of Engage Diversity and Equality Competency*			*Total*
	Low	**Moderate**	**High**	
Yes	21 (52.5%)	67 (41.9%)	50. (48.1%)	138 (45.4%)
No	10 (25.0%)	42 (26.2%)	26 (25.0%)	78 (25.7%)
May be	9 (22.5%)	51 (31.9%)	28 (26.9%)	88 (28.9%)
Total	**40 (100.0%)**	**160 (100.0%)**	**104 (100.0%)**	**304 (100.0%)**

The above table shows the respondents' competency to deal with community problems and level of engage diversity and equality competency. Of the respondents who are competent to deal with community problems, 52.5% possess low level of engage diversity and equality competency, 48.1% and 41.9% possess high and moderate level of engage diversity and equality competency. Of the respondents who are not competent to deal with community problems, 26.2% possess moderate level of engage diversity and equality competency, 25% possess high and low level of engage diversity and equality competency each. Of the respondents who might possess the competency to deal with the community problems, 31.9% possess moderate level of engage diversity and equality competency, 26.9% possess high level and 22.5% possess low level of engage diversity and equality competency. It can be inferred from the above table that the invariable of competency to deal with community problem, the respondents majorly possess moderate level of engage diversity and equality competency followed by high and low level of engage diversity and equality competency.

CHAPTER 10

Level of Rights, Justice and Economic Wellbeing Competency

This chapter involves the analysis and interpretation of level of rights, justice and economic wellbeing competency and demographic variable, reason for choosing social work, perception, career ambition, aspiration, criticism faced and social worker skills.

Table 10.1: Age of the Respondents and the Level of Rights, Justice and Economic Wellbeing Competency

Age of the Respondents	*Level of Rights, Justice and Economic Wellbeing Competency*			*Total*
	Low	*Moderate*	*High*	
Below 21	16 (53.3%)	51 (48.1%)	85 (50.6%)	152 (50.0%)
21–25	13 (43.3%)	51 (48.1%)	75 (44.6%)	139 (45.7%)
25–29	1 (3.3%)	4 (3.8%)	8 (4.8%)	13 (4.3%)
Total	**30 (100.0%)**	**106 (100.0%)**	**168 (100.0%)**	**304 (100.0%)**

The above table represents the level of rights, justice and economic well-being with regards to the respondent's age. The level of rights, justice and economic well-being is low for 53.3% respondents of age below 21 years. The level of rights, justice and economic well-being is high for 50% respondents of age below 21 years. The level of rights, justice and economic well-being is moderate for 48.1% respondents of age below 21 years. 48.1% respondents of age between 21 to 25 years with moderate level of rights justice and economic wellbeing competency. 44.6% respondents age between 21 and 25 years with high level of rights justice and economic wellbeing competency. 43.3% respondents age between 21 and 25 years with low level of rights justice and economic wellbeing competency. 4.8% respondents age between 25 and 29 years with high level of rights justice and economic wellbeing competency. 3.8% respondents age between 25 and 29 years with moderate level of rights justice and economic wellbeing competency. 3.3% respondents age between 25 and 29 years with low level of rights justice and economic wellbeing competency.

Table 10.2: Gender of the Respondents and the Level of Rights, Justice and Economic Wellbeing Competency

Gender of the Respondents	*Level of Rights, Justice and Economic Wellbeing Competency*			*Total*
	Low	*Moderate*	*High*	
Prefer not to say	0 (0.0%)	0 (0.0%)	1 (0.6%)	1 (0.3%)
Female	14 (46.7%)	69 (65.1%)	115 (68.5%)	198 (65.1%)
Male	16 (53.3%)	37 (34.9%)	52 (31.0%)	105 (34.5%)
Total	**30 (100.0%)**	**106 (100.0%)**	**168 (100.0%)**	**304 (100.0%)**

This table depicts the level of right, justice and economic well-being competency of the respondents based on the gender. 68.5% of the women respondents have high level of right, justice and economic well-being competency. 65.1% of the women respondents who have moderate level of right, justice and economic well-being competency. 46.7% of the women respondents have low level of right, justice and economic well-being competency. 53.3% of the men respondents have low level of right, justice and economic well-being competency. 34.9% of the men respondents have moderate level of right, justice and economic well-being and 31% of the men respondents have high level of right, justice and economic well-being competency. 0.6% who prefer not to say the gender have high level of right, justice and economic well-being competency.

Table 10.3: Educational Qualification of the Respondents and the Level of Rights, Justice and Economic Wellbeing Competency

Educational Qualification of the Respondents	*Level of Rights, Justice and Economic Wellbeing Competency*			*Total*
	Low	*Moderate*	*High*	
II & III BSW	19 (63.3%)	51 (48.1%)	82 (48.8%)	152 (50.0%)
II MSW	11 (36.7%)	55 (51.9%)	86 (51.2%)	152 (50.0%)
Total	**30 (100.0%)**	**106 (100.0%)**	**168 (100.0%)**	**304 (100.0%)**

This table depicts the level of right, justice and economic well-being competency based on the educational qualification of the respondents. Among the respondents pursuing II- and III-year BSW, 63.3% of the respondents possess low level, 48.8% of the respondents possess high level and 48.1% of the respondents possess moderate level of rights, justice and economic wellbeing competency. Among the respondents pursuing II-year MSW, 51.9% of the respondents possess moderate level, 51.2% of the respondent's high level and 36.7% of the respondents possess low level of rights, justice and economic wellbeing competency.

Table 10.4: Post Graduate Respondents Under-graduation and the Level of Rights, Justice and Economic Wellbeing Competency

Post Graduate Respondents Under-graduation	*Level of Rights, Justice and Economic Wellbeing Competency*			*Total*
	Low	*Moderate*	*High*	
BSW	3 (10.0%)	24 (22.6%)	42 (25.0%)	69 (22.7%)
OTHER DEGREE	8 (26.7%)	31 (29.2%)	44 (26.2%)	83 (27.3%)
Not Applicable (Under Graduate Respondents)	19 (63.3%)	51 (48.1%)	82 (48.8%)	152 (50.0%)
Total	**30 (100.0%)**	**106 (100.0%)**	**168 (100.0%)**	**304 (100.0%)**

The table 10.4 represents the level of right, justice and economic well-being in accordance with the post graduate respondent's under-graduation. 25% of BSW graduates, possess high level of right, justice and economic well-being competency. 22.6% of BSW graduates, possess moderate level of right, justice and economic well-being competency. 10% of BSW graduates, possess low level of right, justice and economic well-being competency. 29.2% of the respondents pursued other than social work possesses moderate level, 26.7% of the respondents possess low level and 26.2% of the respondents possess high level of right, justice and economic well-being competency.

Table 10.5: Domicile of the Respondents and the Level of Rights, Justice and Economic Wellbeing Competency

Domicile of the Respondents	*Level of Rights, Justice and Economic Wellbeing Competency*			*Total*
	Low	*Moderate*	*High*	
Tamil Nadu	25 (83.3%)	91 (85.8%)	141 (83.9%)	257 (84.5%)
Outside Tamil Nadu	5 (16.7%)	15 (14.2%)	27 (16.1%)	47 (15.5%)
Total	**30 (100.0%)**	**106 (100.0%)**	**168 (100.0%)**	**304 (100.0%)**

This table shows the level of rights, justice and economic well-being competency based on the domicile of the respondents. Among the respondents from Tamilnadu, 85.8% respondents possess moderate level, 83.9% possess high level and 83.3% of the respondents possess low level of rights, justice and economic well-being competency. Among the respondents outside Tamilnadu, 16.7% possess low level, 16.1% possess high level and 14.2% of the respondents possess moderate level of rights, justice and economic wellbeing competency.

Table 10.6: Major Subjects Studied by the Respondents during 12th Standard and the Level of Rights, Justice and Economic Wellbeing Competency

Major Subjects Studied by the Respondents during 12th Standard	*Level of Rights, Justice and Economic Wellbeing Competency*			*Total*
	Low	*Moderate*	*High*	
Bio-Maths	4 (13.3%)	15 (14.2%)	40 (23.8%)	59 (19.4%)
Computer Sciences	5 (16.7%)	23 (21.7%)	24 (14.3%)	52 (17.1%)
Commerce	18 (60.0%)	55 (51.9%)	81 (48.2%)	154 (50.7%)
Humanities	3 (10.0%)	13 (12.3%)	23 (13.7%)	39 (12.8%)
Total	**30 (100.0%)**	**106 (100.0%)**	**168 (100.0%)**	**304 (100.0%)**

The table shows the level of right, justice and economic well-being competency based on the major subjects studied by the respondents during 12th standard.23.8% respondents who studied Bio-Maths, possess high level of right, justice and economic well-being competency. 14.2% studied Bio-Maths, who have moderate level of right, justice and economic well-being competency. 13.3% who studied Bio-Maths, possess low level of right, justice and economic well-being competency. 21.7% respondents studied computer sciences, possess moderate level of right, justice and economic well-being. 16.7% respondents studied computer sciences, possess low level of right, justice and economic well-being. 14.3% respondents studied computer sciences, possess high level of right, justice and economic well-being competency. Among the respondents who studied commerce during 12th standard, 60% of the respondents possess low level, 51.9% possess moderate level and 48.2% of the respondents possess high level of rights, justice and economic wellbeing competency. Among the respondents pursued humanities during 12th standard, 13.7% respondents possess high level, 12.3% of the respondents possess moderate level and 10% possess low level of rights, justice and economic wellbeing competency.

Table 10.7: Respondents Reasons for Choosing Social Work and the Level of Rights, Justice and Economic Wellbeing Competency

Respondents' Reasons for Choosing Social Work	*Level of Rights, Justice and Economic Wellbeing*			*Total*
	Low	*Moderate*	*High*	
Own Interest	17 (56.7%)	63 (59.4%)	107 (63.7%)	187 (61.5%)
Parents/Relatives Recommendation	13 (43.3%)	41 (38.7%)	57 (33.9%)	111 (36.5%)
Siblings Studied/Influence	0 (0.0%)	2 (1.9%)	4 (2.4%)	6 (2.0%)
Total	**30 (100.0%)**	**106 (100.0%)**	**168 (100.0%)**	**304 (100.0%)**

This table depicts the level of right, justice and economic well-being competency based on the reason for choosing social work as their undergraduate discipline. Among the respondents chosen social work on their own interest, 63.7% of the respondents possess high level, 59.44% respondents possess moderate level and 56.7% of the respondents possess low level of rights, justice and economic wellbeing competency. 43.3% respondents who chose social work because of parents/relative's recommendation possess low level of right, justice and economic well-being competency. 38.7% respondents who chose social work because of parents/relatives recommendation possess moderate level of right, justice and economic well-being competency. 33.9% respondents who chose social work because of their parents/relatives recommendation possess high level of right, justice and economic well-being competency. Among the respondents who chosen social work because of the siblings studied social work/ influence, 2.4% respondents possess high level and 1.9% respondents possess moderate level of right, justice and economic well-being competency.

Table 10.8: Respondents Perception about Social Work and the Level of Rights, Justice and Economic Wellbeing Competency

Respondents Perception about Social Work	*Level of Rights, Justice and Economic Wellbeing Competency*			*Total*
	Low	*Moderate*	*High*	
Practise Based Profession	4 (13.3%)	15 (14.2%)	40 (23.8%)	59 (19.4%)
Value Oriented Subject	5 (16.7%)	23 (21.7%)	24 (14.3%)	52 (17.1%)
Helping Profession	18 (60.0%)	55 (51.9%)	81 (48.2%)	154 (50.7%)
Art Course	3 (10.0%)	13 (12.3%)	23 (13.7%)	39 (12.8%)
Total	**30 (100.0%)**	**106 (100.0%)**	**168 (100.0%)**	**304 (100.0%)**

The table states the level of right, justice and economic well-being competency based on the perception about social work. Among the respondents who perceived social work as practice-based profession, 23.8% possess high level, 14.2% possess moderate level and 13.3% of the respondents possess low level of right, justice and economic wellbeing competency. Among the respondents who perceived social work as value-oriented subject, 21.7% respondents possess moderate level, 16.7% of the respondents possess low level and 14.3% of the respondents possess high level of rights, justice and economic wellbeing competency. 60% who perceived it as helping profession, possess low level of right, justice and economic wellbeing competency. 51.9% who perceived it as helping profession, possess moderate level of right, justice and economic wellbeing competency. 48.2% who perceived it as helping profession, possess high level of right, justice and economic wellbeing competency. Among the respondents who perceived social work as art course, 13.7% respondents possess high level, 12.3% respondents possess moderate level and 10% of the respondents possess low level of rights, justice and economic wellbeing competency.

Table 10.9: Family Members of the Respondents Studied Social Work and the Level of Rights, Justice and Economic Wellbeing Competency

Family Members of the Respondents Studied Social Work	*Level of Rights, Justice and Economic Wellbeing Competency*			*Total*
	Low	*Moderate*	*High*	
Yes	3 (10.0%)	20 (18.9%)	24 (14.3%)	47 (15.5%)
No	27 (90.0%)	86 (81.1%)	144 (85.7%)	257 (84.5%)
Total	**30 (100.0%)**	**106 (100.0%)**	**168 (100.0%)**	**304 (100.0%)**

This table represents the level of right, justice and economic well-being competency with respect to the family members of the respondents studied social work. 18.9% respondents whose family members studied social work, possess moderate level of right, justice and economic well-being competency. 14.3% respondents whose family members studied social work, possess high level of right, justice and economic well-being competency. 10% respondents whose family members studied social work, possess low level of right, justice and economic well-being competency. Among the respondents whose have not pursued social work, 90% of the respondents possess low level, 85.7% possess high level and 81.1% of the respondents possess moderate level of rights, justice and economic wellbeing competency.

Table 10.10: Career Ambition of the Respondents and the Level of Rights, Justice and Economic Wellbeing Competency

Career Ambition of the Respondents	*Level of Rights, Justice and Economic Wellbeing Competency*			*Total*
	Low	*Moderate*	*High*	
Professional Social Worker	9 (30.0%)	31 (29.2%)	49 (29.2%)	89 (29.3%)
Psychiatric/Medical Social Worker/Mental Health/Counsellor	10 (33.3%)	38 (35.8%)	63 (37.5%)	111 (36.5%)

Career Ambition of the Respondents	*Level of Rights, Justice and Economic Wellbeing Competency*			*Total*
	Low	*Moderate*	*High*	
N.G.O/Orphan Homes	1 (3.3%)	9 (8.5%)	13 (7.7%)	23 (7.6%)
H.R.	5 (16.7%)	16 (15.1%)	25 (14.9%)	46 (15.1%)
Government Jobs	3 (10.0%)	8 (7.5%)	13 (7.7%)	24 (7.9%)
Professor	2 (6.7%)	4 (3.8%)	5 (3.0%)	11 (3.6%)
Total	**30 (100.0%)**	**106 (100.0%)**	**168 (100.0%)**	**304 (100.0%)**

The above table represents the level of right, justice and economic well-being competency based on the career ambition of the respondents. 30% respondents whose career ambition is to become a professional social worker, 33.3% respondents whose ambition is to become Psychiatric/Medical Social Worker/Mental Health/ Counsellor, 3.3% respondents whose ambition is to set up an NGO/Orphanage, 16.7% respondents whose aim is to become an HR, 10% respondents who prefer government jobs and 16.7% respondents' ambition is becoming a professor possess low level of right, justice and economic well-being competency.29.2% respondents whose career ambition is to become a professional social worker, 35.8% respondents whose ambition is to become Psychiatric/Medical Social Worker/Mental Health/Counsellor, 8.5% respondents whose ambition is to set up an NGO/Orphanage, 15.1% respondents whose aim is to become an HR, 7.5% respondents who prefer government jobs and 3.8% respondents' ambition is becoming a professor possess moderate level of right, justice and economic well-being competency. 29.2% respondents whose career ambition is to become a professional social worker, 37.5% respondents whose ambition is to become Psychiatric/Medical Social Worker/Mental Health/Counsellor, 7.7% respondents whose ambition is to set up an NGO/Orphanage, 14.9% respondents whose aim is to become an HR, 7.7% respondents who prefer government jobs and 3% respondents' ambition is becoming a professor possess high level of right, justice and economic well-being competency.

Table 10.11: Aspiration of the Respondents and the Level of Rights, Justice and Economic Wellbeing Competency

Aspiration of the Respondents	*Level of Rights, Justice and Economic Wellbeing Competency*			*Total*
	Low	*Moderate*	*High*	
Social Worker/Counsellor/HR/	16 (53.3%)	50 (47.2%)	87 (51.8%)	153 (50.3%)
UPSC	8 (26.7%)	37 (34.9%)	50 (29.8%)	95 (31.2%)
No Idea	6 (20.0%)	19 (17.9%)	31 (18.5%)	56 (18.4%)
Total	**30 (100.0%)**	**106 (100.0%)**	**168 (100.0%)**	**304 (100.0%)**

This table shows that level of right, justice and economic well-being competency in accordance with the aspiration of the respondents. 53.3% respondents who aspired for Social Work/HR/Counsellor, possess low level of right, justice and economic well-being competency. 51.8% respondents who aspired for Social Work/HR/Counsellor, possess high level of right, justice and economic well-being competency. 47.2% respondents who aspired for Social Work/HR/Counsellor, possess moderate level of right, justice and economic well-being competency. 34.9% respondents who aspired for union public service commission (UPSC) possess moderate level of right, justice and economic well-being competency. 29.8% respondents who aspired for union public service commission (UPSC) possess high level of right, justice and economic well-being competency. 26.7% respondents who aspired for union public service commission (UPSC) possess low level of right, justice and economic well-being competency. Among the respondents those without any idea about their aspiration, 20% respondents possess high level, 18.5% possess high level and 17.9% of the respondents possess moderate level of right, justice and economic well-being competency.

Table 10.12: Respondent's Awareness about Social Work as a Professional Course and the Level of Rights, Justice and Economic Wellbeing Competency

Respondent's Awareness about Social Work as a Professional Course	*Level of Rights, Justice and Economic Wellbeing Competency*			*Total*
	Low	*Moderate*	*High*	
Yes	22 (73.3%)	77 (72.6%)	132 (78.6%)	231 (76.0%)
No	5 (16.7%)	20 (18.9%)	21 (12.5%)	46 (15.1%)
No idea	3 (10.0%)	9 (8.5%)	15 (8.9%)	27 (8.9%)
Total	**30 (100.0%)**	**106 (100.0%)**	**168 (100.0%)**	**304 (100.0%)**

This table shows about the level of right, justice and economic well-being competency based on the respondents' awareness about social work as a professional course. Among the respondents who are aware of social work as a professional course, 78.6% respondents possess high level, 73.3% respondents possess low level and 72.6% possess moderate level of right, justice and economic well-being competency. Among the respondents who were not aware that social work is a professional course, 18.9% respondents possess moderate level, 16.7% of the respondents possess low level and 12.5% possess high level of right, justice and economic well-being competency. Among the respondents who may or may not aware that social work is a professional course, 10% of the respondents possess low level, 8.9% respondent's possess high level and 8.5% of the respondents possess moderate level of right, justice and economic well-being competency.

Table 10.13: Respondents Faced Criticism for Taking Social Work as their Graduation and Level of Rights, Justice and Economic Wellbeing Competency

Respondents Faced Criticism for Taking Social Work as Their Graduation	*Level of Rights, Justice and Economic Wellbeing Competency*			*Total*
	Low	*Moderate*	*High*	
Yes	18 (60.0%)	62 (58.5%)	95 (56.5%)	175 (57.6%)
No	10 (33.3%)	33 (31.1%)	59 (35.1%)	102 (33.6%)
May be	2 (6.7%)	11 (10.4%)	14 (8.3%)	27 (8.9%)
Total	**30 (100.0%)**	**106 (100.0%)**	**168 (100.0%)**	**304 (100.0%)**

The above table depicts the level of right, justice and economic well-being with respect to the criticism faced by the respondents for taking social work as their graduation. Among the respondents who faced criticism for taking social work as their graduation, 60% respondents possess low level, 58.5% possess moderate level and 56.5% of the respondents possess high level of rights, justice and economic well-being competency. Among the respondents who haven't faced any criticism for taking social work as their graduation, 35.1% of the respondents possess high level, 33.3% of the respondents possess low level and 31.1% of the respondents possess moderate level of rights, justice and economic wellbeing competency. Among the respondents who may or may not faced criticism for taking social work as their graduation, 10.4% respondents possess moderate level, 8.3% respondents possess high level and 6.7% of the respondents possess low level of rights, justice and economic well-being competency.

Table 10.14: Kind of Criticism Faced by the Respondents for Taking Social Work as Their Graduation and the Level of Rights, Justice and Economic Wellbeing Competency

Kind of Criticism Faced by the Respondents for Taking Social Work as their Graduation	*Level of Rights, Justice and Economic Wellbeing Competency*			*Total*
	Low	*Moderate*	*High*	
No	13 (43.3%)	49 (46.2%)	83 (49.4%)	145 (47.7%)
Positive Criticism	2 (6.7%)	5 (4.7%)	9 (5.4%)	16 (5.3%)
Negative Criticism	15 (50.0%)	52 (49.1%)	76 (45.2%)	143 (47.0%)
Total	**30 (100.0%)**	**106 (100.0%)**	**168 (100.0%)**	**304 (100.0%)**

The above table represents the level of right, justice and economic well-being competency based on the kind of criticism faced by the respondents for taking social work as their graduation. 49.4% respondents who doesn't faced any criticism, possess high level, 46.2% respondents who doesn't faced any criticism, possess moderate level and 43.3% respondents who doesn't faced any criticism, possess low level of right, justice and economic well-being. Among the respondents who faced positive criticism for taking social work as their graduation, 6.7% respondents possess low level, 5.4% of the respondents possess high level and 4.7% of the respondents possess low level of right, justice and economic well-being competency. Among the respondents who faced negative criticism for taking social work as their graduation, 50% of the respondents possess low level, 49.1% respondents possess moderate level and 45.2% of the respondents possess high level of rights, justice and economic well-being competency.

Table 10.15: Respondents Feeling of Competent with Regard to Social Work Profession and the Level of Rights, Justice and Economic Wellbeing Competency

Respondents Feeling of Competent with Regard to Social Work Profession	*Level of Rights, Justice and Economic Wellbeing Competency*			*Total*
	Low	*Moderate*	*High*	
Yes	13 (43.3%)	48 (45.3%)	86 (51.2%)	147 (48.4%)
No	0 (0.0%)	2 (1.9%)	4 (2.4%)	6 (2.0%)
May be	17 (56.7%)	56 (52.8%)	78 (46.4%)	151 (49.7%)
Total	**30 (100.0%)**	**106 (100.0%)**	**168 (100.0%)**	**304 (100.0%)**

The above table depicts the level of right, justice and economic well-being competency based on the respondents' feeling of competent with regard to social work profession. 51.2% respondents who feels competent with high level of right, justice and economic well-being competency. 45.3% respondents who feels competent with moderate level of right, justice and economic well-being competency. 43.3% respondents who feels competent with low level of right, justice and economic well-being competency. Among the respondents who are feeling not competent with regard to social work, 2.4% of the respondents possess high level and 1.9% of the respondents possess moderate level of right, justice and economic well-being competency. Among the respondents who may or may not be competent with regard to social work profession, 56.7% of the respondents possess low level, 52.8% of the respondents possess moderate level and 46.4% of the respondents possess high level of right, justice and economic well-being competency.

Table 10.16: List of Skills and the Level of Rights, Justice and Economic Wellbeing Competency

List of Skills	*Level of Rights, Justice and Economic Wellbeing Competency*			*Total*
	Low	*Moderate*	*High*	
Communication Skill	10 (33.3%)	42 (39.6%)	71 (42.3%)	123 (40.5%)
Active Listening	7 (23.3%)	24 (22.6%)	41 (24.4%)	72 (23.7%)
Responsible	4 (13.3%)	23 (21.7%)	24 (14.3%)	51 (16.8%)
No Idea	9 (30.0%)	17 (16.0%)	32 (19.0%)	58 (19.1%)
Total	**30 (100.0%)**	**106 (100.0%)**	**168 (100.0%)**	**304 (100.0%)**

This table shows the level of right, justice and economic well-being competency based on the respondent's skills. Among the respondents who possess communication skills, 42.3% respondents have high level, 39.6% of the respondents have moderate level and 33.3% of the respondents have low level of rights, justice and economic well-being competency. Among the respondents who possess active listening skill, 24.4% of the respondents have high level, 23.3% of the respondents possess low level and 22.6% of the respondents possess moderate level of rights, justice and economic well-being competency. Among the respondents who feels they are responsible, 21% of the respondents possess moderate level, 14.3% possess high level and 13.3% possess low level of rights, justice and economic well-being competency. 30% respondents who have no idea possess low level of right, justice and economic well-being competency. 19% respondents who have no idea possess high level of right, justice and economic well-being competency and 16% respondents who have no idea possess moderate level of right, justice and economic well-being competency.

Table 10.17: Respondents Competent to deal with the Problems of Individuals and the Level of Rights, Justice and Economic Wellbeing Competency

Respondents Competent to Deal with the Problems of Individuals	*Level of Rights, Justice and Economic Wellbeing Competency*			*Total*
	Low	*Moderate*	*High*	
Yes	20 (66.7%)	68 (64.2%)	103 (61.3%)	191 (62.8%)
No	2 (6.7%)	9 (8.5%)	24 (14.3%)	35 (11.5%)
May be	8 (26.7%)	29 (27.4%)	41 (24.4%)	78 (25.7%)
Total	**30 (100.0%)**	**106 (100.0%)**	**168 (100.0%)**	**304 (100.0%)**

The above table represents the level of right, justice and economic well-being competency with respect to the respondents competent to deal with the individuals' problems. Among the respondents who feels competent to deal with individual's problems, 66.7% respondents possess low level, 64.2% of the respondents possess moderate level and 61.3% of the respondents possess high level of right, justice and economic well-being competency. Among the respondents who feels not competent to deal with individual problems, 14.3% of the respondents possess high level, 8.5% of the respondents possess moderate level and 6.7% of the respondents possess low level of right, justice and economic well-being competency. Among the respondents who may or may not be competent to deal with individual problems, 27.4% of the respondents possess moderate level, 26.7% of the respondents possess low level and 24.4% of the respondents' high level of right, justice and economic well-being competency.

Table 10.18: Respondents Competent to deal with the Group Problems and the Level of Rights, Justice and Economic Wellbeing Competency

Respondents Competent to Deal with the Group Problems	*Level of Rights, Justice and Economic Wellbeing Competency*			*Total*
	Low	*Moderate*	*High*	
Yes	17 (56.7%)	57 (53.8%)	95 (56.5%)	169 (55.6%)
No	1 (3.3%)	4 (3.8%)	18 (10.7%)	23 (7.6%)
May be	12 (40.0%)	45 (42.5%)	55 (32.7%)	112 (36.8%)
Total	**30 (100.0%)**	**106 (100.0%)**	**168 (100.0%)**	**304 (100.0%)**

This table depicts the level of right, justice and economic well-being competency based on the respondents competent to deal with group problems. 56.7% respondents who had competent to deal with group problems possess low level of right, justice and economic well-being competency. 56.5% respondents who had competent possess high level of right, justice and economic well-being competency. 53.8% respondents who had competent possess moderate level of right, justice and economic well-being competency. Among the respondents who feels not competent to deal with group problems, 10.7% respondents possess high level, 3.8% possess moderate level and 3.3% of the respondents possess low level of rights, justice and economic well-being competency. Among the respondents who may or may not be competent to deal with group problems, 42.5% of the respondents possess moderate level, 40% respondents possess low level and 32.7% of the respondents possess high level of right, justice and economic well-being competency.

Table 10.19: Respondents Competent to Deal with the Community Problems and the Level of Rights, Justice and Economic Wellbeing Competency

Respondents Competent to Deal with the Community Problems	*Level of Rights, Justice and Economic Wellbeing Competency*			*Total*
	Low	*Moderate*	*High*	
Yes	13 (43.3%)	49 (46.2%)	76 (45.2%)	138 (45.4%)
No	7 (23.3%)	29 (27.4%)	42 (25.0%)	78 (25.7%)
May be	10 (33.3%)	28 (26.4%)	50 (29.8%)	88 (28.9%)
Total	**30 (100.0%)**	**106 (100.0%)**	**168 (100.0%)**	**304 (100.0%)**

This table depicts the level of right, justice and economic well-being competency based on the respondents competent to deal with community problems. 46.2% respondents who feel competent to deal with community problems possess moderate level of right, justice and economic well-being competency. 45.2% respondents who feels competent, possess high level of right, justice and economic well-being competency.43.3% respondents who feels competent, possess low level of right, justice and economic well-being competency. Among the respondents who feels not competent to deal with community problems, 27.4% of the respondents possess moderate level, 25% of the respondents possess high level and 23.3% of the respondents possess low level of rights, justice and economic wellbeing competency. Among the respondents who may or may not be competent to deal with community problems, 33.3% respondents possess low level, 29.8% of the respondents possess high level and 26.4% of the respondents possess moderate level of rights, justice and economic well-being competency.

CHAPTER 11

Level of Knowledge about Human Behaviour Competency

This chapter involves the analysis and interpretation of level of knowledge about human behaviour competency and demographic variable, reason for choosing social work, perception, career ambition, aspiration, criticism faced and social worker skills.

Table 11.1: Age and Level of Knowledge about Human Behaviour Competency of the Respondents

Age of the Respondents	*Level of Knowledge about Human Behaviour Competency*			*Total*
	Low	*Moderate*	*High*	
Below 21	20 (52.6%)	86 (50.0%)	46 (48.9%)	152 (50.0%)
21–25	17 (44.7%)	76 (44.2%)	46 (48.9%)	139 (45.7%)
25–29	1 (2.6%)	10 (5.8%)	2 (2.1%)	13 (4.3%)
Total	**38 (100.0%)**	**172 (100.0%)**	**94 (100.0%)**	**304 (100.0%)**

The above table talks about the level of knowledge about human behaviour competency with regards to the respondent's age. Among the respondents below 21 years of age, 52.6% low level of knowledge about human behaviour competency, 50% of the have moderate level of knowledge about human behaviour competency and 48.9% of the respondents have high level of knowledge about human behaviour competency. 21–25 of the respondents have (48.9%) have high level of knowledge about human behaviour competency (44.7%) have low level of knowledge about human behaviour competency (44.2%) have moderate level of knowledge about human behaviour competency. 25–29 of the respondents have (5.8%) have moderate level of knowledge about human behaviour competency (2.6%) have low level of knowledge about human behaviour competency (2.1%) have high level of knowledge about human behaviour competency.

Table 11.2: Gender and Level of Knowledge about Human Behaviour Competency of the Respondents

Gender of the Respondents	*Level of Knowledge about Human Behaviour Competency*			*Total*
	Low	*Moderate*	*High*	
Female	21 (55.3%)	110 (64.0%)	67 (71.3%)	198 (65.1%)
Male	17 (44.7%)	62 (36.0%)	26 (27.7%)	105 (34.5%)
Prefer not to say	0 (0.0%)	0 (0.0%)	1 (1.1%)	1 (0.3%)
Total	**38 (100.0%)**	**172 (100.0%)**	**94 (100.0%)**	**304 (100.0%)**

This table depicts the level of knowledge about human behaviour competency based on the gender. 71.3% of the women respondents have high-level of knowledge about human behaviour competency, 64% have moderate level of knowledge about human behaviour competency. And 55.3% have low level of knowledge about human behaviour competency. Among the male respondents 44.7% have low level of knowledge about human behaviour competency, 36% have moderate level and 27.7% have high level of knowledge about human behaviour competency. 1.1% of the respondent prefer not to say the gender possess high level of knowledge about human behaviour competency.

Table 11.3: Educational Qualification and Level of Knowledge about Human Behaviour Competency of the Respondents

Educational Qualification of the Respondents	*Level of Knowledge about Human Behaviour Competency*			*Total*
	Low	Moderate	*High*	
II & III BSW	26 (68.4%)	84 (48.8%)	42 (44.7%)	152 (50.0%)
II MSW	12 (31.6%)	88 (51.2%)	52 (55.3%)	152 (50.0%)
Total	**38 (100.0%)**	**172 (100.0%)**	**94 (100.0%)**	**304 (100.0%)**

This above table of education qualification and level of knowledge about human behaviour competency of the respondents. Among the second year and third year BSW respondents 68.4% have low level of knowledge about human behaviour competency, 48.8% of the respondents have moderate level and 44.7% have high level of knowledge about human behaviour competency of the respondents 55.3% of the respondents have knowledge about human behaviour of the respondents 51.2% of the respondents have moderate level of knowledge about human behaviour competency of the respondents 31.6% of the second year MSW have low level of knowledge about human behaviour competency of the respondents.

Table 11.4: Post Graduate Respondents under Graduate Degree and Level of Knowledge about Human Behaviour Competency of the Respondents

Post Graduate Respondents Under Graduate Degree	*Level of Knowledge about Human Behaviour Competency*			*Total*
	Low	*Moderate*	*High*	
BSW	5 (13.2%)	38 (22.1%)	26 (27.7%)	69 (22.7%)
OTHER DEGREE	7 (18.4%)	50 (29.1%)	26 (27.7%)	83 (27.3%)

Post Graduate Respondents Under Graduate Degree	*Level of Knowledge about Human Behaviour Competency*			*Total*
	Low	*Moderate*	*High*	
Not Applicable (Under Graduate Respondents)	26 (68.4%)	84 (48.8%)	42 (44.7%)	152 (50.0%)
Total	**38 (100.0%)**	**172 (100.0%)**	**94 (100.0%)**	**304 (100.0%)**

This table depicts the level of knowledge about human behaviour competency of the respondents based on the post graduate respondents under graduation. Among the respondents pursued social work in under graduation, 27.7% of the respondents have high level of knowledge about human behaviour competency, 22.1% have moderate level and 13.2% of the respondents have low level of knowledge about human behaviour competency. Among the respondents pursued other degree apart from social work, 29.1% of the respondents possess moderate level of knowledge about human behaviour competency, 27.7% have high level of and 18.4% low level of knowledge about human behaviour competency.

Table 11.5: Domicile and Level of Knowledge about Human Behaviour Competency of the Respondents

Domicile of the Respondents	*Level of Knowledge About Human Behaviour Competency*			*Total*
	Low	*Moderate*	*High*	
Tamilnadu	35 (92.1%)	140 (81.4%)	82 (87.2%)	257 (84.5%)
Outside Tamilnadu	3 (7.9%)	32 (18.6%)	12 (12.8%)	47 (15.5%)
Total	**38 (100.0%)**	**172 (100.0%)**	**94 (100.0%)**	**304 (100.0%)**

This table shows the level of knowledge about human behaviour competency based on the domicile of the respondents. Among the respondents from Tamilnadu, 92.1% low level of knowledge about human behaviour competency, 87.2%. of respondents have high level and 81.4% of the respondents have moderate level of knowledge about human behaviour competency. Among the respondents outside Tamilnadu, 18.6% of the respondents have moderate level of knowledge about human behaviour competency, 12.8% of respondents have high level and 7.9% of respondents have low level of knowledge about human behaviour competency.

Table 11.6: Major Subjects Studied during 12th Standard and Level of Knowledge about Human Behaviour of the Respondents

Major Subjects Studied by the Respondents during 12th Standard	*Level of Knowledge about Human Behaviour Competency*			*Total*
	Low	*Moderate*	*High*	
Bio-Maths	4 (10.5%)	32 (18.6%)	23 (24.5%)	59 (19.4%)
Computer Sciences	5 (13.2%)	34 (19.8%)	13 (13.8%)	52 (17.1%)
Commerce	22 (57.9%)	85 (49.4%)	47 (50.0%)	154 (50.7%)
Humanities	7 (18.4%)	21 (12.2%)	11 (11.7%)	39 (12.8%)
Total	**38 (100.0%)**	**172 (100.0%)**	**94 (100.0%)**	**304 (100.0%)**

The above table shows the level of knowledge about human behaviour competency based on the major subjects studied by the respondents during 12th standard. Among the respondents who studied Bio-Maths, 24.5% have high level of knowledge about human behaviour competency, 18.6% have moderate level and 10.5% have low level of knowledge about human behaviour competency. Among the respondents who studied Computer Sciences, 19.8% have moderate level of knowledge about human behaviour competency, 13.8% of the respondents have high level and 13.2% of the respondents have low level of knowledge about human behaviour competency. Among the respondents who studied Commerce, 57.9%

of the respondents have low level of knowledge about human behaviour competency, 50% of the respondents have high level and 49.4% of the respondents have moderate level of knowledge about human behaviour competency. Among the respondents who studied humanities, 18.4% of the respondents have low level of knowledge about human behaviour competency, 12.2% of the respondents have moderate level and 11.7% of the respondents have high-level of knowledge about human behaviour competency.

Table 11.7: Reason for Choosing Social Work and Level of Knowledge about Human Behaviour Competency of the Respondents

Respondents' Reasons for Choosing Social Work	*Level of Knowledge about Human Behaviour Competency*			*Total*
	Low	*Moderate*	*High*	
Own Interest	24 (63.2%)	100 (58.1%)	63 (67.0%)	187 (61.5%)
Parents/Relatives Recommendation	14 (36.8%)	67 (39.0%)	30 (31.9%)	111 (36.5%)
Siblings Studied/Influence	0 (0.0%)	5 (2.9%)	1 (1.1%)	6 (2.0%)
Total	**38 (100.0%)**	**172 (100.0%)**	**94 (100.0%)**	**304 (100.0%)**

This table depicts the level of knowledge about human behaviour competency based on the reason for choosing social work. Among the respondents who chose social work on their interest, 67% respondents possess high level of knowledge about human behaviour competency, 63.2% respondents have low level and 58.1% respondents have moderate level of knowledge about human behaviour competency. Among the respondents who chose social work based on the parents/relative's recommendation, 39% of the respondents have moderate level, 31.9%of the respondents have high level and 36.8% of the respondents have low level knowledge about human behaviour competency. Among the respondents who chose social work based on their sibling studied/influenced, 2.9% respondents have moderate level of knowledge about human behaviour competency and 1.1% of the respondents have high level knowledge about human behaviour competency.

Table 11.8: Perception about Social Work and Level of Knowledge about Human Behaviour Competency of the Respondents

Respondents Perception about Social Work	*Level of Knowledge about Human Behaviour Competency*			*Total*
	Low	*Moderate*	*High*	
Practice Based Profession	4 (10.5%)	32 (18.6%)	23 (24.5%)	59 (19.4%)
Value Oriented Subject	5 (13.2%)	34 (19.8%)	13 (13.8%)	52 917.1%)
Helping Profession	22 (57.9%)	85 (49.4%)	47 (50.0%)	154 (50.7%)
Art Course	7 (18.4%)	21 (12.2%)	11 (11.7%)	39 (12.8%)
Total	**38 (100.0%)**	**172 (100.0%)**	**94 (100.0%)**	**304 (100.0%)**

The above table states the level of knowledge about human behaviour competency based on the perception about social work. Among the respondents who perceive social work as practice-based profession, 24.5% of the respondents have high Level of knowledge about human behaviour competency, 18.6% of the respondents have moderate level and 10.5% of the respondents have low Level of knowledge about human behaviour competency. Among the respondents who perceive social work as value-oriented subject, 19.8% have moderate level of knowledge about human behaviour competency, 13.8% of the respondents have high level and 13.2% of the respondents have low level of knowledge about human behaviour competency. Among the respondents who perceive social as helping profession, 57.9% of the respondents have low level of knowledge about human behaviour competency, 50% of the respondents have high-level and 49.4% of the respondents have moderate level of knowledge about human behaviour competency. Among the respondents who perceive social work as art course, 18.4% of the respondents have low level of knowledge about human behaviour competency, 12.2% of the respondents have moderate level and 11.7% of the respondents have high level of knowledge about human behaviour competency.

Table 11.9: Family Members of the Respondents Studied Social Work and Level of Knowledge about Human Behaviour Competency of the Respondents

Family Members of the Respondents Studied Social Work	*Level of Knowledge about Human Behaviour Competency*			*Total*
	Low	*Moderate*	*High*	
Yes	4 (10.5%)	32 (18.6%)	11 (11.7%)	47 (15.5%)
No	34 (89.5%)	140 (81.4%)	83 (88.3%)	257 (84.5%)
Total	**38 (100.0%)**	**172 (100.0%)**	**94 (100.0%)**	**304 (100.0%)**

This above table represents the level of knowledge about human behaviour competency with respect to the family members of the respondents studied social work. Among the respondents whose family members studied social work, 18.6% of the respondents have moderate-level of knowledge about human behaviour competency, 11.7% respondents have high-level and 10.5% respondents have low-level of knowledge about human behaviour competency. Among of the respondents whose family not studied social work, 89.5% respondents have low-level of knowledge about human behaviour competency, 88.3% respondents have high-level and 81.4% of the respondents have moderate level knowledge about human behaviour competency.

Table 11.10: Career Ambition and Level of Knowledge about Human Behaviour Competency of the Respondents

Career Ambition of the Respondents	*Level of Knowledge about Human Behaviour Competency*			*Total*
	Low	*Moderate*	*High*	
Professional Social Worker	11 (28.9%)	48 (27.9%)	30 (31.9%)	89 (29.3%)
Psychiatry/Medical Social Worker/Mental Health/Counsellor	13 (34.2%)	65 (37.8%)	33 (35.1%)	111 (36.5%)

Career Ambition of the Respondents	*Level of Knowledge about Human Behaviour Competency*			*Total*
	Low	*Moderate*	*High*	
N.G.O/Orphan homes	4 (10.5%)	10 (5.8%)	9 (9.6%)	23 (7.6%)
H.R.	5 (13.2%)	28 (16.3%)	13 (13.8%)	46 (15.1%)
Government Jobs	2 (5.3%)	14 (8.1%)	8 (8.5%)	24 (7.9%)
Professor	3 (7.9%)	7 (4.1%)	1 (1.1%)	11 (3.6%)
Total	**38 (100.0%)**	**172 (100.0%)**	**94 (100.0%)**	**304 (100.0%)**

The above table represents the level of knowledge about human behaviour competency based on the career ambition of the respondents. 31.9% respondents whose career ambition is to become a professional social worker with high Level of knowledge about human behaviour competency. 28.9% respondents whose career ambition is to become a professional social worker with low Level of knowledge about human behaviour competency. 27.9% respondents whose career ambition is to become a professional social worker with moderate Level of knowledge about human behaviour competency. 37.8% respondents whose ambition is to become Psychiatric/Medical Social Worker/Mental Health/Counsellor with moderate level of knowledge about human behaviour competency. 35.1% respondents whose ambition is to become Psychiatric/Medical Social Worker/ Mental Health/Counsellor with high level of knowledge about human behaviour competency. 34.2% respondents whose ambition is to become Psychiatric/Medical Social Worker/Mental Health/ Counsellor with low level of knowledge about human behaviour competency. 10.5% respondents whose ambition is to set up an NGO/Orphanage, with low level of knowledge about human behaviour competency.9.6% respondents whose ambition is to set up an NGO/Orphanage, with high level of knowledge about human behaviour competency. 5.8% respondents whose ambition is to set up an NGO/Orphanage, with moderate level of knowledge about human behaviour competency. 16.3% respondents whose aim is to become an HR, with moderate level of Knowledge about Human.13.8% respondents whose aim is to become an HR, with high level of knowledge about human behaviour competency. 13.2% respondents whose aim is to become an HR, with low level of Knowledge about Human. 8.5% respondents who prefer government jobs with high level of knowledge of human behaviour. 8.1% respondents who prefer government jobs with moderate level of knowledge of human behaviour. 5.3% respondents who prefer government jobs with low level of knowledge of human behaviour. 7.9% respondents' ambition is becoming a professor have low level of knowledge about human behaviour competency. 4.1% respondents' ambition is becoming a professor have moderate-level of knowledge about human behaviour competency. 1.1% respondents' ambition is becoming a professor have high-level of knowledge about human behaviour competency.

Table 11.11: Aspiration and Level of Knowledge about Human Behaviour Competency of the Respondents

Aspiration of the Respondents	*Level of Knowledge About Human Behaviour Competency*			*Total*
	Low	*Moderate*	*High*	
Social Worker/Counsellor/HR	22 (57.9%)	84 (48.8%)	47 (50.0%)	153 (50.3%)
UPSC	9 (23.7%)	55 (32.0%)	31 (33.0%)	95 (31.2%)
No Idea	7 (18.4%)	33 (19.2%)	16 (17.0%)	56 (18.4%)
Total	**38 (100.0%)**	**172 (100.0%)**	**94 (100.0%)**	**304 (100.0%)**

This table shows that level of knowledge about human behaviour competency in accordance with the aspiration of the respondents. Among the respondents who aspire to become Social Worker/ Counsellor/HR, 57.9% possess low level, 50% possess high level and 48.8% possess moderate level of knowledge about human behaviour competency. Among the respondents who aspire to serve Union

Public Service Commission, 33% possess high level, 32% possess moderate level and 23.7% possess low level of knowledge about human behaviour competency. Among the respondents who doesn't have any idea, 19.2% possess moderate level, 18.4% possess low level and 17% possess high level of knowledge about human behaviour competency.

Table 11.12: Respondent's Awareness about Social Work as a Professional Courseand Their Level of Knowledge about Human Behaviour Competency

Respondents' Awareness about Social Work as a Professional Course	*Level of Knowledge about Human Behaviour Competency*			*Total*
	Low	*Moderate*	*High*	
Yes	30 (78.9%)	130 (75.6%)	71 (75.5%)	231 (76.0%)
No	5 (13.2%)	27 (15.7%)	14 (14.9%)	46 (15.1%)
May be	3 (7.9%)	15 (8.7%)	9 (9.6%)	27 (8.9%)
Total	**38 (100.0%)**	**172 (100.0%)**	**94 (100.0%)**	**304 (100.0%)**

This table talks about the level of knowledge about human behaviour competency based on the respondents' awareness about social work as a professional course. Among the respondents who are aware that social work as a professional course, 78.9% possess low level and 75.5% possess high level of knowledge about human behaviour competency. Among the respondents who are not aware that social work is a professional course, 15.7% possess moderate level, 14.9% possess high level and 13.2% possess low level of knowledge about human behaviour competency. Among the respondents who may or may not aware that social work is a professional course, 9.6% possess high level, 8.7% possess moderate level and 7.9% possess low level of knowledge about human behaviour competency.

Table 11.13: Respondents Faced Criticism for Taking Social Work as Their Graduation and Their Level of Knowledge about Human Behaviour Competency

Respondents Faced Criticism for Taking Social Work as their Graduation	*Level of Knowledge About Human Behaviour Competency*			*Total*
	Low	*Moderate*	*High*	
Yes	20 (52.6%)	108 (62.8%)	47 (50.0%)	175 (57.6%)
No	15 (39.5%)	49 (28.5%)	38 (40.4%)	102 (33.6%)
May be	3 (7.9%)	15 (8.7%)	9 (9.6%)	27 (8.9%)
Total	**38 (100.0%)**	**172 (100.0%)**	**94 (100.0%)**	**304 (100.0%)**

The above table depicts the level of knowledge about human behaviour competency with respect to the criticism faced by the respondents for taking social work as their graduation. 62.8% of the respondents who faced criticism with moderate level of knowledge about human behaviour competency. 52.6% of the respondents who faced criticism with low level of knowledge about human behaviour competency. 50% respondents who faced criticism with high level of knowledge about human behaviour competency. 40.4% of the respondents not faced criticism have high level of knowledge about human behaviour. 39.5% of the respondents not faced criticism have low level of knowledge about human behaviour. 28.5% of the respondents not faced criticism have moderate level of knowledge about human behaviour competency. 9.6% of the respondents who may or may not face criticism have high level of knowledge about human behaviour competency. 8.7% respondents who may or may not face criticism have moderate level of knowledge about human behaviour competency. 7.9% respondents who may or may not face criticism with low level of knowledge about human behaviour competency.

Table 11.14: Kind of Criticism Faced by the Respondents for Taking Social Work as Their Graduation and their Level of Knowledge about Human Behaviour Competency

Kind of Criticism Faced by the Respondents for Taking Social Work as Their Graduation	*Level of Knowledge about Human Behaviour Competency*			*Total*
	Low	*Moderate*	*High*	
No	19 (50.0%)	76 (44.2%)	50 (53.2%)	145 (47.7%)
Positive Criticism	3 (7.9%)	7 (4.1%)	6 (6.4%)	16 (5.3%)
Negative Criticism	16 (42.1%)	89 (51.7%)	38 (40.4%)	143 (47.0%)
Total	**38 (100.0%)**	**172 (100.0%)**	**94 (100.0%)**	**304 (100.0%)**

This above table represents the level of knowledge about human behaviour competency based on the kind of criticism faced by the respondents for taking social work as their graduation. 53.2% of respondents who doesn't face any criticism, with high level of knowledge about human behaviour competency. 50% of respondents who doesn't face any criticism, with low level of knowledge about human behaviour competency. 44.2% of respondents who doesn't face any criticism, with moderate level of knowledge about human behaviour competency. 7.9% of respondents who faced positive criticism with low level of knowledge about human behaviour competency. 6.4% of respondents who faced positive criticism with high level of knowledge about human behaviour competency. 4.1% of respondents who faced positive criticism with moderate level of knowledge about human behaviour competency. 51.7% of respondents who faced negative criticism have moderate level of knowledge about human behaviour competency. 42.1% of respondents who faced negative criticism have low level of knowledge about human behaviour competency. 40.4% respondents who faced negative criticism have high level of knowledge about human behaviour competency.

Table 11.15: Respondents Feeling of Competent with Regard to Social Work Profession and their Level of Knowledge about Human Behaviour Competency

Respondents Feeling of Competent with Regard to Social Work Profession	*Level of Knowledge About Human Behaviour Competency*			*Total*
	Low	*Moderate*	*High*	
Yes	21 (55.3%)	81 (47.1%)	45 (47.9%)	147 (48.4%)
No	0 (0.0%)	5 (2.9%)	1 (1.1%)	6 (2.0%)
Maybe	17 (44.7%)	86 (50.0%)	48 (51.1%)	151 (49.7%)
Total	**38 (100.0%)**	**172 (100.0%)**	**94 (100.0%)**	**304 (100.0%)**

The above table depicts the level of knowledge about human behaviour competency based on the respondents feeling of competent with regard to social work profession. 55.3% respondents who feels competent possess low level of knowledge about human behaviour competency. 47.9% respondents who feels competent possess high level of knowledge about human behaviour competency. 47.1% respondents who feels competent possess moderate Level of knowledge about human behaviour competency. 2.9% respondents who doesn't feel competent possess moderate level of knowledge about human behaviour competency. 1.1% respondents who doesn't feel competent possess high level of knowledge about human behaviour competency. Among the respondents who may or not be competent with regard to social work profession, 51.1% respondents possess high level of knowledge about human behaviour competency, 50% respondents possess moderate level and 44.7% respondents possess low level of knowledge about human behaviour competency.

Table 11.16: List of Skills and the Level of Knowledge about Human Behaviour Competency of the Respondents

List of Skills	*Level of Knowledge About Human Behaviour Competency*			*Total*
	Low	*Moderate*	*High*	
Communication Skill	17 (44.7%)	62 (36.0%)	44 (46.8%)	123 (40.5%)
Active Listening	11 (28.9%)	38 (22.1%)	23 (24.5%)	72 (23.7%)
Responsible	5 (13.2%)	34 (19.8%)	12 (12.8%)	51 (16.8%)
No Idea	5 (13.2%)	38 (22.1%)	15 (16.0%)	58 (19.1%)
Total	**38 (100.0%)**	**172 (100.0%)**	**94 (100.0%)**	**304 (100.0%)**

This above table shows the level of knowledge about human behaviour competency based on the competencies. 46.8% respondents who had communication skill, possess high-level of knowledge about human behaviour competency. 44.7% respondents who had communication skill, possess low-level of knowledge about human behaviour competency. 36% respondents who had communication skill, possess moderate-level of knowledge about human behaviour competency. 28.9% respondents who had active listening skill, possess low-level of knowledge about human behaviour competency. 24.5% respondents who had active listening skill, possess high-level of knowledge about human behaviour competency. 22.1% respondents who had active listening skill, possess moderate of Knowledge about Human Behaviour. 19.8% respondents who have responsibility skill possess moderate of Knowledge about Human Behaviour. 13.2% respondents who have responsibility skill possess low of Knowledge about Human Behaviour. 12.8% respondents who have responsibility skill possess high of Knowledge about Human Behaviour. 22.1% respondents who have no idea have moderate level of knowledge. 16% respondents who have no idea have high level of knowledge. 13.2% respondents who have no idea have low level of knowledge.

Table 11.17: Respondents Competent to Deal with the Problems of Individuals and their Level of Knowledge about Human Behaviour Competency

Respondents Competent to Deal with the Problems of Individuals	*Level of Knowledge about Human Behaviour Competency*			*Total*
	Low	*Moderate*	*High*	
Yes	23 (60.5%)	105 (61.0%)	63 (67.0%)	191 (62.8%)
No	2 (5.3%)	24 (14.0%)	9 (9.6%)	35 (11.5%)
May be	13 (34.2%)	43 (25.0%)	22 (23.4%)	78 (25.7%)
Total	**38 (100.0%)**	**172 (100.0%)**	**94 (100.0%)**	**304 (100.0%)**

The above table represents the level of knowledge about human behaviour competency and respondent's competency to deal with individuals' problems. 67% respondents who feels competent, possess high level of knowledge about human behaviour competency. 61% respondents who feels competent, possess moderate level of knowledge about human behaviour competency. 60.5% respondents who feel competent, possess low level of knowledge about human behaviour competency. Among the respondents who doesn't feel competent to deal with individuals' problems, 14% respondents possess moderate level of knowledge about human behaviour competency, 9.6% respondents possess high level and 5.3% respondents possess low level of knowledge about human behaviour competency. Among the respondents who doesn't feel confident about their competency to deal with individual's problems, 34.2% respondents possess low level of knowledge, 25% respondents possess moderate level and23.4% respondents possess high level of knowledge about human behaviour competency.

Table 11.18: Respondents Competent to Deal with the Group Problems and their Level of Knowledge about Human Behaviour Competency

Respondents Competent to Deal with the Group Problems	*Level of Knowledge about Human Behaviour Competency*			*Total*
	Low	*Moderate*	*High*	
Yes	18 (47.4%)	97 (56.4%)	54 (57.4%)	169 (55.6%)
No	1 (2.6%)	15 (8.7%)	7 (7.4%)	23 (7.6%)
May be	19 (50.0%)	60 (34.9%)	33 (35.1%)	112 (36.8%)
Total	**38 (100.0%)**	**172 (100.0%)**	**94 (100.0%)**	**304 (100.0%)**

This table depicts the level of knowledge about human behaviour competency based on the respondents' competent to deal with group problems. Among the respondents who feel competent to deal with group problems, 57.4% respondents possess high level of knowledge about human behaviour competency, 56.4% respondents possess moderate level and 47.4% respondents possess low level of knowledge about human behaviour competency. 8.7% respondents who doesn't feel competent, possess moderate level of knowledge about human behaviour competency, 7.4% respondents possess high level and 2.6% respondents possess low level of knowledge about human behaviour competency. Among the respondents who may or may not be competent to deal with group problems, 50% respondents possess low level of knowledge about human behaviour competency, 35.1% respondents possess high-level and34.9% respondents possess moderate-level of knowledge about human behaviour competency.

Table 11.19: Respondents Competent to Deal with the Community Problems and their Level of Knowledge about Human Behaviour Competency

Respondents Competent to Deal with the Community Problems	*Level of Knowledge about Human Behaviour Competency*			*Total*
	Low	*Moderate*	*High*	
Yes	15 (39.5%)	71 (41.3%)	52 (55.3%)	138 (45.4%)
No	11 (28.9%)	51 (29.7%)	16 (17.0%)	78 (25.7%)
May be	12 (31.6%)	50 (29.1%)	26 (27.7%)	88 (28.9%)
Total	**38 (100.0%)**	**172 (100.0%)**	**94 (100.0%)**	**304 (100.0%)**

This table depicts the level of knowledge about human behaviour competency based on the respondents' competent to deal with community problems. Among the respondents who feel competent to deal with community problems, 55.3% respondents possess high level, 41.3% respondents possess moderate level and 39.5% respondents possess low level of knowledge about human behaviour competency. Among the respondents who doesn't feel competent to deal with community problems, 29.7% respondents possess moderate level, 28.9% respondents possess low level and 17% respondents possess high level of knowledge about human behaviour competency. Among the respondents who may or may not be competent to deal with community problems, 31.6% of the respondents possess low level, 29.1% of the respondents possess moderate-level and 27.7% of the respondents possess high-level of knowledge about human behaviour competency.

CHAPTER 12

Level of Critical Thinking and Analysis Competency

This chapter involves the analysis and interpretation of level of critical thinking and analysis competency and demographic variable, reason for choosing social work, perception, career ambition, aspiration, criticism faced and social worker skills.

Table 12.1: Age of the Respondents and their Level of Critical Thinking and Analysis Competency

Age of the Respondents	*Level of Critical Thinking and Analysis Competency*			*Total*
	Low	*Moderate*	*High*	
Below 21	20 (52.6%)	47 (43.1%)	85 (54.1%)	152 (50.0%)
21–25	17 (44.7%)	54 (49.5%)	68 (43.3%)	139 (45.7%)
25–29	1 (2.6%)	8 (7.3%)	4 (2.5%)	13 (4.3%)
Total	**38 (100.0%)**	**109 (100.0%)**	**157 (100.0%)**	**304 (100.0%)**

The above table shows age and their level of critical thinking and analysis competency. More than half (54.1%) of the respondents below the age 21 years, possess high level of critical thinking and analysis competency, whereas 52.6% of the respondents possess low level and 43.1% of the respondents possess moderate level of competency. Between the age of 21 and 25 years, 49.5% of the respondents possess moderate level of competency with regard to critical thinking and analysis, 44.7% of the respondents possess low level and 43.3% of the respondents possess high of level of critical thinking and analysis competency. Between the age category of 25 and 29 years, 7.3% of the respondents possess moderate level of critical thinking and analysis competency, whereas 2.6% and 2.5% of the respondents possess low and high level of critical thinking and analysis competency respectively. It can be inferred from the above table that most of the respondents invariable of age possess high level of critical thinking and analysis competency, whereas equally there are respondents who possess low level of critical thinking and analysis competency.

Table 12.2: Gender of the Respondents and their Level of Critical Thinking and Analysis Competency

Gender of the Respondents	*Level of Critical Thinking and Analysis Competency*			*Total*
	Low	*Moderate*	*High*	
Prefer not to say	0 (0.0%)	0 (0.0%)	1 (0.6%)	1 (0.3%)
Female	22 (57.9%)	71 (65.1%)	105 (66.9%)	198 (65.1%)
Male	16 (42.1%)	38 (34.9%)	51 (32.5%)	105 (34.5%)
Total	**38 (100.0%)**	**109 (100.0%)**	**157 (100.0%)**	**304 (100.0%)**

The above table shows the Gender of the respondents and Level of critical thinking and analysis. Among the female respondents, 66.9% of the respondents possess high level of critical thinking and analysis, 65.1% possess moderate level of critical thinking and analysis and 57.9% possess low level of critical thinking and analysis. In the Male respondents, 34.9% of the respondents reflect moderate level of critical thinking and analysis, 32.5% of the respondents possess high level of critical thinking and analysis and 42.1% of the respondents possess low level of critical thinking and analysis.0.6% of the respondents with high level of critical thinking and analysis preferred not to say regarding their gender. It can be inferred from the table that irrespective of the gender, the respondents possess high level, moderate level and low level of critical thinking and analysis competency.

Table 12.3: Educational Qualification of the Respondents and their Level of Critical Thinking and Analysis Competency

Educational Qualification of the Respondents	*Level of Critical Thinking and Analysis Competency*			*Total*
	Low	*Moderate*	*High*	
II & III BSW	20 (52.6%)	51 (46.8%)	81 (51.6%)	152 (50.0%)
II MSW	18 (47.4%)	58 (53.2%)	76 (48.4%)	152 (50.0%)
Total	**38 (100.0%)**	**109 (100.0%)**	**157 (100.0%)**	**304 (100.0%)**

The above table shows the educational qualification of the respondents and the level of critical thinking and analysis. Among the respondents those who pursue II- and III-year BSW course, 52.6% possess low level, 51.6% possess high level and 46.8% possess moderate level of critical thinking and analysis competency. Among the respondents those who pursue II-year MSW course, 53.2% possess moderate level, 48.4% possess high level and 47.7% possess low level of critical thinking and analysis competency.

Table 12.4: Post Graduate Respondents Under-Graduate Degree and their Level of Critical Thinking and Analysis Competency

Post Graduate Respondents Under-Graduate Degree	*Level of Critical Thinking and Analysis Competency*			*Total*
	Low	*Moderate*	*High*	
BSW	4 (10.5%)	27 (24.8%)	38 (24.2%)	69 (22.7%)
OTHER DEGREE	14 (36.8%)	31 (28.4%)	38 (24.2%)	83 (27.3%)
Not Applicable (Under-Graduates)	20 (52.6%)	51 (46.8%)	81 (51.6%)	152 (50.0%)
Total	**38 (100.0%)**	**109 (100.0%)**	**157 (100.0%)**	**304 (100.0%)**

The table 12.4 shows the respondents under graduate degree and level of critical thinking and analysis. From the BSW Degree, 24.8% of the respondents possess moderate level of critical thinking and analysis, 24.2% and 10.5% possess high level and low level of critical thinking and analysis respectively. From the Other degree, 36.8% possess low level of critical thinking and analysis, 28.4% and 24.2% possess moderate level and high level of critical thinking and analysis competency respectively. In the not applicable undergraduates, 52.6% of the respondents possess low level of critical thinking and analysis, 51.6% possess high level of critical thinking and analysis and 46.8% of the respondents possess moderate level of critical thinking and analysis. Irrespective of the respondents' degree, they possess high level of critical thinking and analysis. Similarly, the respondents irrespective of the degree also possessed moderate and low level of the critical thinking and analysis competency.

Table 12.5: Domicile of the Respondents and their Level of Critical thinking and Analysis Competency

Domicile of the Respondents	*Level of Critical Thinking and Analysis Competency*			*Total*
	Low	*Moderate*	*High*	
Tamil Nadu	31 (81.6%)	91 (83.5%)	135 (86.0%)	257 (84.5%)
Outside Tamil Nadu	7 (18.4%)	18 (16.5%)	22 (14.0%)	47 (15.5%)
Total	**38 (100.0%)**	**109 (100.0%)**	**157 (100.0%)**	**304 (100.0%)**

The above table shows the Domicile of the respondents and their level of critical thinking and analysis. Among the respondents from Tamilnadu, 86% possess high level, 83.5% possess moderate level and 81.6% possess low level of critical thinking and analysis competency. Among the respondents from outside Tamilnadu, 18.4% possess low level, 16.5% possess moderate level and 14% possess high level of critical thinking and analysis competency.

Table 12.6: Major Subjects Studied by the Respondents during 12th Standard and Their Level of Critical Thinking and Analysis Competency

Major Subjects Studied by the Respondents During 12th Standard	*Level of Critical Thinking and Analysis Competency*			*Total*
	Low	*Moderate*	*High*	
Bio-Maths	8 (21.1%)	20 (18.3%)	31 (19.7%)	59 (19.4%)
Computer Sciences	8 (21.1%)	19 (17.4%)	25 (15.9%)	52 (17.1%)
Commerce	18 (47.4%)	53 (48.6%)	83 (52.9%)	154 (50.7%)
Humanities	4 (10.5%)	17 (15.6%)	18 (11.5%)	39 (12.8%)
Total	**38 (100.0%)**	**109 (100.0%)**	**157 (100.0%)**	**304 (100.0%)**

Above table shows the major subjects studied by the respondents during the 12th standard and level of critical thinking and analysis. In Bio-Maths, 21.1% of the respondents possess low level of critical thinking and analysis, 19.7% and 18.3% of the respondents possess high level and moderate level of critical thinking and analysis respectively. In Computer science, 21.1% of the respondents possess low level of critical thinking and analysis, 17.4% of the respondents possess moderate level of critical thinking and analysis and 15.9% of the respondents possess high level of critical thinking and analysis. From the commerce background, 52.9% of the respondents possess high level of critical thinking and analysis, 48.6% of the respondents possess moderate level of critical thinking and analysis and 47.4% of the respondents possess low level of critical thinking and analysis. From the Humanities background, 15.6% of the respondents possess moderate level of critical thinking and analysis, 11.5% and 10.5% of the respondents possess high and low level of critical thinking and analysis respectively. From the above table it can be inferred that Irrespective of the major subjects undertook in 12th standard, the respondents have high level of critical thinking and analysis. Similarly, the respondents also possess moderate and low level of critical thinking and analysis.

Table 12.7: Respondent's Reasons for Choosing Social Work and their Level of Critical Thinking and Analysis Competency

Respondents' Reasons for Choosing Social Work	*Level of Critical Thinking and Analysis Competency*			*Total*
	Low	*Moderate*	*High*	
Own Interest	21 (55.3%)	73 (67.0%)	93 (59.2%)	187 (61.5%)
Parents/Relatives Recommendation	17 (44.7%)	34 (31.2%)	60 (38.2%)	111 (36.5%)
Siblings Studied/ Influence	0 (0.0%)	2 (1.8%)	4 (2.5%)	6 (2.0%)
Total	**38 (100.0%)**	**109 (100.0%)**	**157 (100.0%)**	**304 (100.0%)**

The table shows the respondents' reason for choosing social work and level of critical thinking and analysis competency. About 67% of the respondents of moderate level, 59.2% of the respondents of high level and 55.3% of the respondents of low level of critical thinking and analysis competency have chosen social work on their own interest. Among the respondents chosen social work by the parents or relatives' recommendation, 44.7% of the respondents possess low level of critical thinking and analysis, 38.2% of the respondents possess high level of critical thinking and analysis and 31.2% of the respondents possess moderate level of critical thinking and analysis. Among the respondents chosen social work by the siblings studied/influence, 2.5% of the respondents possess high level and 1.8% of the respondents possess moderate level of critical thinking and analysis competency.

Table 12.8: Respondents Perception about Social Work and Their Level of Critical thinking and Analysis Competency

Respondents Perception about Social Work	*Level of Critical Thinking and Analysis Competency*			*Total*
	Low	*Moderate*	*High*	
Practise Based Profession	8 (21.1%)	20 (18.3%)	31 (19.7%)	59 (19.4%)
Value Oriented Subject	8 (21.1%)	19 (17.4%)	25 (15.9%)	52 (17.1%)
Helping Profession	18 (47.4%)	53 (48.6%)	83 (52.9%)	154 (50.7%)
Art Course	4 (10.5%)	17 (15.6%)	18 (11.5%)	39 (12.8%)
Total	**38 (100.0%)**	**109 (100.0%)**	**157 (100.0%)**	**304 (100.0%)**

The above table shows the respondents' perception about social work and critical thinking and analysis. With the perception of Practice based profession, 21.1% of the respondents possess low level of critical thinking and analysis, 19.7% of the respondents possess high level of critical thinking and analysis and 18.3% of the respondents possess moderate level of critical thinking and analysis. In respondents with the perception of value-oriented subject, 21.1% of the respondents possess low level of critical thinking and analysis, 17.4% and 15.9% with moderate and high level of critical thinking and analysis respectively. With the perception of helping profession, 52.9% of the respondents possess high level of critical thinking and analysis, 48.6% and 47.4% of the respondents possess moderate level and low level of critical thinking and analysis. With the perception of Art course, 15.6% of the respondents possess moderate level of critical thinking and analysis, 11.5% and 10.5% of the respondents possess high and low level of critical thinking and analysis competency. From the table it can be inferred that irrespective of the different perceptions the respondents possess, the respondents have high level, moderate level and low level of critical thinking and analysis competency.

Table 12.9: Family Members of the Respondents Studied Social Work and Level of Critical Thinking and Analysis of the Respondents

Family Members of the Respondents Studied Social Work	*Level of Critical Thinking and Analysis Competency*			*Total*
	Low	*Moderate*	*High*	
Yes	2 (5.3%)	20 (18.3%)	25 (15.9%)	47 (15.5%)
No	36 (94.7%)	89 (81.7%)	132 (84.1%)	257 (84.5%)
Total	**38 (100.0%)**	**109 (100.0%)**	**157 (100.0%)**	**304 (100.0%)**

The above table shows the family members of the respondents studied social work. For the respondents whose family members have studied social work, 18.3% of the respondents possess moderate level of Level of Critical thinking and Analysis, 15.9% possess high level of Level of Critical thinking and Analysis and 5.3% possess low Level of Critical thinking and Analysis. The respondents whose family members have not studied social work, 94.7% of the respondents possess low level of Critical thinking and Analysis, 84.1% and 81.7% of the respondents possess high and moderate level of Critical thinking and Analysis competency. From the above table it can be inferred that, irrespective of the family members studied social work, the respondents have high, moderate and low level of Critical thinking and Analysis competency.

Table 12.10: Career Ambition and the Level of Critical Thinking and Analysis Competency of the Respondents

Career Ambition of the Respondents	*Level of Critical Thinking and Analysis Competency*			*Total*
	Low	*Moderate*	*High*	
Professional Social Worker	9 (23.7%)	36 (33.0%)	44 (28.0%)	89 (29.3%)
Psychiatry/Medical Social Worker/Mental Health/Counsellor	13 (34.2%)	42 (38.5%)	56 (35.7%)	111 (36.5%)

Career Ambition of the Respondents	*Level of Critical Thinking and Analysis Competency*			*Total*
	Low	*Moderate*	*High*	
N.G.O/Orphan Homes	3 (7.9%)	6 (5.5%)	14 (8.9%)	23 (7.6%)
H.R.	5 (13.2%)	15 (13.8%)	26 (16.6%)	46 (15.1%)
Government Jobs	3 (7.9%)	8 (7.3%)	13 (8.3%)	24 (7.9%)
Professor	5 (13.2%)	2 (1.8%)	4 (2.5%)	11 (3.6%)
Total	**38 (100.0%)**	**109 (100.0%)**	**157 (100.0%)**	**304 (100.0%)**

The above table shows the career ambition of the respondents and level of Critical thinking and Analysis. The respondents whose career ambition is to become professional social worker, 33% possess moderate level of Critical thinking and Analysis, 28% and 23.7% possess high and low level of Critical thinking and Analysis competency respectively. From the respondents whose career ambition is to become Psychiatric/Medical Social Worker/Mental Health/ Counsellor, 38.5% possess moderate level, 35.7% possess high level and 34.2% possess low level of critical thinking and analysis competencies. From the respondents whose ambition is to work/open NGO/Orphanage, 8.9% possess high level of critical thinking and analysis competency, 7.9% possess low level of critical thinking and analysis competency and 5.5% possess moderate level of critical thinking and analysis competency. From the respondents whose ambition is to become HR, 16.6% possess high level of critical thinking and analysis competency, 13.8% and 13.2% possess moderate and low level of critical thinking and analysis competency respectively. From the respondents whose career ambition is to have Government job, 8.3% possess high level of critical thinking and analysis competency and 7.9% and 7.3% possess low and moderate level of critical thinking and analysis competency respectively. From the respondents whose career ambition is to become a professor, 13.2% of the respondents possess low level of critical thinking and analysis competency, 2.5% possess high level of critical thinking and analysis competency and 1.8% possesses moderate level of critical thinking and analysis competency. From the above table it can be inferred that, irrespective of the career ambition, the respondents had high, moderate and low level of critical thinking and analysis competencies.

Table 12.11: Aspiration of the Respondents and Level of Critical Thinking and Analysis Competency

Aspiration of the Respondents	*Level of Critical Thinking and Analysis Competency*			*Total*
	Low	*Moderate*	*High*	
Social Worker/Counsellor/HR	22 (57.9%)	54 (49.5%)	77 (49.0%)	153 (50.3%)
UPSC	8 (21.1%)	37 (33.9%)	50 (31.8%)	95 (31.2%)
No Idea	8 (21.1%)	18 (16.5%)	30 (19.1%)	56 (18.4%)
Total	**38 (100.0%)**	**109 (100.0%)**	**157 (100.0%)**	**304 (100.0%)**

The above table shows the aspiration of respondents and level of critical thinking and analysis. From the respondents who aspire to become social worker/counsellor/HR, 57.9% of the respondents possess low level of critical thinking and analysis, 49.5% possess moderate level of critical thinking and analysis and 49% possess high level of critical thinking and analysis. From the respondents who aspire to become UPSC aspirants, 33.9% of the respondents possess moderate level of critical thinking and analysis, 31.8% of the respondents possess high level of critical thinking and analysis and 21.1% of the respondents possess low level of critical thinking and analysis. From the respondents who had no idea, 21.1% of the respondents possess low level of critical thinking and analysis, 19.1% and 16.5% of the respondents possess high and moderate level of critical thinking and analysis. From the above table it can be inferred that irrespective of the aspirations the respondents possess high, moderate and low level of critical thinking and analysis.

Table 12.12: Respondent's Awareness about Social Work as a Professional Course and Level of Critical Thinking and Analysis Competency

Respondent's Awareness about Social Works as a Professional Course	*Level of Critical Thinking and Analysis Competency*			*Total*
	Low	*Moderate*	*High*	
Yes	30 (78.9%)	85 (78.0%)	116 (73.9%)	231 (76.0%)
No	5 (13.2%)	17 (15.6%)	24 (15.3%)	46 (15.1%)
May be	3 (7.9%)	7 (6.4%)	17 (10.8%)	27 (8.9%)
Total	**38 (100.0%)**	**109 (100.0%)**	**157 (100.0%)**	**304 (100.0%)**

The above table shows the respondents' awareness about social work as a professional course and level of critical thinking and analysis. From the respondents who have awareness that social work as professional course, 78.9% and 78% of the respondents possess low and moderate level of critical thinking and analysis respectively and 73.9% possess high level of critical thinking and analysis. From the respondents who doesn't have awareness on social work as professional course, 15.6% and 15.3% of the respondents possess high and moderate level of critical thinking and analysis and 13.2% possess low level of critical thinking and analysis. From the table it shows irrespective of the awareness on the social work as professional course the respondents possess high, low and moderate level of critical thinking and analysis.

Table 12.13: Respondents Faced Criticism for Taking Social Work as Their Graduation and Level of Critical Thinking and Analysis Competency

Respondents Faced Criticism for Taking Social Work as their Graduation	*Level of Critical Thinking and Analysis Competency*			*Total*
	Low	*Moderate*	*High*	
Yes	21 (55.3%)	67 (61.5%)	87 (55.4%)	175 (57.6%)

No	15 (39.5%)	33 (30.3%)	54 (34.4%)	102 (33.6%)
May be	2 (5.3%)	9 (8.3%)	16 (10.2%)	27 (8.9%)
Total	**38 (100.0%)**	**109 (100.0%)**	**157 (100.0%)**	**304 (100.0%)**

The above table shows that respondents faced criticism for taking social work as their graduation and level of critical thinking and analysis. In the respondents faced criticism for taking social work graduation 61.5% of the respondents possess moderate level of critical thinking and analysis. 55.4% and 55.3% of the respondents possess high and low level of critical thinking and analysis. In the respondents' who has not faced criticism for taking social work graduation, 39.5% of the respondents possess low level of critical thinking and analysis, 34.4% and 30.3% possess high and moderate level of critical thinking and analysis. It can be inferred from the above passage that invariable of the criticisms faced for taking social work as their graduation, the respondents showed high level of critical thinking and analysis followed by moderate and low level of critical thinking and analysis competencies.

Table 12.14: Kind of Criticism Faced by the Respondents for Taking Social Work as Their Graduation and Level of Critical Thinking and Analysis Competency

Kind of Criticism Faced by the Respondents for Taking Social Work as Their Graduation	*Level of Critical Thinking and Analysis Competency*			*Total*
	Low	*Moderate*	*High*	
No	17 (44.7%)	51 (46.8%)	77 (49.0%)	145 (47.7%)
Positive Criticism	3 (7.9%)	5 (4.6%)	8 (5.1%)	16 (5.3%)
Negative Criticism	18 (47.4%)	53 (48.6%)	72 (45.9%)	143 (47.0%)
Total	**38 (100.0%)**	**109 (100.0%)**	**157 (100.0%)**	**304 (100.0%)**

The table 12.14 shows the kind of criticism faced by the respondents for taking social work as their graduation and level of critical thinking and analysis. About 47.7% respondents have not faced criticism in which 44.7% possess low level of critical thinking and analysis, 46.8% moderate level of critical thinking and analysis and 49% high level of critical thinking and analysis. In the respondents' who has faced positive criticism, 7.9% possess level of critical thinking and analysis, 5.1% possess level of critical thinking and analysis and 4.6% possess level of critical thinking and analysis. From the respondents' who has faced negative criticism, 48.6% possess moderate level of critical thinking and analysis, 47.4% possess low level of critical thinking and analysis and 45.9% possess high level of critical thinking and analysis. From the above table it can be inferred that invariable of the kind of criticism, the respondents possess high level of critical thinking and analysis followed by moderate and low level of critical thinking and analysis competency.

Table 12.15: Respondents Feeling of Competent with Regard to Social Work Profession and Level of Critical Thinking and Analysis Competency

Respondents Feeling of Competent with Regard to Social Work Profession	*Level of Critical Thinking and Analysis Competency*			*Total*
	Low	*Moderate*	*High*	
Yes	20 (52.6%)	55 (50.5%)	72 (45.9%)	147 (48.4%)
No	0 (0.0%)	2 (1.8%)	4 (2.5%)	6 (2.0%)
May be	18 (47.4%)	52 (47.7%)	81 (51.6%)	151 (49.7%)
Total	**38 (100.0%)**	**109 (100.0%)**	**157 (100.0%)**	**304 (100.0%)**

The above table shows the respondents' feeling of competent with regard to social work profession and level of critical thinking and analysis competency. Among the respondents who feel competent with regards to social work profession, 52.6% and 50.5% possess low and moderate level of critical thinking and analysis respectively. 45.9% of the respondents possess high level of critical thinking and analysis. In the respondents who don't feel competent with regard to social work profession, 2.5% possess high level of critical thinking and analysis competency and 1.8% possesses moderate level of critical thinking and analysis. From the table, it can be inferred that, invariable of the respondents' feeling of competent with regard to social work profession, the respondents possess high level of critical thinking and analysis followed by moderate and low level of critical thinking and analysis competencies.

Table 12.16: List of Skills and the Level of Critical Thinking and Analysis Competency of the Respondents

List of Skills	*Level of Critical Thinking and Analysis Competency*			*Total*
	Low	*Moderate*	*High*	
Communication Skill	13 (34.2%)	44 (40.4%)	66 (42.0%)	123 (40.5%)
Active Listening	10 (26.3%)	25 (22.9%)	37 (23.6%)	72 (23.7%)
Responsible	6 (15.8%)	22 (20.2%)	23 (14.6%)	51 (16.8%)
No Idea	9 (23.7%)	18 (16.5%)	31 (19.7%)	58 (19.1%)
Total	**38 (100.0%)**	**109 (100.0%)**	**157 (100.0%)**	**304 (100.0%)**

The above table shows the list of competencies and level of critical thinking and analysis. From the respondents with communication as list of skills, 42% possess high level of critical thinking and analysis, 40.4% possess moderate level of critical thinking and analysis and 34.2% possess low level of critical thinking and analysis. From the respondents with active listening as list of skills, 26.3% possess low level of critical thinking and analysis, 23.6% possess high level of critical thinking and analysis and 22.9% possess moderate level of critical thinking and analysis. From the respondents with responsible as list of skills, 20.2% possess moderate level of critical thinking and analysis, 15.8% and 14.6% possess low and high level of critical thinking and analysis respectively. From the respondents with no idea regarding the list of skills, 23.7% possess low level of critical thinking and analysis, 19.7% possess high level of critical thinking and analysis and 16.5% possess moderate level of critical thinking and analysis competency. From the above table it can be inferred that irrespective of the list of skills, the respondents possess high competency followed by moderate and low level of critical thinking and analysis.

Table 12.17: Respondents Competent to Deal with the Problems of Individuals and Level of Critical Thinking and Analysis Competency

Respondents Competent to Deal with the Problems of Individual	*Level of Critical Thinking and Analysis Competency*			*Total*
	Low	*Moderate*	*High*	
Yes	27 (71.1%)	68 (62.4%)	96 (61.1%)	191 (62.8%)
No	4 (10.5%)	9 (8.3%)	22 (14.0%)	35 (11.5%)
May be	7 (18.4%)	32 (29.4%)	39 (24.8%)	78 (25.7%)
Total	**38 (100.0%)**	**109 (100.0%)**	**157 (100.0%)**	**304 (100.0%)**

The above table shows the respondents' competent to deal with the problems of individual and level of critical thinking and analysis. Of the respondents competent to deal with problems of individual, 71.1% possess low level of critical thinking and analysis, 62.4% and 61.1% of the respondents possess moderate and high level of critical thinking and analysis respectively. Of the respondents who are not competent to deal with the problems of individual, 14% possess high level of critical thinking and analysis, 10.5% low level and 8.3% moderate level of critical thinking and analysis. Of the respondents who may or may not be competent to deal with the problems of the individual, 29.4% of the respondents possess moderate level of critical thinking and analysis, 24.8% of the respondents possess high level of critical thinking and analysis and 18.4% possess low level of critical thinking and analysis. From the above table it can be inferred that irrespective of competency to deal with the problems of the individual the respondents possess high level of critical thinking and analysis followed by moderate and low level of critical thinking and analysis competency.

Table 12.18: Respondents Competent to Deal with the Group Problems and Level of Critical Thinking and Analysis Competency

Respondents Competent to Deal with Group Problems	*Level of Critical Thinking and Analysis Competency*			*Total*
	Low	*Moderate*	*High*	
Yes	23 (60.5%)	58 (53.2%)	88 (56.1%)	169 955.6%)
No	1 (2.6%)	11 (10.1%)	11 (7.0%)	23 (7.6%)
May be	14 (36.8%)	40 (36.7%)	58 (36.9%)	112 (36.8%)
Total	**38 (100.0%)**	**109 (100.0%)**	**157 (100.0%)**	**304 (100.0%)**

The above table the respondents' competency to deal with group problems and level of critical thinking and analysis. Of the respondents competent to deal with group problem, 60.5% possess low level of critical thinking and analysis, 56.1% high level and 53.2% possess moderate level of critical thinking and analysis. Of the respondents who are not competent to deal with the group problems, 10.1% possess moderate level of critical thinking and analysis, 7% possess high level of critical thinking and analysis and 2.6% possess low level of critical thinking and analysis. Of the respondents who may or may not be competent to deal with the problems of the group, 36.9% possess high level, 36.8% possess low level and 36.7% possess moderate level of critical thinking and analysis. From the above table it can be inferred that irrespective of the competency to deal with problems of the group, the respondents possess high level of critical thinking and analysis followed by moderate and low level of critical thinking and analysis competency.

Table 12.19: Respondents Competent to Deal with the Community Problems and Level of Critical Thinking and Analysis Competency

Respondent's Competency to Deal with the Community Problems	*Level of Critical Thinking and Analysis Competency*			*Total*
	Low	*Moderate*	*High*	
Yes	16 (42.1%)	47 (43.1%)	75 (47.8%)	138 (45.4%)
No	12 (31.6%)	29 (26.6%)	37 (23.6%)	78 (25.7%)
May be	10 (26.3%)	33 (30.3%)	45 (28.7%)	88 (28.9%)
Total	**38 (100.0%)**	**109 (100.0%)**	**157 (100.0%)**	**304 (100.0%)**

The above table shows the respondents' competency to deal with the community problems and level of critical thinking and analysis. Of the respondents who are competent to deal with community problems, 47.8% possess high level of critical thinking and analysis, 43.1% possess moderate level of critical thinking and analysis and 42.1% possess low level of critical thinking and analysis. Of the respondents who are not competent to deal with the problems of community, 31.6% possess low level of critical thinking and analysis, 26.6% possess moderate level of critical thinking and analysis and 23.6% possess high level of critical thinking and analysis. Of the respondents who may or may not be competent to deal with the problems of the community, 30.3% possess moderate level of critical thinking and analysis, 28.7% possess high level of critical thinking and analysis and 26.3% possess low level of critical thinking and analysis. From the above table it can be inferred that irrespective of the competency to deal with problems of the community, the respondents possess high level of critical thinking and analysis followed by moderate and low level of critical thinking and analysis competencies.

CHAPTER 13

Level of Intervention and Skills Competency

This chapter involves the analysis and interpretation of level of intervention and skills competency and demographic variable, reason for choosing social work, perception, career ambition, aspiration, criticism faced and social worker skills.

Table 13.1: Age of the Respondents and Level of Intervention and Skills Competency

Age of the Respondents	*Level of Intervention and Skills Competency*			*Total*
	Low	*Moderate*	*High*	
Below 21	11 (50.0%)	90 (51.7%)	51 (47.2%)	152 (50.0%)
21–25	10 (45.5%)	77 (44.3%)	52 (48.1%)	139 (45.7%)
25–29	1 (4.5%)	7 (4.0%)	5 (4.6%)	13 (4.3%)
Total	**22 (100.0%)**	**174 (100.0%)**	**108 (100.0%)**	**304 (100.0%)**

The above table represents the level of intervention and skills based on the respondent's age. Among the age group of the respondents below 21 years 51.7% respondents possess moderate, 50% respondents possess low, 47.2% respondents possess high level of intervention and skills competency. Between the age group 21- and 25-years age of respondents, 48.1% respondents possess high, 45.5% respondents possess low and 44.3% respondents possess moderate level of intervention and skills competency. Between the age group of 25- and 29-years of respondents 4.6% possess high, 4.5% of respondents possess low and 4% of the respondents possess moderate level of intervention and skills competency.

Table 13.2: Gender of the Respondents and the Level of Intervention and Skills Competency

Gender of the Respondents	*Level of Intervention and Skills Competency*			*Total*
	Low	*Moderate*	*High*	
Prefer not to say	0 (0.0%)	0 (0.0%)	1 (0.9%)	1 (0.3%)
Female	12 (54.5%)	115 (66.1%)	71 (65.7%)	198 (65.1%)
Male	10 (45.5%)	58 (33.9%)	36 (33.3%)	105 (34.5%)
Total	**22 (100.0%)**	**174 (100.0%)**	**108 (100.0%)**	**304 (100.0%)**

This table implies the level of intervention and skill among the respondents based on gender. The respondents who prefer not to say their gender have 0.9% of the respondents possess high level of intervention and skills competency. The respondents of the female gender have 66.1% moderate level, 65.7% high level and 54.5% low level of intervention and skills competency. Among the respondents of the male gender, 45.5% possess low level, 33.9% possess moderate level and 33.3% possess high level of intervention and skills competency.

Table 13.3: Educational Qualification of the Respondents and the Level of Intervention and Skills Competency

Educational Qualification of the Respondents	*Level of Intervention and Skills Competency*			*Total*
	Low	*Moderate*	*High*	
II & III BSW	13 (59.1%)	86 (49.4%)	53 (49.1%)	152 (50.0%)
II MSW	9 (40.9%)	88 (50.6%)	55 (50.9%)	152 (50.0%)
Total	**22 (100.0%)**	**174 (100.0%)**	**108 (100.0%)**	**304 (100.0%)**

The above table depicts the level of intervention and skills competency in accordance with the respondent's educational quail-fication. Among the respondents pursuing II & III BSW 59.1% of the respondents possess low level, 49.4% possess moderate level and

49.1% of the respondents possess high level of intervention and skills competency. Among the respondents pursuing II MSW, 50.9% of respondents possess high level, 50.6% possess moderate level and 40.9% possess low level of intervention and skills competency.

Table 13.4: Post Graduate Respondents Under-graduation and the Level of Intervention and Skills Competency

Post Graduate Respondents Under-graduation	*Level of Intervention and Skills Competency*			*Total*
	Low	*Moderate*	*High*	
BSW	1 (4.5%)	39 (22.4%)	29 (26.9%)	69 (22.7%)
Other degree	8 (36.4%)	49 (28.2%)	26 (24.1%)	83 (27.3%)
Not Applicable (U.G. Respondents)	13 (59.1%)	86 (49.4%)	53 (49.1%)	152 (50.0%)
Total	**22 (100.0%)**	**174 (100.0%)**	**108 (100.0%)**	**304 (100.0%)**

The above table shows the level of intervention and skill competency with respect to post graduate respondent's under-graduation. Among post graduate respondents who pursued BSW as under graduation, 26.9% possess high level, 22.4% possess moderate level and 4.5% possess low level of intervention and skills competency. Among post graduate respondents who pursued other than social work, 36.4% respondents possess low level, 28.2% possess moderate level and 24.1% possess high level of intervention and skills competency.

Table 13.5: Domicile of the Respondents and the Level of Intervention and Skills Competency

Domicile of the Respondents	*Level of Intervention and Skills Competency*			*Total*
	Low	*Moderate*	*High*	
Tamil Nadu	19 (86.4%)	142 (81.6%)	96 (88.9%)	257 (84.5%)
Outside Tamil Nadu	3 (13.6%)	32 (18.4%)	12 (11.1%)	47 (15.5%)
Total	**22 (100.0%)**	**174 (100.0%)**	**108 (100.0%)**	**304 (100.0%)**

The table 13.5 shows the domicile of the respondents and the level of intervention and skills competency. Among the respondents from Tamil Nadu, 88.9% possess high level, 86.4% possess low level and 81.6% possess moderate level of intervention and skills competency. Among the respondents from outside Tamil Nadu 18.4% possess moderate level, 13.6% possess low level and 11.1% Possess high level of intervention and skills competency.

Table 13.6: Major Subjects Studied by the Respondents during 12th Standard and the Level of Intervention and Skills Competency

Major Subjects Studied by the Respondents during 12th Standard	*Level of Intervention and Skills Competency*			*Total*
	Low	*Moderate*	*High*	
Bio Maths	3 (13.6%)	36 (20.7%)	20 (18.5%)	59 (19.4%)
Computer Sciences	2 (9.1%)	35 (20.1%)	15 (13.9%)	52 (17.1%)
Commerce	14 (63.6%)	81 (46.6%)	59 (54.6%)	154 (50.7%)
Humanities	3 (13.6%)	22 (12.6%)	14 (13.0%)	39 (12.8%)
Total	**22 (100.0%)**	**174 (100.0%)**	**108 (100.0%)**	**304 (100.0%)**

The above-mentioned table represents the level of intervention and skills competency based on the major subjects studied by the respondents during 12th standard. The respondents who pursued Bio Math have 20.7% moderate level, 18.5% high level and 13.6% low level of intervention and skills competency. The respondents who pursued computer science have 20.1% moderate level, 13.9% high level and 9.1% low level of intervention and skills competency. Among the respondents who pursued commerce, 63.6% possess low level, 54.6% possess high level and 46.6% possess moderate level of intervention and skills competency. Among the respondents who pursued humanities, 13.6% possess low level, 13% possess high level and 12.6% possess moderate level of intervention and skills competency.

Table 13.7: Respondents Reasons for Choosing Social Work and the Level of Intervention and Skills

Respondent's Reasons for Choosing Social Work	*Level of Intervention and Skills Competency*			*Total*
	Low	*Moderate*	*High*	
Own Interest	14 (63.6%)	103 (59.2%)	70 (64.8%)	187 (61.5%)
Parents/Relatives Recommendation	8 (36.4%)	68 (39.1%)	35 (32.4%)	111 (36.5%)
Siblings Studied/Influence	0 (0.0%)	3 (1.7%)	3 (2.8%)	6 (2.0%)
Total	**22 (100.0%)**	**174 (100.0%)**	**108 (100.0%)**	**304 (10s0.0%)**

This table represents the level of intervention and skills in accordance with the respondents' reason for choosing social work. Among the respondents who chose social work on their own interest, 64.8% possess high level, 63.6% of the respondents possess low level and 59.2% of the respondents possess moderate level of intervention and skills competency. Among the respondents who chose social work based on Parents/Relatives Recommendation, 39.1% possess moderate level, 36.4% possess low level and 32.4% possess high level of intervention and skills competency. Among the respondents who chose social work because of their Siblings Studied/Influence, 2.8% possess high level, 1.7% possess moderate, level of intervention and skills competency.

Table 13.8: Respondents Perception about Social Work and the Level of Intervention and Skills Competency

Respondents Perception about Social Work	*Level of Intervention and Skills Competency*			*Total*
	Low	*Moderate*	*High*	
Practise Based Profession	3 (13.6%)	36 (20.7%)	20 (18.5%)	59 (19.4%)
Value Oriented Subject	2 (9.1%)	35 (20.1%)	15 (13.9%)	52 (17.1%)

Respondents Perception about Social Work	*Level of Intervention and Skills Competency*			*Total*
	Low	*Moderate*	*High*	
Helping Profession	14 (9.1%)	81 (20.1%)	59 (13.9%)	154 (17.1%)
Art Course	3 (13.6%)	22 (12.6%)	14 (13.0%)	39 (12.8%)
Total	**22 (100.0%)**	**174 (100.0%)**	**108 (100.0%)**	**304 (100.0%)**

The above table shows the level of intervention and skills with respect to the respondents' perception about social work. Among the respondents who perceived social work as practice-based profession, 20.7% possess moderate level, 18.5% possess high level and 13.6% possess low level of intervention and skills competency. Among the respondents who perceived social work as Value Oriented Subject, 20.1% possess moderate level, 13.9% possess high level and 9.1% possess low level of intervention and skills competency. Among the respondents who perceived social work as Helping Profession, 20.1% possess moderate level, 13.9% of the respondents possess high level and 9.1% possess low level of intervention and skills competency. Among the respondents who perceived social work as Art course, 13.6% of the respondents possess low level, 13% of the respondents possess high level and 12.6% possess moderate level of intervention and skills competency.

Table 13.9: Family Members of the Respondents Studied Social Work and the Level of Intervention and Skills Competency

Family Members of the Respondents Studied Social Work	*Level of Intervention and Skills Competency*			*Total*
	Low	*Moderate*	*High*	
Yes	2 (9.1%)	33 (19.0%)	12 (11.1%)	47 (15.5%)
No	20 (90.9%)	141 (81.0%)	96 (88.9%)	257 (84.5%)
Total	**22 (100.0%)**	**174 (100.0%)**	**108 (100.0%)**	**304 (100.0%)**

This table 13.9 depicts the level of intervention and skills competency with respect to the family members of the respondents studied social work. Among the respondents whose family members studied social work, 19% possess moderate level, 11.1% possess high level and 9.1% possess low level of intervention and skills competency. Among the respondents whose family members haven't studied social work, 90.9% of the respondents possess low level, 88.9% of the respondents possess high level and 81% of the respondents possess moderate level of intervention and skills competency.

Table 13.10: Career Ambition of the Respondents and the Level of Intervention and Skills Competency

Career Ambition of the Respondents	*Level of Intervention and Skills Competency*			*Total*
	Low	*Moderate*	*High*	
Professional Social Worker	8 (36.4%)	49 (28.2%)	32 (29.6%)	89 (29.3%)
Psychiatric/Medical Social Worker/Mental Health/Counsellor	8 (36.4%)	66 (37.9%)	37 (34.3%)	111 (36.5%)
N.G.O/Orphan Homes	1 (4.5%)	12 (6.9%)	10 (9.3%)	23 (7.6%)
H.R.	2 (9.1%)	27 (15.5%)	17 (15.7%)	46 (15.1%)
Government Jobs	1 (4.5%)	13 (7.5%)	10 (9.3%)	24 (7.9%)
Professor	2 (9.1%)	7 (4.0%)	2 (1.9%)	11 (3.6%)
Total	**22 (100.0%)**	**174 (100.0%)**	**108 (100.0%)**	**304 (100.0%)**

The above table represents the level of intervention and skills competency based on the career ambition of the respondents. Among the respondents whose ambition is to become a professional social worker, 36.4% of the respondents possess low level, 29.6% of the respondents possess high level and 28.2% of the respondents possess moderate level of intervention and skills competency. Among the respondents whose career ambition is to become a Psychiatric/Medical Social Worker/Mental Health/Counsellor, 37.9% of the respondents possess moderate level, 36.4% of the respondents possess low level and 34.3% of the respondents possess high level of intervention and skills competency. Among the respondents whose career ambition is to work in a N.G.O/Orphan home, 9.3% of the respondents possess high level, 6.9% of the respondents possess moderate level and 4.5% of the respondents possess low level of intervention and skills competency. Among the respondents whose career ambition is to become a human resource manager, 15.7% of the respondents possess high level, 15.5% of the respondents possess moderate level and 9.1% of the respondent's low level of intervention and skills competency. Among the respondents whose career ambition is to get Government Jobs, 9.3% possess high level, 7.5% possess moderate level and 4.5% possess low level of intervention and skills competency. Among the respondents whose career ambition is to become a professor, 9.1% possess low level, 4% possess moderate level and 1.9% possess high level of intervention and skills competency.

Table 13.11: Aspiration of the Respondents and the Level of Intervention and Skills Competency

Aspiration of the Respondents	*Level of Intervention and Skills Competency*			*Total*
	Low	*Moderate*	*High*	
Social Worker/ Counsellor/HR/	13 (59.1%)	82 (47.1%)	58 (53.7%)	153 (50.3%)
UPSC	6 (27.3%)	59 (33.9%)	30 (27.8%)	95 (31.2%)
No Idea	3 (13.6%)	33 (19.0%)	20 (18.5%)	56 (18.4%)
Total	**22 (100.0%)**	**174 (100.0%)**	**108 (100.0%)**	**304 (100.0%)**

The table shows the level of intervention and skills competency in accordance with the aspiration of the respondents. Among the respondents who aspired to become Social Worker/HR/Counsellor, 59.1% of the respondents possess low level, 53.7% of the respondents possess high level and 47.1% of the respondents possess moderate level of intervention and skills competency. Among the respondents who aspire for Union Public Service Commission, 33.9% of the respondents possess moderate level, 27.8% of the respondents possess high level and 27.3% of the respondents possess low level of intervention and skills competency. Among the respondent who doesn't have any idea, 19% of the respondents possess moderate level, 18.5% of the respondents possess high level and 13.6% of the respondents possess low level of intervention and skills competency.

Table 13.12: Respondents Awareness about Social Work as a Professional Course and the Level of Intervention and Skills Competency

Respondent's awareness about Social Work as a Professional Course	*Level of Intervention and Skills Competency*			*Total*
	Low	*Moderate*	*High*	
Yes	18 (81.8%)	131 (75.3%)	82 (75.9%)	231 (76.0%)
No	2 (81.8%)	28 (75.3%)	16 (75.9%)	46 (76.0%)
May be	2 (9.1%)	15 (8.6%)	10 (9.3%)	27 (8.9%)
Total	**22 (100.0%)**	**174 (100.0%)**	**108 (100.0%)**	**304 (100.0%)**

This table shows the level of intervention and skills competency based on the respondent's awareness about social work as a professional course. Among the respondents who were aware about social work as a professional course, 81.8% of the respondents possess low level, 75.9% possess high level and 75.3% possess moderate level of intervention and skills competency. Among the respondents who were not aware that social work is a professional course, 81.8% possess low level, 75.9% possess high level and 75.3% possess moderate level of intervention and skills competency. Among the respondents who may or may not aware that social work is a professional course, 9.3% of the respondents possess high level, 9.1% of the respondents possess low level and 8.6% possess moderate level of intervention and skills competency.

Table 13.13: Respondents Faced Criticism for Taking Social Work as Their Graduation and the Level of Intervention and Skills Competency

Respondents Faced Criticism for Taking Social Work as Their Graduation	*Level of Intervention and Skills Competency*			*Total*
	Low	*Moderate*	*High*	
Yes	12 (54.5%)	106 (60.9%)	57 (52.8%)	175 (57.6%)
No	9 (40.9%)	52 (29.9%)	41 (38.0%)	102 (33.6%)
May be	1 (4.5%)	16 (9.2%)	10 (9.3%)	27 (8.9%)
Total	**22 (100.0%)**	**174 (100.0%)**	**108 (100.0%)**	**304 (100.0%)**

The above table depicts the level of intervention and skills competency with respect to the criticism faced by the respondents for taking social work as their graduation. Among the respondents who faced criticism for taking social work as their graduation, 60.9% of the respondents possess moderate level, 54.5% possess low level and 52.8% possess high-level of intervention and skills competency. Among the respondents who have not faced criticism, 40.9% possess low level, 38% possess high level and 29.9% possess moderate level of intervention and skills competency. Among the respondents who may or may not have faced criticism, 9.3% possess high level, 9.2% possess moderate level and 4.5% possess low-level of intervention and skills competency.

Table 13.14: Kind of Criticism Faced by the Respondents for Taking Social Work as Their Graduation and the Level of Intervention and Skills Competency

Kind of Criticism Faced by the Respondents for Taking Social Work as their Graduation	*Level of Intervention and Skills Competency*			*Total*
	Low	*Moderate*	*High*	
No	10 (45.5%)	79 (45.4%)	56 (51.9%)	145 (47.7%)

Kind of Criticism Faced by the Respondents for Taking Social Work as their Graduation	*Level of Intervention and Skills Competency*			*Total*
	Low	*Moderate*	*High*	
Positive Criticism	2 (9.1%)	6 (3.4%)	8 (7.4%)	16 (5.3%)
Negative Criticism	10 (45.5%)	89 (51.1%)	44 (40.7%)	143 (47.0%)
Total	**22 (100.0%)**	**174 (100.0%)**	**108 (100.0%)**	**304 (100.0%)**

The above table represents the level of intervention and skills competency based on the kind of criticism faced by the respondents for taking social work as their graduation. Among The respondents who doesn't face any criticism, 51.9% possess high level, 45.5% possess low level and 45.4% possess moderate level of intervention and skills competency. Among the respondents who faced positive criticism, 9.1% possess-low level, 7.4% possess high level and 3.4% possess moderate level of intervention and skills competency. Among the respondents who faced negative criticism, 51.9% possess-high level, 45.5% possess low level and 45.4% possess moderate level of intervention and skills competency.

Table 13.15: Respondents Feeling of Competent with Regard to Social Work Profession and the Level of Intervention and Skills Competency

Respondents Feeling of Competent with Regard to Social Work Profession	*Level of Intervention and Skills Competency*			*Total*
	Low	*Moderate*	*High*	
Yes	9 (40.9%)	87 (50.0%)	51 (47.2%)	147 (48.4%)
No	0 (0.0%)	3 (1.7%)	3 (2.8%)	6 (2.0%)
May be	13 (59.1%)	84 (48.3%)	54 (50.0%)	151 (49.7%)
Total	**22 (100.0%)**	**174 (100.0%)**	**108 (100.0%)**	**304 (100.0%)**

The table 13.15 depicts the level of intervention and skills competency based on the respondents feeling of competent with regard to social work profession. Among The respondents who feels competent, 50% of the respondents possess moderate level, 47.2% of the respondents possess high level and 40.9% of the respondents possess low-level of intervention and skills competency. Among the respondents who doesn't feels competent 2.8% possess moderate level, 47.2% possess high level and 40.9% possess low-level of intervention and skills competency. Among the respondents who may or may not feel competent, 59.1% of the respondents possess low level, 50% of the respondents possess high level and 48.3% possess low-level of intervention and skills competency.

Table 13.16: List of Skills and the Level of Intervention and Skills Competency

List of Skills	*Level of Intervention and Skills Competency*			*Total*
	Low	*Moderate*	*High*	
Communication Skill	*7(31.8%)*	*67(38.5%)*	*49(45.4%)*	*123(40.5%)*
Active Listening	8 (36.4%)	38 (21.8%)	26 (24.1%)	72 (23.7%)
Responsible	1 (4.5%)	34 (19.5%)	16 (14.8%)	51 (16.8%)
No Idea	6 (27.3%)	35 (20.1%)	17 (15.7%)	58 (19.1%)
Total	**22 (100.0%)**	**174 (100.0%)**	**108 (100.0%)**	**304 (100.0%)**

The table shows the level of intervention and skills competency based on the respondent's skills. Among the respondents who possess communication skill, 45.4% have high level, 38.5% have moderate level and 31.8% have low level of intervention and skills competency. The respondents who possess active listening, 36.4% of the respondents have low level, 24.1% of the respondents have high level and 21.8% of the respondents have moderate level of intervention and skills competency. Among the respondents who feels being responsible as their skill, 19.5% possess moderate level, 14.8% possess high level and 4.5% of the respondents possess low level of intervention and skills competency. Among the respondents who had no idea, 27.3% possess low level, 20.1% of the respondents possess moderate level and 15.7% of the respondents possess high level of intervention and skills competency.

Table 13.17: Respondents Competent to Deal with the Problems of Individuals and the Level of Intervention and Skills Competency

Respondents Competent to Deal with the Problems of Individuals	*Level of Intervention and Skills Competency*			*Total*
	Low	*Moderate*	*High*	
Yes	16 (72.7%)	106 (60.9%)	69 (63.9%)	191 (62.8%)
No	1 (4.5%)	23 (13.2%)	11 (10.2%)	35 (11.5%)
May be	5 (22.7%)	45 (25.9%)	28 (25.9%)	78 (25.7%)
Total	**22 (100.0%)**	**174 (100.0%)**	**108 (100.0%)**	**304 (100.0%)**

The above table represents the level of intervention and skills competency with respect to the respondents competent to deal with the individual's problems. Among the respondents who feels competent to deal with individual problems, 72.7% possess low level, 63.9% possess high level and 60.9% possess moderate level of intervention and skills competency. Among the respondents who doesn't feel competent to deal with individual problems, 13.2% possess moderate level, 10.2% possess high level and 4.5% possess low level of intervention and skills competency. Among the respondents who may or may not competent, 25.9% possess moderate level, 25.9% possess high level and 22.7%possess low-level of intervention and skills competency.

Table 13.18: Respondents Competent to Deal with the Group Problems and the Level of Intervention and Skills Competency

Respondents Competent to Deal with the Group Problems	*Level of Intervention and Skills Competency*			*Total*
	Low	*Moderate*	*High*	
Yes	12 (54.5%)	100 (57.5%)	57 (52.8%)	169 (55.6%)
No	1 (4.5%)	12 (6.9%)	10 (9.3%)	23 (7.6%)
May be	9 (40.9%)	62 (35.6%)	41 (38.0%)	112 (36.8%)
Total	**22 (100.0%)**	**174 (100.0%)**	**108 (100.0%)**	**304 (100.0%)**

The table depicts the level of intervention and skills competency based on the respondents competent to deal with group problems. Among the respondents who feel competent to deal with group problems, 57.5% possess moderate level, 54.5% possess low level, 52.8% possess high level of intervention and skills competency. Among the respondents who doesn't feel competent, 9.3% possess high level, 6.9% possess moderate level and 4.5%possess low-level of intervention and skills competency. Among the respondents who may or may not competent, 40.9% possess low level, 38% possess high level and 35.69%possess low-level of intervention and skills competency.

Table 13.19: Respondents Competent to Deal with the Community Problems and the Level of Intervention and Skills Competency

Respondents Competent to Deal with the Group Problems	*Level of Intervention and Skills Competency*			*Total*
	Low	*Moderate*	*High*	
Yes	9 (40.9%)	75 (43.1%)	54 (50.0%)	138 (45.4%)
No	8 (36.4%)	47 (27.0%)	23 (21.3%)	78 (25.7%)

Respondents Competent to Deal with the Group Problems	*Level of Intervention and Skills Competency*			*Total*
	Low	*Moderate*	*High*	
May be	5 (22.7%)	52 (29.9%)	31 (28.7%)	38 (28.9%)
Total	**22 (100.0%)**	**174 (100.0%)**	**108 (100.0%)**	**304 (100.0%)**

The table depicts the level of intervention and skills competency based on the respondents competent to deal with community problems. Among the respondents who feels competent to deal with community problems, 50% possess high level, 43.1% possess moderate level and 40.9%possess low-level of intervention and skills competency. Among the respondents who doesn't feel competent, 36.4% of the respondents possess low level, 27% possess moderate level and 21.3% possess-high level of intervention and skills competency. Among the respondents who may or may not feel competent, 29.9% of the respondents possess moderate level, 28.7% possess high level and 22.7% of the respondents possess-low-level of intervention and skills competency.

CHAPTER 14

Level of Contexts and Organisation Competency

This chapter involves the analysis and interpretation of level of contexts and organisation competency and demographic variable, reason for choosing social work, perception, career ambition, aspiration, criticism faced and social worker skills.

Table 14.1: Age-wise Distribution of Level of Contexts and Organisation Competency

Age of the Respondent	*Level of Contexts and Organizations Competency*			*Total*
	Low	*Moderate*	*High*	
Below 21	15 (53.6%)	53 (46.5%)	84 (51.9%)	152 (50.0%)
21–25	12 (42.9%)	56 (49.1%)	71 (43.8%)	139 (45.7%)
25-29	1 (3.6%)	5 (4.4%)	7 (4.3%)	13 (4.3%)
Total	**28 (100.0%)**	**114 (100.0%)**	**162 (100.0%)**	**304 (100.0%)**

The above table represents the level of context and organizations competency based on the age of the respondents. Among the respondents below the age of 21 years, 53.6% possess low level, 51.9% possess high level and 46.5% possess moderate level of context and organizations competency. Among the respondents between the age of 21 and 25 years, 49.1% of the respondents possess moderate level, 43.8% possess high level and 42.9% of the respondents possess low level of context and organizations competency. Among the respondents between the age of 25 and 29 years, 4.4% possess moderate level, 4.3% possess high level and 3.6% possess low level of context and organizations competency.

Table 14.2: Gender of the Respondents and the Level of Contexts and Organisations Competency

Gender of the Respondents	*Level of Contexts and Organizations Competency*			*Total*
	Low	*Moderate*	*High*	
Prefer not to say	0 (0.0%)	0 (0.0%)	1 (0.6%)	1 (0.3%)
Female	16 (57.1%)	81 (71.1%)	101 (62.3%)	198 (65.1%)
Male	12 (42.9%)	33 (28.9%)	60 (37.0%)	105 (34.5%)
Total	**28 (100.0%)**	**114 (100.0%)**	**162 (100.0%)**	**304 (100.0%)**

The above table represents the level of contexts and organisation competency based on the gender of the respondents. 0.6% of the respondents who prefer not to say the gender, possess high level of context and organizations competency. Among the female respondents, 71.1% of the respondents possess moderate level, 62.3% of the respondents possess high level and 57.1% of the respondents possess low level of context and organizations competency. Among the male respondents, 42.9% of the respondents possess low level, 37% possess high level and 28.9% possess moderate level of context and organizations competency.

Table 14.3: Educational Qualification of the Respondents and the Level of Contexts and Organisations Competency

Educational Qualification of the Respondents	*Level of Contexts and Organizations Competency*			*Total*
	Low	*Moderate*	*High*	
II & III BSW	14 (50.0%)	60 (52.6%)	78 (48.1%)	152 (50.0%)
II MSW	14 (50.0%)	54 (47.4%)	84 (51.9%)	152 (50.0%)
Total	**28 (100.0%)**	**114 (100.0%)**	**162 (100.0%)**	**304 (100.0%)**

The table 14.3 represents the level of contexts and organisation competency based on the educational qualification of the respondents. Among the respondents who are pursuing II- and III-year BSW, 52.6% of the respondents possess moderate level, 50% of the respondents possess low level and 48.1% possess high level of context and organizations competency. Among the respondents who are pursuing II-year MSW, 51.9% possess high level, 50% possess low level and 47.4% possess moderate level of context and organizations competency.

Table 14.4: Post Graduate Respondents Under-Graduation and the Level of Contexts and Organisations Competency.

Post Graduate Respondents Under-Graduation	*Level of Contexts and Organizations Competency*			*Total*
	Low	*Moderate*	*High*	
BSW	5 (17.9%)	20 (17.5%)	44 (27.2%)	69 (22.7%)
OTHER DEGREE	9 (32.1%)	34 (29.8%)	40 (24.7%)	83 (27.3%)
Not Applicable (Respondents pursuing under graduate)	14 (50.0%)	60 (52.6%)	78 (48.1%)	152 (50.0%)
Total	**28 (100.0%)**	**114 (100.0%)**	**162 (100.0%)**	**304 (100.0%)**

The above table represents the level of contexts and organisation competency based on post graduate respondents under graduation. Among the respondents who pursued social work during their under graduation, 27.2% possess high level, 17.9% possess low level and 17.5% possess moderate level of context and organizations competency. Among the respondents who pursued subjects other than social work during their under graduation, 32.1% possess low level, 29.8% possess moderate level and 24.7% possess high level of context and organizations competency.

Table 14.5: Domicile of the Respondents and the Level of Contexts and Organisations Competency

Domicile of the Respondents	*Level of Contexts and Organizations Competency*			*Total*
	Low	*Moderate*	*High*	
Tamil Nadu	24 (85.7%)	98 (86.0%)	135 (83.3%)	257 (84.5%)
Outside Tamil Nadu	4 (14.3%)	16 (14.0%)	27 (16.7%)	47 (15.5%)
Total	**28 (100.0%)**	**114 (100.0%)**	**162 (100.0%)**	**304 (100.0%)**

The above table represents the level of contexts and organisation competency based on respondent's domicile. Among the respondents from Tamilnadu, 86% of the respondents possess moderate level, 85.7% of the respondents possess low level and 83.3% possess high level of context and organizations competency. Among the respondents from outside Tamilnadu, 16.7% possess high level, 14.3% possess low level and 14% possess moderate level of context and organizations competency.

Table 14.6: Major Subjects Studied by the Respondents During 12th Standard and the Level of Contexts and Organisations Competency

Major Subjects Studied by the Respondents during 12th Standard	*Level of Contexts and Organizations Competency*			*Total*
	Low	*Moderate*	*High*	
Bio Maths	4 (14.3%)	21 (18.4%)	34 (21.0%)	59 (19.4%)
Computer Sciences	4 (14.3%)	24 (21.1%)	24 (14.8%)	52 (17.1%)
Commerce	17 (60.7%)	54 (47.4%)	83 (51.2%)	154 (50.7%)
Humanities	3 (10.7%)	15 (13.2%)	21 (13.0%)	39 (12.8%)
Total	**28 (100.0%)**	**114 (100.0%)**	**162 (100.0%)**	**304 (100.0%)**

The table 14.6 represents the level of contexts and organisation based on the major subjects studied by the respondents during 12th standard. Among the respondents who studied Bio-maths during 12th standard, 21% possess high level, 18.4% possess moderate level and 14.3% possess low level of context and organizations competency. Among the respondents who pursued Computer Sciences during 12th standard, 21.1% of the respondents possess moderate level, 14.8% of the respondents possess high level and 14.3% of the respondents possess low level of context and organizations competency. Among the respondents who studied Commerce during 12th standard, 60.7% possess low level, 51.2% possess high level and 47.4% possess moderate level of context and organizations competency. Among the respondents who studied humanities during 12th standard, 13.2% possess moderate level, 13% possess high level and 10.7% possess low level of context and organizations competency.

Table 14.7: Respondents Reasons for Choosing Social Work and the Level of Contexts and Organisations Competency

Respondent's Reasons for Choosing Social Work	*Level of Contexts and Organizations Competency*			*Total*
	Low	*Moderate*	*High*	
Own Interest	18 (64.3%)	67 (58.8%)	102 (63.0%)	187 (61.5%)
Parents/Relatives Recommendation	10 (35.7%)	45 (39.5%)	56 (34.6%)	111 (36.5%)
Siblings Studied/Influence	0 (0.0%)	2 (1.8%)	4 (2.5%)	6 (2.0%)
Total	**28 (100.0%)**	**114 (100.0%)**	**162 (100.0%)**	**304 (100.0)**

The above table represents the level of contexts and organisation competency based on respondents' reasons for choosing social work. Among the respondents who chose social work on their own interest, 64.3% of the respondents possess low level, 63% of the respondents possess high level and 58.8% of the respondents possess moderate level of context and organizations competency. Among the respondents who chose social work based on their parents/relatives recommendation,

39.5% of the respondents possess moderate level, 35.7% possess low level and 34.6% of the respondents possess high level of context and organizations competency. Among the respondents who chose social work based on their sibling studied social work/influenced, 2.5% of the respondents possess high level and 1.8% of the respondents possess moderate level of context and organizations competency.

Table 14.8: Respondents Perception about Social Work and the Level of Contexts and Organisations Competency

Respondents Perception about Social Work	*Level of Contexts and Organizations Competency*			*Total*
	Low	*Moderate*	*High*	
Practise Based Profession	4 (14.3%)	21 (18.4%)	34 (21.0%)	59 (19.4%)
Value Oriented Subject	4 (14.3%)	24 (21.1%)	24 (14.8%)	52 (17.1%)
Helping Profession	17 (60.7%)	54 (47.4%)	83 (51.2%)	154 (50.7%)
Art Course	3 (10.7%)	15 (13.2%)	21 (13.0%)	39 (12.8%)
Total	**28 (100.0%)**	**114 (100.0%)**	**162 (100.0%)**	**304 (100.0%)**

The above table represents the level of contexts and organisation competency based on respondent's perception about social work. Among the respondents who perceive social work as practice-based profession, 21% possess high level, 18.4% possess moderate level and 14.3% possess low level of context and organizations competency. Among the respondents who perceive social work as value-oriented subject, 21.1% possess moderate level, 14.8% possess high level and 14.3% possess low level of context and organizations competency. Among the respondents who perceive social work as helping profession, 60.7% respondents possess low level, 51.2% respondents possess high level and 47.4% possess moderate level of context and organizations competency. Among the respondents who perceive social work as art course, 13.2% of the respondents possess moderate level, 13% of the respondents possess high level and 10.7% possess low level of context and organizations competency.

Table 14.9: Family Members of the Respondents Studied Social Work and the Level of Contexts and Organisations Competency

Family Members of the Respondents Studied Social Work	*Level of Contexts and Organizations Competency*			*Total*
	Low	*Moderate*	*High*	
Yes	2 (7.1%)	23 (20.2%)	22 (13.6%)	47 (15.5%)
No	26 (92.9%)	91 (79.8%)	140 (86.4%)	257 (84.5%)
Total	**28 (100.0%)**	**114 (100.0%)**	**162 (100.0%)**	**304 (100.0%)**

The above table represents the level of contexts and organisation competency based on respondents' family members studied social work. Among the respondents whose family members studied social work, 20.2% possess moderate level, 13.6% of the respondents possess high level and 7.1% of the respondents possess low level of context and organizations competency. Among the respondents whose family members not studied social work, 92.9% of the respondents possess low level, 86.4% of the respondents possess high level and 79.8% of the respondents possess moderate level of context and organizations competency.

Table 14.10: Career Ambition of the Respondents and the Level of Contexts and Organisations Competency

Career Ambition of the Respondent	*Level of Contexts and Organizations Competency*			*Total*
	Low	*Moderate*	*High*	
Professional Social Worker	7 (25.0%)	36 (31.6%)	46 (28.4%)	89 (29.3%)
Psychiatric/Medical Social Worker/Mental Health/Counsellor	12 (42.9%)	43 (37.7%)	56 (34.6%)	111 (36.5%)
N.G.O/Orphan Homes	2 (7.1%)	7 (6.1%)	14 (8.6%)	23 (7.6%)
H.R	4	15	27	46

Career Ambition of the Respondent	*Level of Contexts and Organizations Competency*			*Total*
	Low	*Moderate*	*High*	
	(14.3%)	(13.2%)	(16.7%)	(15.1%)
Government Jobs	1 (3.6%)	11 (9.6%)	12 (7.4%)	24 (7.9%)
Professor	2 (7.1%)	2 (1.8%)	7 (4.3%)	11 (3.6%)
Total	**28 (100.0%)**	**114 (100.0%)**	**162 (100.0%)**	**304 (100.0%)**

The above table represents the level of contexts and organisation competency based on respondents' career ambition. Among the respondents whose ambition is to become professional social worker, 31.6% of the respondents possess moderate level, 28.4% of the respondents possess high level and 25% of the respondents possess low level of context and organizations competency. Among the respondents whose ambition is to become psychiatric/medical social worker/mental health/counsellor, 42.9% possess low level, 37.7% possess moderate level and 34.6% possess high level of context and organizations competency.

Among the respondents whose ambition to work in non-governmental organization/orphan homes, 8.6% possess high level, 7.1% possess low level and 6.1% possess moderate level of context and organizations competency. Among the respondents whose ambition is to become human resource managers, 16.7% possess high level, 14.3% possess low level and 13.2% possess moderate level of context and organizations competency. Among the respondents whose ambition is to get Government jobs, 9.6% of the respondents possess moderate level, 7.4% of the respondents possess high level and 3.6% possess low level of context and organizations competency. Among the respondents whose ambition is to become professor, 7.1% possess low level, 4.3% possess high level and 1.8% possess moderate level of context and organizations competency.

Table 14.11: Aspiration of the Respondents and the Level of Contexts and Organisations Competency

Aspiration of the Respondents	*Level of Contexts and Organizations Competency*			*Total*
	Low	*Moderate*	*High*	
Social Worker/Counsellor/HR	14 (50.0%)	59 (51.8%)	80 (49.4%)	153 (50.3%)
UPSC	8 (28.6%)	37 (32.5%)	50 (30.9%)	95 (31.2%)
No Idea	6 (21.4%)	18 (15.8%)	32 (19.8%)	56 (18.4%)
Total	**28 (100.0%)**	**114 (100.0%)**	**162 (100.0%)**	**304 (100.0%)**

The above table represents the level of contexts and organisation competency based on respondents' aspiration. Among the respondents who aspire to become social worker/counsellor/HR, 51.8% of the respondents possess moderate level, 50% possess low level and 49.4% possess high level of context and organizations competency. Among the respondents who aspire to write union public service commission, 32.5% possess moderate level, 30.9% possess high level and 28.6% possess low level of context and organizations competency. Among the respondents who doesn't have any idea, 21.4% possess low level, 19.8% possess high level and 15.8% of the respondents possess moderate level of context and organizations competency.

Table 14.12: Respondents Awareness about Social Work as a Professional Course and the Level of Contexts and Organisations Competency

Respondent's Awareness about Social Work as a Professional Course	*Level of Contexts and Organizations Competency*			*Total*
	Low	*Moderate*	*High*	
Yes	22 (78.6%)	85 (74.6%)	124 (76.5%)	231 (76.0%)
No	4 (14.3%)	18 (15.8%)	24 (14.8%)	46 (15.1%)

Respondent's Awareness about Social Work as a Professional Course	*Level of Contexts and Organizations Competency*			*Total*
	Low	*Moderate*	*High*	
May be	2 (7.1%)	11 (9.6%)	14 (8.6%)	27 (8.9%)
Total	**28 (100.0%)**	**114 (100.0%)**	**162 (100.0%)**	**304 (100.0%)**

The above table represents the level of contexts and organisation competency based on respondent's awareness about Social Work as a Professional Course. Among the respondents who aware that social work is a professional course, 78.6% of the respondents possess low level, 76.5% of the respondents possess high level and 74.6% of the respondents possess moderate level of context and organizations competency. Among the respondents who are not aware that social work is a professional course, 15.8% possess moderate level, 14.8% possess high level and 14.3% low level of context and organizations competency. Among the respondents who may or may not aware that social work is a professional course, 9.6% possess moderate level, 8.6% possess high level and 7.1% possess low level of context and organizations competency.

Table 14.13: Respondents Faced Criticism for Taking Social Work as their Graduation and the Level of Contexts and Organisations Competency

Respondents Faced Criticism for Taking Social Work as their Graduation	*Level of Contexts and Organizations Competency*			*Total*
	Low	*Moderate*	*High*	
Yes	17 (60.7%)	66 (57.9%)	92 (56.8%)	175 (57.6%)
No	9 (32.1%)	39 (34.2%)	54 (33.3%)	102 (33.6%)
May be	2 (7.1%)	9 (7.9%)	16 (9.9%)	27 (8.9%)
Total	**28 (100.0%)**	**114 (100.0%)**	**162 (100.0%)**	**304 (100.0%)**

The table 14.13 represents the level of contexts and organisation competency based on respondents faced criticism for taking Social Work as their Graduation. Among the respondents who faced criticism for taking social work as their graduation, 60.7% possess low level, 57.9% possess moderate level and 56.8% possess high level of context and organizations competency. Among the respondents who haven't faced criticism, 34.2% possess moderate level, 33.3% possess high level and 32.1% possess low level of context and organizations competency. Among the respondents who may or may not face criticism, 9.9% possess high level, 7.9% possess moderate level and 7.1% possess low level of context and organizations competency.

Table 14.14: Kind of Criticism Faced by the Respondents for Taking Social Work as Their Graduation and the Level of Contexts and Organisations Competency

Kind of Criticism Faced by the Respondents for taking Social Work as their Graduation	*Level of Contexts and Organizations Competency*			*Total*
	Low	*Moderate*	*High*	
No	11 (39.3%)	57 (50.0%)	77 (47.5%)	145 (47.7%)
Positive Criticism	2 (7.1%)	8 (7.0%)	6 (3.7%)	16 (5.3%)
Negative Criticism	15 (53.6%)	49 (43.0%)	79 (48.8%)	143 (47.0%)
Total	**28 (100.0%)**	**114 (100.0%)**	**162 (100.0%)**	**304 (100.0%)**

The above table represents the level of contexts and organisation competency based on the kind of criticism faced by the respondents for taking social work as their graduation. Among the respondents who doesn't face any kind of criticism, 50% possess moderate level, 47.5% possess high level and 39.3% possess low level of context and organizations competency. Among the respondents who faced positive criticism, 7.1% possess low level, 7% possess moderate level and 3.7% possess high level of context and organizations competency. Among the respondents who faced negative criticism 53.6% possess low level, 48.8% possess high level and 43% possess moderate level of context and organizations competency.

Table 14.15: Respondents Feeling of Competent with Regard to Social Work Profession and the Level of Contexts and Organisations Competency

Respondents Feeling of Competent with Regard to Social Work Profession	*Level of Contexts and Organizations Competency*			*Total*
	Low	*Moderate*	*High*	
Yes	15 (53.6%)	58 (50.39%)	74 (45.7%)	147 (48.4%)
No	0 (0.0%)	2 (1.8%)	4 (2.5%)	6 (2.0%)
May be	13 (46.4%)	54 (47.4%)	84 (51.9%)	151 (49.7%)
Total	**28 (100.0%)**	**114 (100.0%)**	**162 (100.0%)**	**304 (100.0%)**

The above table represents the level of contexts and organisation competency based on respondents feeling of Competent with regard to Social Work Profession. Among the respondents who feels competent with regard to social work profession, 53.6% possess low level, 50.39% possess moderate level and 45.7% possess high level of contexts and organisation competency. Among the respondents who doesn't feel competent with regard to social work profession, 2.5% possess high level and 1.8% possess moderate level of contexts and organisation competency. Among the respondents who may or may not be competent, 51.9% possess high level, 47.4% possess moderate level and 46.4% possess low level of contexts and organisation competency.

Table 14.16: List of Skills and the Level of Contexts and Organisations Competency

List of Skills	*Level of Contexts and Organizations Competency*			*Total*
	Low	*Moderate*	*High*	
Communication Skill	10 (35.7%)	48 (42.1%)	65 (40.1%)	123 (40.5%)
Active Listening	9 (32.1%)	23 (20.2%)	40 (24.7%)	72 (23.7%)
Responsible	2 (7.1%)	23 (20.2%)	26 (16.0%)	51 (16.8%)
No Idea	7 (25.0%)	20 (17.5%)	31 (19.1%)	58 (19.1%)
Total	**28 (100.0%)**	**114 (100.0%)**	**162 (100.0%)**	**304 (100.0%)**

The above table represents the level of contexts and rganisation competency based on respondent's skills. Among the respondents who possess communication skills, 42.1% have moderate level, 40.1% have high level and 35.7% possess low level of context and organizations competency. Among the respondents who possess active listening skill, 32.1% possess low level. 24.7% possess high level and 20.2% possess moderate level of context and organizations competency. Among the respondents who feels that being responsible is their skill, 20.2% possess moderate level, 16% possess high level and 7.1% possess low level of context and organizations competency. Among the respondents who doesn't have any idea about their skill, 25% possess low level, 19.1% possess high level and 17.5% possess moderate level of context and organizations competency.

Table 14.17: Respondents Competent to Deal with the Problems of Individuals and the Level of Contexts and Organisations Competency

Respondents Competent to Deal with the Problems of Individuals	*Level of Contexts and Organizations Competency*			*Total*
	Low	*Moderate*	*High*	
Yes	19 (67.9%)	73 (64.0%)	99 (61.1%)	191 (62.8%)
No	2 (7.1%)	11 (9.6%)	22 (13.6%)	35 (11.5%)
May be	7 (25.0%)	30 (26.3%)	41 (25.3%)	78 (25.7%)
Total	**28 (100.0%)**	**114 (100.0%)**	**162 (100.0%)**	**304 (100.0%)**

The above table represents the level of contexts and organisation competency based on respondents competent to deal with the problems of Individuals. Among the respondents who are feeling competent to deal with individual problems, 67.9% possess low level, 64% possess moderate level and 61.1% possess high level of contexts and organisation competency. Among the respondents who doesn't feel competent to deal with individual problems, 13.6% possess high level, 9.6% possess moderate level and 7.1% possess low level of contexts and organisation competency. Among the respondents who may or may not be competent to deal the individual problems, 26.3% possess moderate level, 25.3% possess high level and 25% possess low level of contexts and organisation competency.

Table 14.18: Respondents Competent to Deal with the Group Problems and the Level of Contexts and Organisations Competency

Respondents Competent to Deal with the Group Problem	*Level of Contexts and Organizations Competency*			*Total*
	Low	*Moderate*	*High*	
Yes	14 (50.0%)	68 (59.6%)	87 (53.7%)	169 (55.6%)
No	0 (0.0%)	8 (7.0%)	15 (9.3%)	23 (7.6%)

Respondents Competent to Deal with the Group Problem	*Level of Contexts and Organizations Competency*			*Total*
	Low	*Moderate*	*High*	
May be	14 (50.0%)	38 (33.3%)	60 (37.0%)	112 (36.8%)
Total	**28 (100.0%)**	**114 (100.0%)**	**162 (100.0%)**	**304 (100.0%)**

The above table represents the level of contexts and organisation competency based on respondent's competency to deal with group problems. Among the respondents who are competent to deal with the group problems, 59.6% possess moderate level, 53.7% possess high level and 50% possess low level of contexts and organisation competency. Among the respondents who doesn't feel competent to deal with group problems, 9.3% possess high level and 7% possess moderate level of contexts and organisation competency. Among the respondents who may or may not feel competent to deal with group problems, 50% possess low level, 37% possess high level and 33.3% possess moderate level of contexts and organisation competency.

Table 14.19: Respondents Competent to Deal with the Community Problems and the Level of Contexts and Organisations Competency

Respondents Competent to Deal with the Community Problems	*Level of Contexts and Organizations Competency*			*Total*
	Low	*Moderate*	*High*	
Yes	14 (50.0%)	55 (48.2%)	69 (42.6%)	138 (45.4%)
No	7 (25.0%)	25 (21.9%)	46 (28.4%)	78 (25.7%)
May be	7 (25.0%)	34 (29.8%)	47 (29.0%)	88 (28.9%)
Total	**28 (100.0%)**	**114 (100.0%)**	**162 (100.0%)**	**304 (100.0%)**

The above table represents the level of contexts and organisation competency based on respondents competent to deal with community problems. Among the respondents who feels competent to deal with community problems, 50% of the respondents possess low level, 48.2% possess moderate level and 42.6% of the respondents possess high level of contexts and organisation competency. Among the respondents who are not feeling competent to deal with community problems, 28.4% possess high level, 25% possess low level and 21.9% possess moderate level of contexts and organisation competency. Among the respondents who may or may not feeling competent to deal the problems of community, 29.8% possess moderate level, 29% possess high level and 25% possess low level of contexts and organisation competency.

CHAPTER 15

Level of Professional Leadership Competency

This chapter involves the analysis and interpretation of level of professional leadership competency and demographic variable, reason for choosing social work, perception, career ambition, aspiration, criticism faced and social worker skills.

Table 15.1: Age of the Respondents and their Level of Professional Leadership Competency

Age of the Respondents	*Level of Professional Leadership Competency*			*Total*
	Low	*Moderate*	*High*	
Below 21	12 (57.1%)	59 (50.9%)	81 (48.5%)	152 (50.0%)
21–25	8 (38.1%)	54 (46.6%)	77 (46.1%)	139 (45.7%)
25-29	1 (4.8%)	3 (2.6%)	9 (5.4%)	13 (4.3%)
Total	**21 (100.0%)**	**116 (100.0%)**	**167 (100.0%)**	**304 (100.0%)**

The above table represents the level of Professional Leadership Competency based on respondents' age. Among the respondents below the age of 21 years 57.1% of the respondents possess low level of Professional Leadership Competency, 50.9% of the respondents possess moderate level and 48.5% of the respondents possess high level of Professional Leadership Competency Among the respondents between the age of 21 and 25 years, 46.6% possess moderate level,

46.1% of the respondents possess high level and 38.1% of the respondents possess low level of Professional Leadership Competency Among the respondents between the age of 25 and 29 years, 5.4% of the respondents possess high level, 4.8% of the respondents possess low level and 2.6% of the respondents possess moderate level of Professional Leadership Competency.

Table 15.2: Gender of the Respondents and their Level of Professional Leadership Competency

Gender of the Respondents	*Level of Professional Leadership Competency*			*Total*
	Low	*Moderate*	*High*	
Prefer not to say	0 (0.0%)	0 (0.0%)	1 (0.6%)	1 (0.3%)
Female	10 (47.6%)	73 (62.9%)	115 (68.9%)	198 (65.1%)
Male	11 (52.4%)	43 (37.1%)	51 (30.5%)	105 (34.5%)
Total	**21 (100.0%)**	**116 (100.0%)**	**167 (100.0%)**	**304 (100.0%)**

The above table represents the level of Professional Leadership Competency based on respondents' gender. Among the female respondents,68.9% of the respondents possess high level of Professional Leadership Competency, 62.9% of the respondents possess moderate level and 47.6% of the respondents possess low level of Professional Leadership Competency, Among the male respondents, 52.4% of the respondents possess low level, 37.1% of the respondents possess moderate level and 30.5% of the respondents possess high level of Professional Leadership Competency, 0.6% of the respondents who prefer not to say the gender possess high level of Professional Leadership Competency.

Table 15.3: Educational Qualification of the Respondents and their Level of Professional Leadership Competency

Educational Qualification of the Respondents	*Level of Professional Leadership Competency*			*Total*
	Low	*Moderate*	*High*	
II & III BSW	14 (66.7%)	60 (51.7%)	78 (46.7%)	152 (50.0%)
II MSW	7 (33.3%)	56 (48.3%)	89 (53.3%)	152 (50.0%)
Total	**21 (100.0%)**	**116 (100.0%)**	**167 (100.0%)**	**304 (100.0%)**

The above table represents the level of Professional Leadership Competency based on respondents' educational qualification. Among the respondents of II- and III-year BSW students, 66.7% possess low level, 51.7% possess moderate level and 46.7% possess high level of Professional Leadership Competency. Among the respondents of II-year MSW students, 53.3% of the respondents possess high level, 48.3% possess moderate level and 33.3% of the respondents possess low level of Professional Leadership Competency.

Table 15.4: Post Graduate Respondents under Graduation and Level of Professional Leadership Competency

Post Graduate Respondents Under-Graduation	*Level of Professional Leadership Competency*			*Total*
	Low	*Moderate*	*High*	
BSW	1 (4.8%)	24 (20.7%)	44 (26.3%)	69 (22.7%)
other degree	6 (28.6%)	32 (27.6%)	45 (26.9%)	83 (27.3%)
Not Applicable (U.G. respondents)	14 (66.7%)	60 (51.7%)	78 (46.7%)	152 (50.0%)
Total	**21 (100.0%)**	**116 (100.0%)**	**167 (100.0%)**	**304 (100.0%)**

The above table represents the level of Professional Leadership Competency based on post graduate respondents' under-graduation. Among the respondents who pursued social work as their under graduation, 26.3% possess high level of Professional Leadership Competency, 20.7% possess moderate level and 4.8% of the respondents possess low level of Professional Leadership Competency. Among the respondents who pursued other than social work as their under graduation, 28.6% of the respondents possess low level, 27.6% of the respondents possess moderate level and 26.9% of the respondents possess high level of Professional Leadership Competency.

Table 15.5: Domicile of the Respondents and the Level of Professional Leadership Competency

Domicile of the Respondents	*Level of Professional Leadership Competency*			*Total*
	Low	*Moderate*	*High*	
Tamil Nadu	18 (85.7%)	99 (85.3%)	140 (83.8%)	257 (84.5%)
Outside Tamil Nadu	3 (14.3%)	17 (14.7%)	27 (16.2%)	47 (15.5%)
Total	**21 (100.0%)**	**116 (100.0%)**	**167 (100.0%)**	**304 (100.0%)**

The above table represents the level of Professional Leadership Competency based on respondents' domicile. Among the respondents within Tamilnadu, 85.7% of the respondents possess low level of Professional Leadership Competency 85.3% possess moderate level and 83.8% of the respondents possess high level of Professional Leadership Competency. Among the respondents outside Tamilnadu, 16.2% of the respondents possess high level of Professional Leadership Competency, 14.7% of the respondents possess moderate level and 14.3% of the respondents possess low level of Professional Leadership Competency.

Table 15.6: Major Subjects Studied by the Respondents during 12th Standard and the Level of Professional Leadership Competency

Major Subjects Studied by the Respondents during 12th Standard	*Level of Professional Leadership Competency*			*Total*
	Low	*Moderate*	*High*	
Bio-Maths	3 (14.3%)	21 (18.1%)	35 (21.0%)	59 (19.4%)
Computer Sciences	2 (9.5%)	26 (22.4%)	24 (14.4%)	52 (17.1%)
Commerce	14 (66.7%)	54 (46.6%)	86 (51.5%)	154 (50.7%)
Humanities	2 (9.5%)	15 (12.9%)	22 (13.2%)	39 (12.8%)
Total	**21 (100.0%)**	**116 (100.0%)**	**167 (100.0%)**	**304 (100.0%)**

The above table represents the level of Professional Leadership Competency based on respondents' major subject studied during 12th standard. Among the respondents who pursued bio-maths during 12th standard, 21% possess high level, 18.1% possess moderate and 14.3% of the respondents possess low level of Professional Leadership Competency. Among the respondents who pursued computer sciences during 12th standard, 22.4% of the respondents possess moderate level, 14.4% of the respondents possess high level and 9.5% of the respondents possess low level of Professional Leadership Competency. Among the respondents who pursued commerce during 12th standard, 66.7% of the respondents possess low level, 51.5% possess high level and 46.6% of the respondents possess moderate level of Professional Leadership Competency. Among the respondents who pursued humanities during 12th standard, 13.2% possess high level, 12.9% of the respondents possess moderate level and 9.5% of the respondents possess low level of Professional Leadership Competency.

Table 15.7: Respondents Reasons for Choosing Social Work and the Level of Professional Leadership Competency

Respondent's reasons for choosing Social Work	*Level of Professional Leadership Competency*			*Total*
	Low	*Moderate*	*High*	
Own Interest	14 (66.7%)	69 (59.5%)	104 (62.3%)	187 (61.5%)
Parents/Relatives Recommendation	7 (33.3%)	45 (38.8%)	59 (35.3%)	111 (36.5%)
Siblings Studied/Influence	0 (0.0%)	2 (1.7%)	4 (2.4%)	6 (2.0%)
Total	**21 (100.0%)**	**116 (100.0%)**	**167 (100.0%)**	**304 (100.0%)**

The above table represents the level of Professional Leadership Competency based on respondents' reasons for choosing social work. The level of Professional Leadership Competency is low for 66.7% respondents who chose social work on their own interest. The level of Professional Leadership Competency is high for 62.3% respondents who chose social work on their own interest. The level of Professional Leadership Competency is moderate for 59.5% respondents who chose social work on their own interest. The level of Professional Leadership Competency is moderate for 38.8% respondents who chose social work because of Parents/Relatives Recommendation. The level of Professional Leadership Competency is high for 35.3% respondents who chose social work because of Parents/Relatives Recommendation. The level of Professional Leadership Competency is low for 33.3% respondents who chose social work because of Parents/Relatives Recommendation. The level of Professional Leadership Competency is high for 2.4% respondents of who chose social work because of Siblings Studied/Influence. The level of Professional Leadership Competency is moderate for 1.7% respondents who chose social work because of Siblings Studied/Influence.

Table 15.8: Respondents Perception about Social Work and the Level of Professional Leadership Competency

Respondents Perception about Social Work	*Level of Professional Leadership Competency*			*Total*
	Low	*Moderate*	*High*	
Practise Based Profession	3 (14.3%)	21 (18.1%)	35 (21.0%)	59 (19.4%)
Value Oriented Subject	2 (9.5%)	26 (22.4%)	24 (14.4%)	52 (17.1%)
Helping Profession	14 (66.7%)	54 (46.6%)	86 (51.5%)	154 (50.7%)
Art Course	2 (9.5%)	15 (12.9%)	22 (13.2%)	39 (12.8%)
Total	**21 (100.0%)**	**116 (100.0%)**	**167 (100.0%)**	**304 (100.0%)**

The above table represents the level of Professional Leadership Competency based on respondents' perception about social work. The level of Professional Leadership Competency is high for 21% respondents who perceive social work as practised based profession. The level of Professional Leadership Competency is moderate for 18.1% respondents who perceive social work as practised based profession. The level of Professional Leadership Competency is low for 14.3% respondents who perceive social work as practised based profession. The level of Professional Leadership Competency is moderate for 22.4% respondents who perceive social work as Value Oriented Subject. The level of Professional Leadership Competency is high for 14.4% respondents who perceive social work as Value Oriented Subject. The level of Professional Leadership Competency is low for 9.5% respondents who perceive social work as Value Oriented Subject. The level of Professional Leadership Competency is low for 66.7% respondents who perceive social work as Helping Profession. The level of Professional Leadership Competency is high for 51.5% respondents who perceive social work as Helping Profession. The level of Professional Leadership Competency is moderate for 46.6%

respondents who perceive social work as Helping Profession. The level of Professional Leadership Competency is high for 13.2% respondents who perceive social work as Art Course. The level of Professional Leadership Competency is moderate for 12.9% respondents who perceive social work as Art Course. The level of Professional Leadership Competency is low for 9.5% respondents who perceive social work as Art Course.

Table 15.9: Family Members of the Respondents Studied Social Work and the Level of Professional Leadership Competency

Family Members of the Respondents Studied Social Work	*Level of Professional Leadership Competency*			*Total*
	Low	*Moderate*	*High*	
Yes	2 (9.5%)	22 (19.0%)	23 (13.8%)	47 (15.5%)
No	19 (90.5%)	94 (81.0%)	144 (86.2%)	257 (84.5%)
Total	**21 (100.0%)**	**116 (100.0%)**	**167 (100.0%)**	**304 (100.0%)**

The above table represents the level of Professional Leadership Competency based on respondents' family members studied social work. The level of Professional Leadership Competency is moderate for 19% respondent's whose family members studied social work. The level of Professional Leadership Competency is high for 13.8% respondent's whose family members studied social work. The level of Professional Leadership Competency is moderate for 9.5% respondent's whose family members studied social work. The level of Professional Leadership Competency is low for 90.5% respondent's whose family members not studied social work. The level of Professional Leadership Competency is high for 86.2% respondent's whose family members not studied social work. The level of Professional Leadership Competency is moderate for 81% respondent's whose family members not studied social work.

Table 15.10: Career Ambition of the Respondents and the Level of Professional Leadership Competency

Career Ambition of the Respondents	*Level of Professional Leadership Competency*			*Total*
	Low	*Moderate*	*High*	
Professional Social Worker	5 (23.8%)	30 (25.9%)	54 (32.3%)	89 (29.3%)
Psychiatric/Medical Social Worker/Mental Health/Counsellor	8 (38.1%)	46 (39.7%)	57 (34.1%)	111 (36.5%)
N.G.O/Orphanage	1 (4.8%)	8 (6.9%)	14 (8.4%)	23 (7.6%)
H.R.	3 (14.3%)	18 (15.5%)	25 (15.0%)	46 (15.1%)
Government Jobs	2 (9.5%)	10 (8.6%)	12 (7.2%)	24 (7.9%)
Professor	2 (9.5%)	4 (3.4%)	5 (3.0%)	11 (3.6%)
Total	**21 (100.0%)**	**116 (100.0%)**	**167 (100.0%)**	**304 (100.0%)**

The above table represents the level of Professional Leadership Competency based on respondents' career ambition. The level of Professional Leadership Competency is high for 32.3% respondent's whose ambition is to become professional social worker. The level of Professional Leadership Competency is moderate for 25.9% respondent's whose ambition is to become professional social worker. The level of Professional Leadership Competency is low for 23.8% respondent's whose ambition is to become professional social worker. The level of Professional Leadership Competency is moderate for 39.7% respondent's whose ambition is to become Psychiatric/Medical Social Worker/Mental Health/Counsellor. The level of Professional Leadership Competency is low for 38.1% respondent's whose ambition is to become Psychiatric/Medical Social Worker/Mental Health/Counsellor. The level of Professional Leadership Competency is high for 34.1% respondent's whose ambition is to become Psychiatric/Medical Social Worker/Mental Health/Counsellor. The level of Professional Leadership Competency is high for 8.4% respondent's whose ambition is to work in a N.G.O/Orphanage. The level of Professional Leadership Competency is moderate for 6.9% respondent's whose ambition is to work in a N.G.O/Orphanage. The level of Professional Leadership Competency is low for 4.8% respondent's whose ambition is to work in a N.G.O/Orphanage. The level of Professional Leadership Competency is moderate for 15.5% respondent's whose ambition is to become H.R. The level of Professional Leadership Competency is high for 15% respondent's whose ambition is to become H.R. The level of Professional Leadership Competency is low for 14.3% respondent's whose ambition is to become H.R. The level of Professional Leadership Competency is low for 9.5% respondent's whose ambition is to get Government Jobs. The level of Professional Leadership Competency is moderate for 8.6% respondent's whose ambition is to get Government Jobs. The level of Professional Leadership Competency is high for 7.2% respondent's whose ambition is to get Government Jobs. The level of Professional Leadership Competency is low for 9.5% respondent's whose ambition is to become Professor. The level of Professional Leadership Competency is moderate for 3.4% respondent's whose ambition is to become Professor. The level of Professional Leadership Competency is high for 3% respondent's whose ambition is to become Professor.

Table 15.11: Aspiration of the Respondents and the Level of Professional Leadership Competency

Aspiration of the Respondents	*Level of Professional Leadership Competency*			*Total*
	Low	*Moderate*	*High*	
Social Worker/Counsellor/HR	11 (52.4%)	63 (54.3%)	79 (47.3%)	153 (50.3%)
UPSC	5 (23.8%)	36 (31.0%)	54 (32.3%)	95 (31.2%)
No Idea	5 (23.8%)	17 (14.7%)	34 (20.4%)	56 (18.4%)
Total	**21 (100.0%)**	**116 (100.0%)**	**167 (100.0%)**	**304 (100.0%)**

The above table represents the level of Professional Leadership Competency based on respondents' aspiration. The level of Professional Leadership Competency is moderate for 54.3% respondent's whose aspiration is to become social worker/counsellor/HR. The level of Professional Leadership Competency is low for 52.4% respondent's whose aspiration is to become social worker/counsellor/HR. The level of Professional Leadership Competency is high for 47.3% respondent's whose aspiration is to become social worker/counsellor/HR. The level of Professional Leadership Competency is high for 32.3% respondent's whose aspiration is to write union public service commission (UPSC).The level of Professional Leadership Competency is moderate for 31% respondent's whose aspiration is to write union public service commission (UPSC).The level of Professional Leadership Competency is low for 23.8% respondent's whose aspiration is to write union public service commission (UPSC). Among the respondents without any idea about their aspiration, 23.8% of the respondents possess low level, 20.4% possess high level and 14.7% of the respondents possess moderate level of Professional Leadership Competency.

Table 15.12: Respondents Awareness about Social Work as a Professional Course and Level of Professional Leadership Competency

Respondent's Awareness about Social Work as a Professional Course	*Level of Professional Leadership Competency*			*Total*
	Low	*Moderate*	*High*	
Yes	16 (76.2%)	88 (75.9%)	127 (76.0%)	231 (76.0%)
No	2 (9.5%)	19 (16.4%)	25 (15.0%)	46 (15.1%)
No idea	3 (14.3%)	9 (7.8%)	15 (9.0%)	27 (8.9%)
Total	**21 (100.0%)**	**116 (100.0%)**	**167 (100.0%)**	**304 (100.0%)**

The above table represents the level of Professional Leadership Competency based on respondents' awareness about Social Work as a

Professional Course. The level of Professional Leadership Competency is low for 76.2% respondents who are aware that social work is a professional course. The level of Professional Leadership Competency is high for 76% respondents who are aware that social work is a professional course. The level of Professional Leadership Competency is moderate for 75.9% respondents who are aware that social work is a professional course. Among the respondents who are not aware that social work is a professional course, 16.4% of the respondents possess moderate level, 15% possess high level and 9.5% possess low level of professional leadership competency. The level of Professional Leadership Competency is low for 14.3% respondents who are may or may not be aware. The level of Professional Leadership Competency is high for 9% of the respondents who are may or may not be aware. The level of Professional Leadership Competency is moderate for 7.8% of the respondents who are may or may not be aware.

Table 15.13: Respondents Faced Criticism for Taking Social Work as their Graduation and the Level of Professional Leadership Competency

Respondents Faced Criticism for Taking Social Work as their Graduation	*Level of Professional Leadership Competency*			*Total*
	Low	*Moderate*	*High*	
Yes	12 (57.1%)	66 (56.9%)	97 (58.1%)	175 (57.6%)
No	7 (33.3%)	41 (35.3%)	54 (32.3%)	102 (33.6%)
No idea	2 (9.5%)	9 (7.8%)	16 (9.6%)	27 (8.9%)
Total	**21 (100.0%)**	**116 (100.0%)**	**167 (100.0%)**	**304 (100.0%)**

The above table represents the level of Professional Leadership Competency based on respondents' faced criticism for taking Social Work as their Graduation. The level of Professional Leadership Competency is high for 58.1% respondents who faced criticism. The level of Professional Leadership Competency is low for 57.1% respondents who faced criticism. The level of Professional Leadership

Competency is moderate for 56.9% respondents who faced criticism. The level of Professional Leadership Competency is moderate for 35.3% respondents who are not faced criticism. The level of Professional Leadership Competency is low for 33.3% respondents who are not faced criticism. The level of Professional Leadership Competency is high for 32.3% respondents who are not faced criticism. The level of Professional Leadership Competency is high for 9.6% respondents who may or may not face criticism. The level of Professional Leadership Competency is low for 9.5% respondents who may or may not face criticism. The level of Professional Leadership Competency is moderate for 7.8% respondents who may or may not face criticism.

Table 15.14: Kind of Criticism Faced by the Respondents for Taking Social Work as Their Graduation and the Level of Professional Leadership Competency

Kind of Criticism Faced by the Respondents for Taking Social Work as their Graduation	*Level of Professional Leadership Competency*			*Total*
	Low	*Moderate*	*High*	
No	8 (38.1%)	59 (50.9%)	78 (46.7%)	145 (47.7%)
Positive Criticism	2 (9.5%)	6 (5.2%)	8 (4.8%)	16 (5.3%)
Negative Criticism	11 (52.4%)	51 (44.0%)	81 (48.5%)	143 (47.0%)
Total	**21 (100.0%)**	**116 (100.0%)**	**167 (100.0%)**	**304 (100.0%)**

The above table represents the level of Professional Leadership Competency based on respondents' kind of Criticism faced for taking Social Work as their graduation. The level of Professional Leadership Competency is moderate for 50.9% of respondents who had not faced any criticism. The level of Professional Leadership Competency is high for 46.7% respondents who had not faced any criticism. The level of Professional Leadership Competency is low for 38.1% respondents who had not faced any criticism. The level of Professional Leadership Competency is low for 9.5% respondents who faced positive criticism. The level of Professional Leadership Competency is moderate for 5.2% respondents who faced positive criticism. The level of Professional Leadership Competency is high for 4.8% respondents who faced positive criticism. The level of Professional Leadership Competency is low for 52.4% respondents' who faced negative criticism. The level of Professional Leadership Competency is high for 48.5% respondents who faced negative criticism. The level of Professional Leadership Competency is moderate for 44% respondents' who faced negative criticism.

Table 15.15: Respondents Feeling of Competent with regard to Social Work Profession and the Level of Professional Leadership Competency

Respondents Feeling of Competent with Regard to Social Work Profession	*Level of Professional Leadership Competency*			*Total*
	Low	*Moderate*	*High*	
Yes	11 (52.4%)	60 (51.7%)	76 (45.5%)	147 (48.4%)
No	0 (0.0%)	2 (1.7%)	4 (2.4%)	6 (2.0%)
No idea	10 (47.6%)	54 (46.6%)	87 (52.1%)	151 (49.7%)
Total	**21 (100.0%)**	**116 (100.0%)**	**167 (100.0%)**	**304 (100.0%)**

The above table represents the level of Professional Leadership Competency based on respondents' feeling of Competent with regard to Social Work Profession. The level of Professional Leadership Competency is low for 52.4% respondents who felt competent with regard to social work profession. The level of Professional Leadership Competency is moderate for 51.7% respondents who felt competent with regard to social work profession. The level of Professional Leadership Competency is high for 45.5% respondents who felt competent with regard to social work profession. The level of Professional Leadership Competency is high for 2.4% respondents who are not felt competent with regard to social work profession. The level of Professional Leadership Competency is moderate for 1.7% respondents who are not felt competent with regard to social work profession. Among the respondents who are not confident about their competency with regard to social work profession, 52.1% of the respondents possess high level, 47.6% of the respondents possess low level and 46.6% of the respondents possess moderate level of professional leadership competency.

Table 15.16: List of Skills and the Level of Professional Leadership Competency of the Respondents

List of Skills	*Level of Professional Leadership Competency*			*Total*
	Low	*Moderate*	*High*	
Communication Skill	7 (33.3%)	45 (38.8%)	71 (42.5%)	123 (40.5%)
Active Listening	8 (38.1%)	29 (25.0%)	35 (21.0%)	72 (23.7%)
Responsible	1 (4.8%)	22 (19.0%)	28 (16.8%)	51 (16.8%)
No Idea	5 (23.8%)	20 (17.2%)	33 (19.8%)	58 (19.1%)
Total	**21 (100.0%)**	**116 (100.0%)**	**167 (100.0%)**	**304 (100.0%)**

The above table represents the level of Professional Leadership Competency based on respondent's skills. The level of Professional Leadership Competency is high for 42.5% respondents who possess communication skill. The level of Professional Leadership Competency is moderate for 38.8% respondents who possess communication skill. The level of Professional Leadership Competency is low for 33.3% respondents who possess communication skill. The level of Professional Leadership Competency is low for 38.1% respondents who possess active Listening. The level of Professional Leadership Competency is moderate for 25% respondents who possess active listening. The level of Professional Leadership Competency is high for 21% respondents who possess active listening. The level of Professional

Leadership Competency is moderate for 19% respondents who are responsible. The level of Professional Leadership Competency is high for 16.8% respondents who are responsible. The level of Professional Leadership Competency is low for 4.8% respondents who are Responsible. Among the respondents who doesn't have any idea about their skills, 23.8% of the respondents possess low level, 19.8% of the respondents possess high level and 17.2% of the respondents possess moderate level of professional leadership competency.

Table 15.17: Respondents Competent to Deal with the Problems of Individuals and the Level of Professional Leadership Competency

Respondents Competent to Deal with the Problems of Individuals	*Level of Professional Leadership Competency*			*Total*
	Low	*Moderate*	*High*	
Yes	16 (76.2%)	72 (62.1%)	103 (61.7%)	191 (62.8%)
No	2 (9.5%)	14 (12.1%)	19 (11.4%)	35 (11.5%)
May be	3 (14.3%)	30 (25.9%)	45 (26.9%)	78 (25.7%)
Total	**21 (100.0%)**	**116 (100.0%)**	**167 (100.0%)**	**304 (100.0%)**

The above table represents the level of Professional Leadership Competency based on respondents' Competent to deal with the problems of Individuals. The level of Professional Leadership Competency is low for 76.2% respondents who feels competent to deal with individual problems. The level of Professional Leadership Competency is moderate for 62.1% respondents who feels competent to deal with individual problems. The level of Professional Leadership Competency is high for 61.7% respondents who feels competent to deal with individual problems. The level of Professional Leadership Competency is moderate for 12.1% respondents who feels not competent to deal with individual problems. The level of Professional Leadership Competency is high for 11.4% respondents who feels not competent to deal with individual problems. The level of Professional

Leadership Competency is low for 9.5% respondents who feels not competent to deal with individual problems. Among the respondents who are may or may not be competent to deal with individual problems, 26.9% possess high level, 25.9% possess moderate level and 14.3% possess low level of professional leadership competency.

Table 15.18: Respondents Competent to Deal with the Group Problems and the Level of Professional Leadership Competency

Respondents Competent to Deal with the Group Problems	*Level of Professional Leadership Competency*			*Total*
	Low	*Moderate*	*High*	
Yes	12 (57.1%)	67 (57.8%)	90 (53.9%)	169 (55.6%)
No	0 (0.0%)	8 (6.9%)	15 (9.0%)	23 (7.6%)
May be	9 (42.9%)	41 (35.3%)	62 (37.1%)	112 (36.8%)
Total	**21 (100.0%)**	**116 (100.0%)**	**167 (100.0%)**	**304 (100.0%)**

The above table represents the level of Professional Leadership Competency based on respondents' Competent to deal with the group problems. The level of Professional Leadership Competency is moderate for 57.8% respondents who feels competent to deal with group problems. The level of Professional Leadership Competency is low for 57.1% respondents who feels competent to deal with group problems. The level of Professional Leadership Competency is high for 53.9% respondents who feels competent to deal with group problems. The level of Professional Leadership Competency is high for 9% respondents who feels not competent to deal with group problems. The level of Professional Leadership Competency is moderate for 6.9% respondents who feels not competent to deal with group problems. Among the respondents who are may or may not be competent to deal with group problems, 42.9% of the respondents possess low level, 37.1% of the respondents possess high level and 35.3% of the respondents possess moderate level of professional leadership competency.

Table 15.19: Respondents Competent to Deal with the Community Problems and the Level of Professional Leadership Competency

Respondents Competent to Deal with the Community Problems	*Level of Professional Leadership Competency*			*Total*
	Low	*Moderate*	*High*	
Yes	9 (42.9%)	54 (46.6%)	75 (44.9%)	138 (45.4%)
No	7 (33.3%)	30 (25.9%)	41 (24.6%)	78 (25.7%)
May be	5 (23.8%)	32 (27.6%)	51 (30.5%)	88 (28.9%)
Total	**21 (100.0%)**	**116 (100.0%)**	**167 (100.0%)**	**304 (100.0%)**

The above table represents the level of Professional Leadership Competency based on respondents' Competent to deal with the community problems. The level of Professional Leadership Competency is moderate for 46.6% respondents who feels competent to deal with community problems. The level of Professional Leadership Competency is high for 44.9% respondents who feels competent to deal with community problems. The level of Professional Leadership Competency is low for 42.9% respondents who feels competent to deal with community problems. The level of Professional Leadership Competency is low for 33.3% respondents who feels not competent to deal with community problems. The level of Professional Leadership Competency is moderate for 25.9% respondents who feels not competent to deal with community problems. The level of Professional Leadership Competency is high for 24.6% respondents who feels not competent to deal with community problems. Among the respondents who are may or may not competent to deal with community problems, 30.5% of the respondents possess high level, 27.6% of the respondents possess moderate level and 23.8% of the respondents possess low level of professional leadership competency.

CHAPTER 16

Level of Professional Competencies

This chapter involves the analysis and interpretation of level of professional competencies and demographic variable, reason for choosing social work, perception, career ambition, aspiration, criticism faced and social worker skills.

Table 16.1: Age of the Respondents and the Level of Professional Competencies

Age of the Respondents	*Level of Professional Competencies of Social Work Students*			*Total*
	Low	*Moderate*	*High*	
Below 21	7 (46.7%)	49 (48.5%)	96 (51.1%)	152 (50.0%)
21–25	7 (46.7%)	49 (48.5%)	83 (44.1%)	139 (45.7%)
25-29	1 (6.7%)	3 (3.0%)	9 (4.8%)	13 (4.3%)
Total	**15 (100.0%)**	**101 (100.0%)**	**188 (100.0%)**	**304 (100.0%)**

The above table shows the age of the respondents and level of professional competencies of social work students. Below 21 years, 51.1% of the respondents possess high level, 48.5% and 46.7% respondents possess moderate and low level of professional competencies respectively. Between 21 and 25 years, 48.5% of the respondents possess moderate level, 46.7% and 44.1% possess low and high level of professional competencies respectively. Of the respondents between 25 and 29 years, 6.7% possess low level, 4.8% possess high and 3% possess moderate level of professional competencies. From the table it can be inferred that majority of the respondents possess high level of professional competencies.

Table 16.2: Gender of the Respondents and the Level of Professional Competencies

Gender of the Respondents	*Level of Professional Competencies of Social Work Students*			*Total*
	Low	*Moderate*	*High*	
Prefer not to say	0 (0.0%)	0 (0.0%)	1 (0.5%)	1 (0.3%)
Female	7 (6.7%)	63 (62.4%)	128 (68.1%)	198 (65.1%)
Male	8 (53.3%)	38 (37.6%)	59 (31.4%)	105 (34.5%)
Total	**15 (100.0%)**	**101 (100.0%)**	**188 (100.0%)**	**304 (100.0%)**

The table shows the gender of respondents and level of professional competencies of social work students. Of the respondents who don't. Of the female prefer to say gender, 0.5% possess high level of professional competencies respondents, 68.1% possess high level, 62.4% possess moderate and 6.7% possess low level of professional competencies. Of the male respondents, 53.3% possess low level, 37.6% possess moderate level and 31.4% possess high level of professional competencies. From the above table it is inferred that irrespective of the gender, majority of the respondents possess high level of professional competencies.

Table 16.3: Educational Qualification of the Respondents and the Level of Professional Competencies

Educational Qualification	*Level of Professional Competencies of Social Work Students*			*Total*
	Low	*Moderate*	*High*	
II & III BSW	8 (53.3%)	55 (54.5%)	89 (47.3%)	152 (50.0%)
II MSW	7 (46.7%)	46 (45.5%)	99 (52.7%)	152 (50.0%)
Total	**15 (100.0%)**	**101 (100.0%)**	**188 (100.0%)**	**304 (100.0%)**

The table 16.3 shows the educational qualification of the respondents and level of professional competencies. Of the II & III BSW students, 54.5% and 53.3% possess moderate and low level of professional competencies respectively and 47.3% possess high level of professional competencies. Of the II MSW students, 52.7% possess high level of professional competencies of social work students, 46.7% and 45.5% possess low and moderate level of professional competencies. From the table it can be inferred that irrespective of educational qualification, the respondents possess high level of professional competencies.

Table 16.4: Post Graduate Respondents Under-graduation and the Level of Professional Competencies.

Post Graduate Respondents Under Graduation	*Level of Professional Competencies of Social Work Students*			*Total*
	Low	*Moderate*	*High*	
BSW	1 (6.7%)	21 (20.8%)	47 (25.0%)	69 (22.7%)
OTHER DEGREE	6 (40.0%)	25 (24.8%)	52 (27.7%)	83 (27.3%)
Not Applicable (U.G. Students)	8 (53.3%)	55 (54.5%)	89 (47.3%)	152 (50.0%)
Total	**15 (100.0%)**	**101 (100.0%)**	**188 (100.0%)**	**304 (100.0%)**

The above table shows the post graduate respondents under graduation and level of professional competencies. Of the respondents with social work as their under graduation, 25% possess high level, 20.8% possess moderate and 6.7% possess low level of professional competencies. Of the respondents with other degree during their under graduation, 40% possess low level, 27.7% and 24.8% possess high and moderate level of professional competencies respectively. From the above table it can be inferred that, invariable of the under graduation, the respondents majorly possess high level of professional competencies.

Table 16.5: Domicile of the Respondents and the Level of Professional Competencies

Domicile of Respondents	*Level of Professional Competencies of Social Work Students*			*Total*
	Low	*Moderate*	*High*	
Tamil Nadu	12 (80.0%)	85 (84.2%)	160 (85.1%)	257 (84.5%)
Outside Tamil Nadu	3 (20.0%)	16 (15.8%)	28 (14.9%)	47 (15.5%)
Total	**15 (100.0%)**	**101 (100.0%)**	**188 (100.0%)**	**304 (100.0%)**

The above table shows the domicile of the respondents and level of professional competencies. Of the respondents from Tamilnadu, 85.1%, 84.2% and 80% possess high, moderate and low level of professional competencies respectively. Of the respondents from domicile outside Tamilnadu, 20% possess low level of professional competencies, 15.8% and 14.9% possess moderate and high level of professional competencies respectively. It can be inferred from the above table that irrespective of the domicile of the respondents, they majorly possess high level of professional competencies followed by moderate level of professional competencies.

Table 16.6: Major Subjects Studied by the Respondents during 12th Standard and the Level of Professional Competencies

Major Subjects Studied by the Respondents during 12th Standard	*Level of Professional Competencies of Social Work Students*			*Total*
	Low	*Moderate*	*High*	
Bio-Maths	2 (13.3%)	18 (17.8%)	39 (20.7%)	59 (19.4%)
Computer Sciences	2 (13.3%)	23 (22.8%)	27 (14.4%)	52 (17.1%)
Commerce	8 (53.3%)	49 (48.5%)	97 (51.6%)	154 (50.7%)
Humanities	3 (20.0%)	11 (10.9%)	25 (13.3%)	39 (12.8%)
Total	**15 (100.0%)**	**101 (100.0%)**	**188 (100.0%)**	**304 (100.0%)**

The table 16.6 shows the major subjects studied by respondents during 12th standard and level of professional competencies. Of the respondents with bio maths as main subject during 12th standard, 20.7%, 17.8% & 13.3% possess high, moderate and low level of professional competencies respectively. Of the respondents with computer science as major subject during 12th standard, 22.8% possess moderate level, 14.4% and 13.3% possess high and low level of professional competencies respectively. Of the respondents with commerce as main subject during 12th standard, 53.3% and 51.6% possess low & high level of professional competencies & 48.5% possess moderate level of professional competencies. Of the respondents with humanities as major subject during 12th standard, 20% possess low level, 13.3% possess high level and 10.9% possess moderate level of professional competencies.

Table 16.7: Respondents Reasons for Choosing Social Work and the Level of Professional Competencies

Respondents Reason for Choosing Social Work	*Level of Professional Competencies of Social Work Students*			*Total*
	Low	*Moderate*	*High*	
Own Interest	10 (66.7%)	57 (56.4%)	120 (63.8%)	187 (61.5%)
Parents/Relatives Recommendation	5 (33.3%)	42 (41.6%)	64 (34.0%)	111 (36.5%)
Siblings Studied/Influence	0 (0.0%)	2 (2.0%)	4 (2.1%)	6 (2.0%)
Total	**15 (100.0%)**	**101 (100.0%)**	**188 (100.0%)**	**304 (100.0%)**

The table shows the respondents reason for choosing social work and level of professional competencies. Of the respondents chosen social work on their own interest, 66.7%, 63.8% and 56.4% possess low, high and moderate level of professional competencies respectively. Of the respondents chosen social work because of parents/relatives recommendation, 41.6% possess moderate level, 34% and 33.3% possess high and low level of professional competencies respectively. Of the respondents chosen social work due to sibling's influence, 2.1% and 2% possess high and moderate level of professional competencies respectively.

Table 16.8: Respondents Perception about Social Work and the Level of Professional Competencies

Respondents Perception about Social Work	*Level of Professional Competencies of Social Work Students*			*Total*
	Low	*Moderate*	*High*	
Practice Based Profession	2 (13.3%)	18 (17.8%)	29 (20.7%)	59 (19.4%)
Value Oriented Subject	2 (13.3%)	23 (22.8%)	27 (14.4%)	52 (17.1%)
Helping Profession	8 (53.3%)	49 (48.5%)	97 (51.6%)	154 (50.7%)
Art Course	3 (20.0%)	11 (10.9%)	25 (13.3%)	39 (12.8%)
Total	**15 (100.0%)**	**101 (100.0%)**	**188 (100.0%)**	**304 (100.0%)**

The table shows the respondents perception on social work and level of professional competencies. Of the respondents with perception of social work as practise-based profession, 20.7% possess high level, 17.8% and 13.3% possess moderate and low level of professional competencies. Of the respondents with perception of social work as value oriented subject 22.8%, 14.4% &13.3% possess moderate, high and low level of professional competencies respectively. Of the respondents perceiving social work as helping profession, 53.3% low level, 51.6% high & 48.5% moderate level of professional competencies. Of the respondents perceiving social work as art course, 20% possess low level, 13.3% high &10.9% possess moderate level of professional competencies.

Table 16.9: Family Members of the Respondents studied Social Work and the Level of Professional Competencies

Family Members of the Respondents Studied Social Work	*Level of Professional Competencies of Social Work Students*			*Total*
	Low	*Moderate*	*High*	
Yes	1 (6.7%)	19 (18.8%)	27 (14.4%)	47 (15.5%)
No	14 (93.3%)	82 (81.2%)	161 (85.6%)	257 (84.5%)
Total	**15 (100.0%)**	**101 (100.0%)**	**188 (100.0%)**	**304 (100.0%)**

The above table shows the family members of the respondents studied social work and level of professional competencies. Of the respondents whose family members have studied social work, 18.8% possess moderate level, 14.4% possess high and 6.7% possess low level of professional competencies. Of the respondents whose family members have not studied social work, 93% possess low level, 85.6% and 81.2% possess high and moderate level of professional competencies respectively.

Table 16.10: Career Ambition of the Respondents and the Level of Professional Competencies

Career ambition of the respondents	*Level of Professional Competencies of Social Work Students*			*Total*
	Low	*Moderate*	*High*	
Professional Social Worker	4 (26.7%)	25 (24.8%)	60 (31.9%)	89 (29.3%)
Psychiatric/Medical Social Worker/Mental Health/Counsellor	6 (40.0%)	38 (37.6%)	67 (35.6%)	111 (36.5%)
N.G.O/Orphan homes	1 (6.7%)	7 (6.9%)	15 (8.0%)	23 (7.6%)
H.R.	2 (13.3%)	17 (16.8%)	27 (14.4%)	46 (15.1%)

Career ambition of the respondents	*Level of Professional Competencies of Social Work Students*			*Total*
	Low	*Moderate*	*High*	
Government Jobs	1 (6.7%)	8 (7.9%)	15 (8.0%)	24 (7.9%)
Professor	1 (6.7%)	6 (5.9%)	4 (2.1%)	11 (3.6%)
Total	**15 (100.0%)**	**101 (100.0%)**	**188 (100.0%)**	**304 (100.0%)**

The table shows the professional ambition of respondents and level of professional competencies. Of the respondents with ambition of becoming professional social worker, 31.9%, 26.7% and 24.8% possess high, low and moderate level of professional competencies respectively. Of the respondents with ambition Psychiatric/Medical Social Worker/Mental Health/Counsellor, 40%, 37.6% and 35.6% possess low, moderate and high level of professional competencies respectively. Of the respondents with ambition of working in non-governmental organization/orphan homes, 8%, 6.9% and 6.7% possess high, moderate and low level of professional competencies respectively. Of the respondents with ambition to become human resource professional, 16.8% possess moderate level, 14.4% high level and 13.3% possess low level of professional competencies. Of the respondents with ambition getting government jobs, 8% and 7.9% possess high and moderate level of professional competencies respectively and 6.7% possess low level of professional competencies. Of the respondents with ambition to become professor, 6.7%, 5.9% and 2.1% possess low, moderate and high level of professional competencies respectively.

Table 16.11: Aspiration of the Respondents and the Level of Professional Competencies

Aspiration of the Respondents	*Level of Professional Competencies of Social Work Students*			*Total*
	Low	*Moderate*	*High*	
Social Worker/ Counsellor/HR	11 (73.3%)	48 (47.5%)	94 (50.0%)	153 (50.3%)

Aspiration of the Respondents	*Level of Professional Competencies of Social Work Students*			*Total*
	Low	*Moderate*	*High*	
UPSC	2 (13.3%)	31 (30.7%)	62 (33.0%)	95 (31.2%)
No Idea	2 (13.3%)	22 (21.8%)	32 (17.0%)	56 (18.4%)
Total	**15 (100.0%)**	**101 (100.0%)**	**188 (100.0%)**	**304 (100.0%)**

The table shows the aspirations of the respondents and level of professional competencies. Of the respondents aspiring to become social worker/counsellor/HR, around 73.3% possess low level, 50% and 47.5% possess high and moderate level of professional competencies respectively. Of the respondents aspiring for union public service commission (UPSC), 33% possess high level, 30.7% possess moderate and 13.3% possess low level of professional competencies. Of the respondents who have no idea, 21.8% possess moderate level, 17% possess high and 13.3% possess low level of professional competencies.

Table 16.12: Respondents Awareness about Social Work as a Professional Course and the Level of Professional Competencies

Respondent's Awareness about Social Work as Profession	*Level of Professional Competencies of Social Work Students*			*Total*
	Low	*Moderate*	*High*	
Yes	12 (80.0%)	75 (74.3%)	144 (76.6%)	231 (76.0%)
No	2 (13.3%)	18 (17.8%)	26 (13.8%)	46 (15.1%)
May be	1 (6.7%)	8 (7.9%)	18 (9.6%)	27 (8.9%)
Total	**15 (100.0%)**	**101 (100.0%)**	**188 (100.0%)**	**304 (100.0%)**

The table 16.12 shows the respondents awareness about social work as professional course and level of professional competencies. Of the respondents who are aware, 80% possess low level, 76.6% and 74.3% possess high and moderate level of professional competencies respectively. Of the respondents who are not aware, 17.8% possess moderate level, 13.8% possess high and 13.3% possess low level of professional competencies. Of the respondents who may or may not aware, 9.6% possess high level, 7.9% possess moderate level and 6.7% possess low level of professional competencies.

Table 16.13: Respondents Faced Criticism for Taking Social Work as their Graduation and the Level of Professional Competencies

Respondents Faced Criticism for Taking Social Work as Their Graduation	*Level of Professional Competencies of Social Work Students*			*Total*
	Low	*Moderate*	*High*	
Yes	8 (53.3%)	63 (62.4%)	104 (55.3%)	175 (57.6%)
No	7 (46.7%)	29 (28.7%)	66 (35.1%)	102 (33.6%)
May be	0 (0.0%)	9 (8.9%)	18 (9.6%)	27 (8.9%)
Total	**15 (100.0%)**	**101 (100.0%)**	**188 (100.0%)**	**304 (100.0%)**

The table shows the criticism faced by respondents for taking up social work as graduation and level of professional competencies. Of the respondents faced criticism, 62.4% possess moderate level and 55.3% possess high and 53.3% possess low level of professional competencies. Of the respondents who have not faced criticism, 46.7% possess low level, 35.1% possess high level and 28.7% possess moderate level of professional competencies. Of the respondents who might have faced criticism, 9.6% possess high level and 8.9% possess moderate level of professional competencies.

Table 16.14: Kind of Criticism Faced by the Respondents for Taking Social Work as Their Graduation and the Level of Professional Competencies

Kind of Criticism Faced by the Respondents for Taking Social Work as their Graduation	*Level of Professional Competencies of Social Work Students*			*Total*
	Low	*Moderate*	*High*	
No	7 (46.7%)	50 (49.5%)	88 (46.8%)	145 (47.7%)
Positive Criticism	2 (13.3%)	3 (3.0%)	11 (5.9%)	16 (5.3%)
Negative Criticism	4 (40.0%)	48 (47.5%)	89 (47.3%)	143 (47.0%)
Total	**15 (100.0%)**	**101 (100.0%)**	**188 (100.0%)**	**304 (100.0%)**

The table shows the kind of criticism faced by the respondents and level of professional competencies. Of the respondents who have not faced any kind of criticism, 49.5%, 46.8% and 46.7% possess moderate, high and low level of professional competencies respectively. Of the respondents who have faced positive criticism, 13.3% possess low level, around 5.9% possess high and 3% possess moderate level of professional competencies. Of the respondents faced negative criticism, 47.5% and 47.3% possess moderate and high level of professional competencies respectively and 40% possess low level of professional competencies. From the above table it can be inferred that invariable of the kind of criticism, the respondents possess high level of professional competencies followed by moderate and low level of professional competencies.

Table 16.15: Respondents Feeling of Competent with Regard to Social Work Profession and the Level of Professional Competencies

Respondents Feeling Competent with Regard to Social Work Profession	*Level of Professional Competencies of Social Work Students*			*Total*
	Low	*Moderate*	*High*	
Yes	8 (53.3%)	49 (48.5%)	90 (47.9%)	147 (48.4%)
No	0 (0.0%)	2 (2.0%)	4 (2.1%)	6 (2.0%)
May be	7 (46.7%)	50 (49.5%)	94 (50.0%)	151 (49.7%)
Total	**15 (100.0%)**	**101 (100.0%)**	**188 (100.0%)**	**304 (100.0%)**

The table shows the respondent feeling of competent with regard to social work profession and level of professional competencies. Of the respondents feeling competent, 53.3% possess low level, 48.5% possess moderate level and 47.9% possess high level of professional competencies. Of the respondents not feeling competent 2.1% and 2% possess moderate and high level of professional competencies respectively. Of the respondents may or may not feel competent, 50% possess high level, 49.5% possess moderate level and 46.7% possess low level of professional competencies.

Table 16.16: List of Skills and the Level of Professional Competencies

List of Skills	*Level of Professional Competencies of Social Work Students*			*Total*
	Low	*Moderate*	*High*	
Communication Skill	5 (33.3%)	39 (38.6%)	79 (42.0%)	123 (40.5%)
Active Listening	6 (40.0%)	19 (18.8%)	47 (25.0%)	72 (23.7%)
Responsible	1 (6.7%)	19 (18.8%)	31 (16.5%)	51 (16.8%)
No Idea	3 (20.0%)	24 (23.8%)	31 (16.5%)	58 (19.1%)
Total	**15 (100.0%)**	**101 (100.0%)**	**188 (100.0%)**	**304 (100.0%)**

The table 16.16 the list of skills and level of professional competencies. Of the respondents feeling communication as competent, 42%, 38.6% and 33.3% possess high, moderate and low level of professional competencies respectively. Of the respondents feeling active listening as competent, 40% possess low level, 25% possess high level and around 18% possess moderate level of professional competencies. Of the respondents feeling responsible as competency, 18.8% possess moderate level, around 16.5% possess high level and 6.7% possess low level of professional competencies. Of the respondents with no idea, 23.8% and 20% possess moderate and low level of professional competencies respectively and 16.5% possess high level of professional competencies. From the above table it can be inferred that invariable of the list of competencies, the respondents possess high level of professional competencies in majority.

Table 16.17: Respondents Competent to Deal with the Problems of Individuals and the Level of Professional Competencies

Respondents Competent to Deal with the Problems of Individuals	*Level of Professional Competencies of Social Work Students*			*Total*
	Low	*Moderate*	*High*	
Yes	12 (80.0%)	61 (60.4%)	118 (62.8%)	191 (62.8%)
No	1 (6.7%)	12 (11.9%)	22 (11.7%)	35 (11.5%)
May be	2 (13.3%)	28 (27.7%)	48 (25.5%)	78 (25.7%)
Total	**15 (100.0%)**	**101 (100.0%)**	**188 (100.0%)**	**304 (100.0%)**

The table shows the respondents competency to deal with individual problems and level of professional competencies. Of the respondents who are competent, 80% possess low level, 62.8% and 60.4% possess high and moderate level of professional competencies respectively. Of the respondents who are not competent, 11.9% and

11.7% possess moderate and high level of professional competencies respectively and 6.7% possess low level of professional competencies. Of the respondents who may be competent to deal with individual problems, 27.7% and 25.5% possess moderate and high level of professional competencies respectively and 13.3% possess low level of professional competencies.

Table 16.18: Respondents Competent to Deal with the Group Problems and the Level of Professional Competencies

Respondents Competent to Deal with Group Problems	*Level of Professional Competencies of Social Work Students*			*Total*
	Low	*Moderate*	*High*	
Yes	8 (53.3%)	58 (57.4%)	103 (54.8%)	169 (55.6%)
No	1 (6.7%)	5 (5.0%)	17 (9.0%)	23 (7.6%)
May be	6 (40.0%)	38 (37.6%)	68 (36.2%)	112 (36.8%)
Total	**15 (100.0%)**	**101 (100.0%)**	**188 (100.0%)**	**304 (100.0%)**

The above table shows the respondents competency to deal with group problems and level of professional competencies. Of the respondents who are competent, 57.4% possess moderate level of professional competencies, 54.8% and 53.3% possess high and low level of professional competencies respectively. Of the respondents who are not competent, 9% possess high level, 6.7% and 5% possess low and moderate level of professional competencies respectively. Of the respondents who may be competent, 40% possess low level, 37.6% possess moderate level and 36.2% possess high level of professional competencies.

Table 16.19: Respondents Competent to Deal with the Community Problems and the Level of Professional Competencies

Respondents Competent to Deal with Community Problems	*Level of Professional Competencies of Social Work Students*			*Total*
	Low	*Moderate*	*High*	
Yes	6 (40.0%)	47 (46.5%)	85 (45.2%)	138 (45.4%)
No	5 (33.3%)	27 (26.7%)	46 (24.5%)	78 (25.7%)
May be	4 (26.7%)	27 (26.7%)	57 (30.3%)	88 (28.9%)
Total	**15 (100.0%)**	**101 (100.0%)**	**188 (100.0%)**	**304 (100.0%)**

The table shows the respondents competency to deal with community problems and level of professional competencies. Of the respondents who are competent, 46.5% possess moderate level of professional competencies, 45.2% and 40% possess high and low level of professional competencies respectively. Of the respondents who are not competent, 33.3% possess low level, 26.7% possess moderate and 24.5% possess high level of professional competencies respectively. Of the respondents who may possess community, 30.3% possess high level and 26.7% possess moderate and low 26.7% level of professional competencies respectively each.

CHAPTER 17

Intervention

This chapter involves the major findings, discussion and intervention required to enhance the professional competencies of social workers. There is tremendous work to be done to improve the professional competency of the social work students. The recommendations in this chapter, however, are directly related to the findings of the current study and the scope of a competency-based educational approach. The following proposals are given in light of the findings:

1. The current study explored that without much knowledge students are choosing social work; hence proper orientation must be given in the beginning.
2. The schools of social work can implement uniform curriculum and must be based on the competency model.
3. Periodic assessment of professional competencies of social workers must be carried out where ever social workers are employed.
4. As illustrated in the CBE framework, curriculum reviewers should make an effort to develop a clear connection between theory and practice.
5. Schools should make an effort to develop indigenous training modules and instructional materials, particularly with regard to the core professional competencies.
6. Tools for assessing and evaluating professional competencies at different levels of social workers must be established.
7. Field work competencies modules must be established to assess and evaluate the practical competencies.
8. Based on the competency the social workers can be provided license to practice, this will take social work profession to next level.
9. For renewal of license the professional competencies can be tested using indigenous tool specific to the field of practice.

The professional competencies of social work students are assessed using the concurrent triangulation method. This method involves the collection of qualitative and quantitative data sat the same time. The quantitative and qualitative data was analysed separately and major findings were compared, integrated and interpreted. Overall professional competencies of social work students are high while comparing the both the methods. Two third of the respondents possess high level of professional competencies, which was also reflected in the in-depth interview and focussed group discussion. Among the nine domains of professional competencies of social work students, the following domains reflected well in both the method, Professionalism, Values and Ethical, Rights, Justice and economic well-being, Critical thinking and analysis, Contexts and organization and Professional Leadership. The remaining competencies are less reflected in both the methods. It was also identified from both the method the post graduate students are having the potential to describe the professional competencies of social workers. In both the method most emphasized competency is the values and Ethical, the respondents agreed upon the importance of social workers to possess it. The quantitative data was collected using the tool constructed by the authors, while collecting qualitative data, the respondents was found difficult to describe the professional competencies, few terms are not much familiar. The major objective of the study is to assess the professional competencies of social work students in under graduate and post graduate level. Both the method reveals that the respondents possess high level of professional competencies. But the awareness about different competencies is less. This shows the inefficiency of the curriculum, to teach about the professional competencies, hence it is important to include it in the syllabus and also periodic assessment should be ensured. The assessment of professional competencies must be ensured while employing a social worker in any practice setting.

Social work is an illustrious profession founded on compassion and altruism. It was not considered a profession in its early stages and was frequently criticised. Helping gradually evolved into a profession, and individuals began practising it after receiving professional training. The purpose of this study was to examine social work students' professional competencies. While it is referred to as a profession, many individuals are unaware of its significance. A professional course entails completing an undergraduate degree and a postgraduate degree in the same discipline, as the fundamentals are necessary for understanding postgraduate concepts. However, the study reveals that students who pursued careers other than social work are more numerous than those who pursued social work during their undergraduate years. Students who pursued commerce in the 12th grade opted for social work over bio-maths or computer sciences. Additionally, the study reveals that less than one third (15.1 percent) of respondents are unaware that social work is a profession, and 9% lack confidence in it. As a result, the authors created a tool to evaluate the professional competencies of social work students in this study.

Additionally, the authors were interested in determining why students chose social work. Based on the author's experience, the majority of students chose social work as a result of their parents or relatives. However, this study reveals that over two-thirds of social workers chose their field of work out of personal interest. More over half of respondents consider social work to be a helping profession, while 18% consider it to be an art form.

The authors were interested in determining the goals and ambitions of social work students, as both are necessary for professional development in the chosen field. Except for a few individuals, the study suggests that the majority of students aim to be professional social workers. Due to a lack of information about social work in India, students are chastised for pursuing it as a career. Nearly half of respondents encountered criticism for choosing social work as their field of study. Despite the lack of recognition and knowledge of social work, students continue to pursue it, and the majority of respondents believe they are able to deal with individual, group, and community problems. More than two third of the respondent's report having a good level of overall professional competencies.

According to the authors, the existing model of social work education in India provides significant potential for implementing the competency-based education. The majority of schools of social work have recognised the importance of outcome-based education, which includes a comprehensive list of papers and practicums that social work programmes must cover. Equally to curriculum development the assessment part should be based on competency outcome. In this view the authors attempted to create a tool to measure the professional competency of the social workers.

Nowadays, social work students' professionalism is in decline, which is contributing to the decline in students' passion. To meet the demands of the Indian population, Indian social workers have fallen short of the world norm. Unskilled social workers serve individuals in the globalised age without having the necessary training, knowledge, and experience. The majority of students, gain entry to the programme without any relevant abilities, and they will finish it with nothing. Is it because the students aren't prepared, or because they lack training? Is this sufficient for the job? regardless of the result of the admission. Social work students' competency is at a crossroads.

To safeguard the dignity of the social work profession, this is the appropriate time to help our students become better members of society, as well as workers in industry, by providing them professional competent knowledge. All institutions must awaken and focus on providing training and assessment based on the professional competency. Periodic assessment can be done in-order to improve professional identity, values and ethical principles, engaging in engage diversity and equality, knowledge about rights, justice and economic well-being, knowledge about human behaviour, critical thinking and analysis, intervention and skills, context and organization and professional leadership.

This study focussed on the establishment and assessment of professional competencies of social work students. Further research can be conducted in establishing separate tools for assessing the competencies at different level of social workers like, entry level, experienced, senior social workers etc., Moreover Indigenous tools can be established to assess the professional competencies based on specialization area and specific to the field of practice.

References

(n.d.). Retrieved from https://connect.springerpub.com/content/book/978-0-8261-7853-4/part/part01/chapter/ch01#bid_1_7

[1] Alexander, J.S. (2017). A Competency based Framework for Social Work Education in India. *International Journal of Recent Scientific Research.*

[2] Bogo, M.R. (2002). Establishing the Reliability and Validity of a Competency Based Evaluation Tool to Assess M.S.W. Students' Performance in Field Practicum. *Research Institute for Evidence based Social Work research, University of Toronto.*

[3] Britany Swinton, A.F. (2019). Elevating Competence in Social Work. *The New Social Worker :the social work career magazine.*

[4] Chee Liee Chin, M.L. (2013). *The National Social Work Competency Framework.* Singapore.

[5] *Cultural-historical activity theory.* (n.d.). Retrieved from Wikipedia: https://en.wikipedia.org/wiki/Cultural-historical_activity_theory

[6] Davletkaliev1, D.K. (2015). Professional Competence Development of the Social Work Specialists in the Period of Study in the System of Additional Education. *International Education Studies.*

[7] Drisko, J.W. (2016). Competencies and Their Assessment. *Journal of Social Work Education.*

[8] Drisko., J. (17th July 2014). Competencies and their assessments by James.W. Drisko. *Journal of social work education*, 414–426.

[9] Education, C.f. (2015). *National Educational policy 2015.* USA: Council on Social Work Education.

[10] Lymbery, E.F., M. (2003). Negotiating the contradictions between competence and creativity in social work education. *SAGE.*

[11] Molodtsova, L.A. (2019). Technologies of Organization of Students' Independent Work in Studying Pedagogical Disciplines at Classic Universities. In *Modern Technologies for Teaching and Learning in Socio-Humanitarian Disciplines* (p. 29). IGI Global Publisher of Timely knoweldge.

[12] Nair, T.K. (2015). Social Work in India—A Semi Profession. *Social Work Foot Prints—Samajakaryada Hejjegalu.*

[13] Olswang, K.A. (2017). Building Competence: A Historical Perspective of Competency-Based Education. In P.N. Karen Rasmussen,

Handbook of Research on Competency-Based Education in University Settings (p. 13).

[14] Poulin, J.P. (2019). *Social Work Practice A Competency based practice.* Springer Publishing Company. Retrieved from https://connect.springerpub.com/content/book/978-0-8261-7853-4/part/part01/chapter/ch01#bid_1_21

[15] Premraj, M.P. (2017). A Case Study on Competency of Professional Social Work Students in Social Work Education, Research and Training. *Research on Humanities and Social Sciences*, 152–156.

[16] Regulators, C.C. (2012). *Entry Level competency profile for social work profession in canada.* Canada: Canadian Council of Social Work Regulators.

[17] Regulators, C.C. (2012). *Entry level competency profile for the social work profession in Canada.* Canda: Canadian council of social work regulators.

[18] Shajahan, P.K., P.L. (n.d.). Competencies Needed for Social Work Practice in Family Studies.

[19] Siddiqui, H.Y. (n.d.). Towards a Competency based education for Social Work. *International Journal oF Social Work.*

[21] Stier, J. (2004). Intercultural Competencies as a Means to Manage Intercultural Interactions. (J. Allwood, Ed.) *Intercultural Communication* (issue 7.).

[22] Workers, B.A. (2018). *BASW The professional association for social work and social workers.* Retrieved from https://www.basw.co.uk/social-work-training/professional-capabilities-framework-pcf

[23] ying, Y.-W. (2013). Contribution of Self Compassion to competence and mental health in social work students. *Journal of Social Work Education*, 309–323.

[24] Yu Guo, S. L.-C. (2018). Core Competency Education of Social Work Students: An Empirical Assessment Through Scale Development. *International Journal of Social Work*, 59–77.